DISCARDED

The Hispanic Contribution to the State of Colorado

The Hispanic Contribution to the State of Colorado

edited by José de Onís

Published under the auspices of the
University of Colorado Centennial Commission

Westview Press
Boulder, Colorado

All rights reserved. No part of this publication may be reproduced or transmitted in any form or by any means, electronic or mechanical, including photocopy, recording or any information storage and retrieval system, without permission in writing from the publisher.

Copyright © 1976 by the Board of Regents, University of Colorado.

Published 1976 in the United States of America by

>Westview Press, Inc.
>1898 Flatiron Court
>Boulder, Colorado 80301
>Frederick A. Praeger, Publisher and Editorial Director

Published under the auspices of the University of Colorado Centennial Commission.

Library of Congress Cataloging in Publication Data
Main entry under title:
The Hispanic contribution to the State of Colorado

(University of Colorado Centennial publication)
Bibliography: p. 209
Includes index.
 1. Spanish Americans in Colorado—Addresses, essays, lectures.
2. Colorado—History—Addresses, essays, lectures. I. De Onís, José.
II. Series: Colorado. University. University of Colorado Centennial publication.
F785.S75H57   978.8'004'68   76-7014
ISBN 0-89158-100-6

Printed and bound in the United States of America.

*To Stuart Cuthbertson, for many
years Head of the Department of Modern
Languages at the University of Colorado,
who devoted his entire life to the study
of the Hispanic heritage in our State and to
the dissemination of this knowledge to
generations of Colorado students*

Preface

This volume on the Hispanic contribution to the State of Colorado, composed of fourteen essays by different authorities in their respective fields of specialization, is being sponsored by the University of Colorado Centennial Commission, which has placed at our disposal its various resources.

The essays make some contribution to the knowledge of the region, but their main function is to achieve perspective and interpretation by presenting a fresh point of view and focusing attention on those aspects of their common theme that seem to have a special interest for the present generation. They also will serve as a reminder of the sometimes forgotten important participation of the native Hispanic people in the development of the State.

The State of Colorado has the distinction of being able to celebrate in 1976 both a centennial of its statehood and a bicentennial of the Independence of our country. And it is only fitting and proper that the Hispanic people of our State should participate in this celebration, since they are neither immigrants into the United States nor the descendants of any such immigrants. This had been their homeland for many years before anyone ever heard of the United States. As stated by Fr. Angélico Chávez "only the aboriginal Indians can rate them as alien newcomers. Whatever trace of their Hispanic language and culture that may have survived is their very own since it grew up apart from that of Mexico and from that of Spain itself."

We are grateful to Eugene Wilson, Chairman of the Centennial Commission, who advised and encouraged us during the preparation of this volume. We are thankful to the members of the Advisory Committee: William Markward of the English Department, University of Colorado; Lynn Wolf of the Fine Arts Department, University of Colorado; William Grupp and Ralph Kite of the Spanish Department, University of Colorado; and particularly Arthur L. Campa of Denver University, who has generously contributed with his great knowledge of the Spanish Southwest. We also should include here the name of J. K. Emery, Director of Publications Service of the University of Colorado, who is responsible for the format and other technical aspects of this book.

José de Onís

Contents

Preface vi

Introduction x

1. Early Spanish Contacts with Colorado   1
Arthur Campa, Denver University

2. The Dominguez-Escalante Expedition of 1776   19
Leroy R. Hafen, Brigham Young University

3. The Adams-Onís Treaty of 1819   33
José de Onís, University of Colorado

4. Spanish and Mexican Land Grants in the Southwest   43
Harold H. Dunham, Denver University

5. Mexican Land Grants in Colorado   65
Charles Vigil, Attorney, Denver

6. Miguel Alona: The Hero of Cochetopa Pass   79
Ann Federici Martin, Writer, Boulder, Colorado

7. Hispanic Folklore in Colorado   91
Arthur Campa, Denver University

8. The Santero Tradition   117
John Wilson, University of Colorado

9. Peasant Religion: Retablos and Penitentes   123
Thomas Steele, S.J., Regis College

10. Alabados of the San Luis Valley   141
Yvonne Guillon Barrett, University of Colorado

11. Tradiciones hispanas en el Valle del Río Grande   153
Arthur Campa, Denver University

12 Aguilar and Its Western Valley of Trujillo Creek 163
Anne Lucero, Writer, Aguilar, Colorado

13 Spanish-Surnamed Americans in the First Hundred Years of Government 183
Charles Vigil, Attorney, Denver

14 The Spanish Language of the San Luis Valley 191
Anthony G. Lozano, University of Colorado

Selected Bibliography 209
Eva Marja Kahiluoto Rudat

Index of Names 227

Introduction

The State of Colorado forms part of what is generally known as the Spanish Southwest. This is a region which has a character all of its own, different from the rest of the nation and also different, in many ways, from neighboring Mexico. Because of its geographic conditions—surrounded by a chain of deserts and wastelands that made communication with the outside precarious—it remained isolated from the rest of the world for centuries, landlocked, in a sort of hinterland.

In the south, it was bordered by the Chihuahua Desert. It took a well-planned yearly caravan to go from Santa Fe to the City of Chihuahua, and beyond here, there was still more desert, cold and wind-swept in the winter, scorching hot in the summer. Let us remember that Don Francisco Vásquez de Coronado first came up by way of the Pacific coast, and then through what is present-day Nogales, a route which presented many problems, but in those days, it was easier than coming by the central plateau. To the west, it was bound by the Mojave Desert. Trying to avoid it on the way to California, the Escalante Trail went north toward the region of the salt lakes, and then turned west and finally came out by Monterey in the Pacific. To the east, there was the Territory of Arkansas and Texas, with its small adobe town of San Antonio, an immense open land that appeared to go nowhere. To the northeast, there was the great undulating prairie known as the Missouri Territory, which some have called the Great American Desert, at one time French, then Spanish, then French again, and finally American. Toward the north and northwest, there was a continuous chain of impenetrable mountains that seemed to go on indefinitely.

The presence of hostile tribes of Indians surrounding them made matters even more hazardous for these dauntless inhabitants and further intensified their isolation. "We have spent 118 years of continuous wars with the thirty-three nations of Gentiles that surround us, and up to the present time we have not lost one span of land within our ancient boundaries," states Pedro Pino in his *Exposition of 1812*.

There were no established roads north of Santa Fe; the Camino Real only went as far as this city. From here on, there were only oxcart trails leading to places like Taos, Mora, and Ratón. In September of every year, these settlers made an expedition to Taos to celebrate the Fair of San Jerónimo, and to trade with the Comanches and other Indians. Beyond here, there was an immense wilderness, always difficult to penetrate. The easiest way out of the region, nonetheless, was by the way of Saint Louis, and then by boat down the Mississippi River to New Orleans. In those early days, water represented an easier mode of travel than land.

The first leg of this trip was what was generally known as the Santa Fe Trail. It would go two ways: northeast diagonally across Kansas, or directly north by Ratón Pass, along the foothills of the Rocky Mountains to the Arkansas River and then due east to the Missouri. The first of these two routes was the shortest and was the one followed by Pedro Vial in 1792. The other, through the present-day State of Colorado, though the longest, had the advantage of being open to the fur trade, which was very important in those early stages of our development. In any event, the distances were tremendous. It took months, sometimes years, to make the round-trip cycle. Many never made it.

Under such adverse conditions, cultural inbreeding was inevitable. Here, in a region isolated from Spain and Mexico for most of 300 years, as it was from the French and Anglo-Saxon influences to the east and northeast, Western Civilization was reduced to its fundamentals. As a result, a distinctive culture developed in the mountain areas and valleys of the State of Colorado that has never been fully explored. Once the "high waters" of the Spanish empire receded, this region was the first to be left stranded, condemned to eternal solitude and plagued by incestuous cultural existence—as if the Spanish imperial galleons of a distant yesterday were left high and dry, surrounded by a limitless ocean of sagebrush and cacti.

Don Pedro Bautista Pino, the Representative to the Spanish Cortes of Cádiz for this region in 1811, in a memoir published in Cádiz one year later entitled *Exposición sucinta y sencilla de la Provincia de Nuevo México,* complained bitterly of their abandonment. In many cases, the attachment and loyalty of this region to the mother country was better known to the citizens of the United States than to those of old Spain. "Aware of the abandonment with which this province has been treated," states Don Pedro, "they have tried to win our favor through various means. Knowing that by possessing this province they would be masters of the other frontier provinces from the North Sea to the South Sea, and that consequently, they would be in a position to intrude into this Kingdom of Mexico, they have tried, with offers of lucrative commerce and promises of gentle and protective laws, to incorporate this valuable portion of territory to that of Louisiana, which has recently been purchased and which borders on our territory. However, neither by this means nor by the threats made by the construction of forts near us, nor by arming the wild tribes against us, have they been able to gain ground; they have realized instead that each of their attempts has been entirely futile."

In the meantime, in the central Mexican plateau two thousand miles to the south, there had developed a great culture comparable to that of the mother country. Great cities like México, Querétaro, Puebla, and Cuernavaca rivaled those of Spain itself. Humboldt called Mexico City "the city of palaces." Here the cultivation of architecture and the fine arts produced the greatest masterpieces this continent had known. Through its schools and colleges, the language was kept fresh and creative. Its literature was the best the New World had to offer. Sor Juana Inés de la Cruz was doubtlessly the greatest poetess America had produced.

The inhabitants of our region, isolated as they were by such long distances and for such a long period of time, did not share in that cultural development. Unlike the baroque culture of Mexico City and Lima, which produced great Renaissance Universities— the University of Mexico and the University of San Marcos— here education was limited to the religious instruction offered by the good Franciscan fathers. For the most part, the people remained illiterate, except for some families who passed on the rudiments of reading and writing from father to son. There was a scarcity of professional men, especially medical doctors. The arts in general were reduced to the most basic fundamentals. Many of the natives had never seen money. There were no great authors. The language remained stagnant, losing many words and current expressions, while preserving archaisms now lost in the mother country.

And yet by 1800, in some respects, conditions here were better than in Mexico. There was very little peonage. Everyone enjoyed sufficient land to enable him to make a living by agriculture, and as a result they did not have the vagrants that, according to Don Pedro Pino, swarmed like ants in the Viceroyalty of Mexico. "I had never seen these conditions until I had occasion to cross the Viceroyalty on my way to the Cortes. My heart was sorely touched upon observing hunger, nakedness, and everywhere the most unhappy conditions in which man can exist." In contrast to this poverty, the towns of New Mexico presented a most agreeable appearance. "A close view discloses the good discipline and the cleanliness of the people." "All the people wear clothes and shoes. The women (to whom nature has granted grace and beauty) wear tunics and mantillas, and comb their hair, as has been customary from remote antiquity, and as do our gypsies of today."

The first settlers of European descent to come to Colorado were these same Spanish-speaking people who came north from New Mexico. The Mexican government in an effort to secure its hold on the region gave large tracts of land to individuals who were both Catholic and Mexican citizens and who promised to defend the frontier from foreign encroachment. Early settlements were made by the Napestle River (the Arkansas) at the foothills of the Spanish Peaks, known then as "Las Tetas," and on the east and west sides of the San Luis Valley. These three regions, as pointed out by Robert Adams, were developed independently of each other. The first was separated by the Culebra Mountains, the other two were separated by the arid central span which divides the San Luis Valley into two parts.

Hispanic settlements east of the Peaks came earlier than in the Valley, but here there was none of any great consequence until about the time of the building of Bent's Fort in 1832, and these were not always permanent.

During the Spanish regime, an effort was made to establish a Comanche model village at the edge of the plains called "San Carlos de los Jupes." On a site not far from present-day Pueblo in July 1787, the Spaniards brought in tools and supplies from Taos and started to instruct the Indians in the growing of wheat. By October, according to A. B. Thomas, they had constructed 19 houses, laying out a typical Spanish village. All went well until January 1788, when a prominent Indian woman died and the Jupes suddenly deserted their settlement and went back to their nomadic lives as hunters. It was their custom that when any person of estimation died, no matter how suitable the habitation, to take up their "rancheríos" and to change sites, going long distances, even to places lacking everything necessary for subsistence. After this, the New Mexican Government considered the possibility of resettling San Carlos with Spanish families, but nothing ever came of it, and more than one-half century was to pass before another settlement was established on Colorado soil.

Bent's Fort, completed in 1832, seems to have attracted the founding of other nearby settlements. Mathew C. Field, a correspondent for the *New Orleans Picayune,* who visited the region in 1839, gives us a colorful description of a small town, five miles above Bent's Fort, called "Pueblo de la Leche." It was constructed of adobes, and it consisted of about 30 houses of small dimensions, "all built compactly together in an oblong square, leaving a large space in the center, and the houses themselves forming the walls of the fort, into which there was but one entrance, through a large and very strong gate." It was inhabited primarily by New Mexicans and French trappers, who had retired there to raise grain, vegetables, horses, mules, and other rudimentary commodities. "The men generally had beards at full length, and long hair flowing over their shoulders, which, together with their dark skin and piercing eyes, gave them a truly wild and ferocious appearance." They were described as being as brave and daring as the Comanches themselves, "of whose wild nature they seemed to partake and they could sally forth and battle successfully with any war party of ordinary numbers." The women were neat and pleasant to look at. "Their dress consisted of just three articles, a common domestic undergarment, a coarse petticoat, and a big narrow shawl thrown over the head." They were well combed and seemed to take delight in showing off their raven black hair. "They were all much taken with us," states

Field, "and crowded about us chattering Spanish in a manner most bewildering to American ears."

Field goes on to describe a delightful pastoral scene that could have been typical of any Spanish settlement in the early southwest. "Dogs, goats, cats, tame cows, tame antelopes, tame buffalo calves, kids, and jackasses were about in all directions and little children were on their backs kicking their heels and playing with the animals. A stout little rascal near us was bellowing 'Madre! Madre!' to come to punish a juvenile buffalo who had hit him a butt and knocked him against the wall."

In the Spanish southwest, the word "plaza" came to mean town. Soon plazas started to appear along the mountains and to the south on the Green Horn River. In 1842, a trading post was established near what is now Pueblo; it soon grew into a large Spanish village. Most of these immigrants came from Taos. Friendly relations developed between Americans and New Mexicans after the Independence of Mexico, and Taos had become the supply base for trappers operating in southern and western Colorado.

The first large Spanish-American town east of the mountains, however, was Santa Trinidad, begun in 1839, when Gabriel Guitérrez and Juan N. Guitérrez settled there. It was named after Trinidad Baca, daughter of Felipe Baca, the most influential citizen in the region.

The eastern side of the San Luis Valley, on the other side of the mountains, was settled shortly afterward. In 1849, a settlement was begun on the Costilla River; in 1851, the town of San Luis was begun by Carlos Beaubien on the Culebra River. The early history of Costilla County seems to have been an extension of Taos. Most of the colonists who settled on the Sangre de Cristo Grant came from there. Other towns followed—San Pedro and San Acacio. These three villages were the first permanent settlements in the state. The town of San Luis, so called because the day of their arrival, June 21, was the Festivity of San Luis, is the oldest town in Colorado. The irrigation ditch which they constructed is the first one of its kind to be built in the state; others soon followed. "The irrigation system of the San Luis District," states Leroy Hafen, "is a good index to the progress in the valley." The first general store in Colorado, owned by the Gallegos family, was started here in 1857.

The western part of the valley had numerous early contacts, although most of them were unfortunate. As early as 1833, colonists from New Mexico tried to settle on the Conejos River in the southwestern corner of the valley, but they were immediately attacked by hostile Indians, and the project was abandoned. Shortly after this, a settlement was made at the confluence of the Conejos and the San Antonio Rivers; the settlement was called "San Francisco." The homesteaders succeeded in planting crops, but they were once again driven out by Indians. There also was founded in 1846 a town named "Santa Margarita," which suffered the same fate as the others. From this time on, the settlers developed the practice of making summer plantings and then abandoning the region when the harvest was over.

In 1851, however, under the leadership of Crescencio Valdez and José María Jacques, families from El Rito and Abiquiú settled near the Conejos River and established the community of Guadalupe. Father Lamy visited the town in 1853 and witnessed the construction of the new chapel. The Indians continued to harass the colonists, and safe homesteading did not become possible in this region until Fort Massachusetts was well established. Archuleta County to the southwest was created some years later.

As a result of these early settlements, there was created in the State of Colorado an elementary culture that was essentially rustic and pastoral. In places such as Tierra Amarilla, the San Luis Valley, and the Sangre de Cristo Mountains, there is still to be found today an indigenous culture in which the values of Western Civilization have been concentrated and simplified, without losing any of their quality or vigor, as it is evident in the unbending faith of the *penitentes*. Here we have a peasant culture, which has become proficient in herding and mining, the two main industries of the State of Colorado.

When the Anglo-Saxons first arrived in this region, they learned much of what they know of these two trades from the Spanish natives who were here long before them. The average North American in 1848 was skilled in a number of occupations, but mining was not one of them. The first American mining followed the course established by the Spaniards and their American successors. They were, according to James H. McClintock, the best prospectors and the closest judges of ore ever known. The Spanish *arrastra,* a machine used for crushing ore, was not an uncommon sight to the early pioneer. One of them still is being exhibited in Central City. Many Spanish mining terms found their way into our Western vernacular: *batea, escoria, bonanza, borrasco,* etc. Many Spanish laws and customs are still accepted practice in the Western States. Even today, most of the coal miners in Colorado are still Mexican-Americans.

When it comes to herding as a way of life, our Spanish heritage here is even stronger than in that of mining. As pointed out by Herbert E. Bolton in the "Epic of Greater America," from the very beginning, there has existed a Hispanic pastoral culture, from the Columbia River to Patagonia, which constitutes one of the most permanent common denominators between the two Americas. The early Hispanic people who came into southern Colorado were agriculturists and grazing country-folk looking for fertile land and good pastures which were scarce to the south. "The Spanish-Americans who ranched along the Huerfano, the Arkansas and the Purgatorio rivers for a generation or more before most of the Anglos arrived were pioneers themselves. They had brought their herds and their families over the Sangre de Cristo Mountains from the Rio Grande Valley and the long-established settlement north of Santa Fe. With them," state Richard Goff and Robert H. McCafree in their book, *Century in the Saddle,* "came their centuries-old customs of land- and livestock-management customs that had been developed in Spain and Mexico to fit this same type of country. They contributed their basic ideas of rangeland law, too, that still persist in the statues of our state."

Such spectacles as *rodéos,* or rodeos, are derived from the Spanish customs of herding and branding mavericks in the spring, a practice that still continues in portions of the state. It was all part of the *Mesta,* a legal system used in herding since medieval times. In this system, the *mesteño,* or mustang, was the unbranded critter. During the round-ups, the cowboys from different ranches came together to show their manliness by doing tricks the others could not accomplish. In a traditional society such as that of the San Luis Valley, the branding of cattle and horses, the shearing of sheep, and the harvesting of wheat and oats were important social events, anticipated with great pleasure and comparable only to the celebration of certain saints' days. It was an occasion for the older folk to meet with their *compadres* to discuss the latest news, and for the younger ones to do some courting, very much as their ancestors had done in Spain prior to their coming to America.

When it came to herding skills, these people were no amateurs. It is said of Coronado, who was a Charro from Salamanca, that when he and his men first saw buffalo, they untied their lariats, lassoed the buffalo, and milked them. According to some critics, the Anglo-Saxons contributed little to the development of cattle raising in the Southwest. "By a curious cultural transmutation," states Carey McWilliams in his book, *North from Mexico,* "Anglo-Americans have long claimed credit for the origin and development of the cattle industry. No folk hero in American life has enjoyed anything like the popularity of the American cowboy. Each week millions of Americans see 'Western' films, and their sons and daughters will probably line up at the box-office years hence to see cowboys ride, rope, and shoot on the screen. Yet, with the exception of the capital provided to expand the industry, there seems to have been nothing the American rancher or cowboy contributed to the development of cattle-raising in the Southwest."

The *Mesta,* of course, included the grazing of both cattle and sheep, and the *pastor* or sheep herder was perhaps even more important than the *vaquero*. Some of the herds in Colorado were so large that there were individuals who made a living by following the herds and gathering the *pencos,* the young lambs that had become separated from their mothers. These were known as *penqueros*. The shepherd became synonymous with the entire culture. In a lonely, isolated land, he, more than anyone else, became the personification of all patience and resignation. To overcome his loneliness, he sang ancient songs that he had learned from his father, and his father, in turn, from his father's father. Many were songs sung in Spain by their ancestors prior to their coming to America, like the verses of "Mal de amores," sung by the Charro shepherds of Salamanca and by the shepherds of the San Luis Valley.

Si acaso yo me muriere,
no me entierren en sagrado,
entiérrenme en campo verde,
donde me pise el ganado,
con un letrero que diga
aquí murió un malhadado;
no murió de tabardillo,
ni un dolor de costado,
pues murió de mal de amores
que le dio desenfrenado.

Pastoreo, herding, included other animals as well—goats, pigs, donkeys, etc. It had its own vocabulary, based on generations of practical experience. Many of these terms were indispensable, as attested by the fact that many of our expressions in the cattle and sheep industries used today were originally Spanish: *hackamore, cinch, remuda, latigo, dogie, rodeo, stampede, chaps, lariat, buckaroo, mustang,* and other herding-country terms such as *ramada, chaparral, mesa, siesta, adobe, cayon, vigilante, arroyo, vamus.* Even the word *ranch* comes from the Spanish.

The Anglo-Saxon pioneers who came from the East were from regions where growing conditions and climate were different from ours, yet, according to Richard Goff and Robert McCafree, they adapted quickly by taking advantage of the great knowledge and tradition of the Hispanic people that had preceded them. "They saw the Spanish system of handling cattle, branding and of organization, and they adopted it because it worked."

The Hispanic natives also contributed the basic concepts of rangeland law that still endure in Colorado. These laws, according to these authors, have persisted "because they were practical, they were simple, and they were eminently fair." They were founded on the principle that the first comers were entitled to the protection from the encroachment of late comers, and the laws were applicable to both land and water.

This basic idea of "first in use, first in law" is best exemplified in the priority rights of our irrigation laws. Many of our earliest ditch rights for water go back to early Spanish development work along the streams of southern Colorado.

Even our present fence laws are still based on the Spanish concept of rangeland usage. Here in Colorado the basic differences between English law and Spanish law first met head-on. On several occasions conflicts have arisen between these two legal philosophies that brought the issue either to a vote or to the courts. So far, the Spanish law has always prevailed.

To simplify the two ideas and reduce them to bare essentials, the difference is merely this: English law held that the owner of livestock was responsible for his cattle and he was expected to fence them in. Spanish law, on the other hand, assumed that range land was open to all and that the owner of crop land was himself responsible for the protection of his crops. The farmer who raised a garden or grain crop was therefore expected to fence cattle off his land, if he wanted to protect it from the destruction of roving livestock. Thus, English law held that the cattle owner should fence cattle in, Spanish law compelled the land owner to fence them out.

Essentially this same philosophy is incorporated into our present day fence laws.

The Spanish contributed the fundamental ideas for our modern brand laws, too. At one of the first meetings of the Association, members were urged to come and register their brands with the organization. As the direct result of this early organization, Colorado has probably the most effective brand laws in the nation today.

Such institutions as the *Juez de Campo* and other types of cattle justice are still part of our tradition. According to William H. Dusenberry, the responsibilities of these officials have been transferred upon justices of the peace and certain county officers. "Laws relating to ranching, which are essentially similar to ordinances of the *Mesta,* have been embodied in the constitutional and legal systems of states in the West. Modern stock laws are but variations and adaptations of legislations which controlled ranching in colonial Mexico. The influence of the *Mesta* on the administration of ranching persists to this day."

Caught between the former Spanish provinces of Missouri and New Mexico, Colorado was the heartland of what some historians have called the "Adobe Empire." In the plains just north of Denver, along the banks of the South Platte, with Longs Peak in the background, these two groups of settlers eventually converged and contributed some of our most interesting historical monuments: Fort Vasquez, founded by the son of a Spaniard, Luis Vasquez, who had come down from Missouri; and Fort Saint Vrain, founded by Ceran Saint Vrain, a one-time Mexican citizen, whose father, Jacques Lássus, and uncle, Charles Auguste Lássus, had fled to Spain after the French Revolution and there became acculturated to Spanish ways. In Spain, Charles Auguste served as an officer in the guard of Charles IV, rising high in the King's esteem; he eventually was to come to America, where he was appointed Lieutenant Governor of Louisiana in 1799. The rivalry in this region north of Denver was between Missourians and New Mexicans from Taos, but most of them had a similar background; both had become Hispanized prior to their coming.

Much of the participation of the Spanish-surnamed inhabitants of Colorado nonetheless has remained anonymous, such as in the case of the story of Miguel Alona included in this volume. We are, however, constantly surrounded by reminders of the history of these early days in the many Spanish names which are abundantly scattered over the map of the state. Spanish influence, as stated by Leroy Hafen, can be readily observed in the place names of this region. "Such peaks and mountain ranges as the La Plata, San Miguel, Blanca, and Sangre de Christo remind us of the Spanish explorers, miners, missionaries, and soldiers who early visited this country and left behind these musical appellations. In addition to the Río Grande, the Huérfano, Cucharas, Las Animas, La Plata, Florida, Dolores, and Conejos are streams with Spanish names. A few of the many towns and cities whose names are redolent of old Spanish are Pueblo, Trinidad, Antonito, Los Cerritos, Durango, Del Norte, La Junta, Los Pinos, San Pablo, and La Plaza de los Leones (later known as Walsenburg). Many of the counties in the southern and western Colorado have Spanish names: Las Animas, Alamosa, Archuleta, Dolores, Otero, Conejos, Costilla, Baca Mesa, and San Juan."

Even the French and English names in the state often have a Spanish connection. Kit Carson, Saint Vrain, and a host of trappers from Taos, New Mexico, set their traps for beaver and other valuable pelts as far north as the Big Thompson and its tributaries. In the sunny days of winter, they would come down from the frozen mountains to thaw out in protected places such as what is now Lyons, at the foot of the mountains. This is how this town was first settled.

Old Main in the University of Colorado was built by the descendants of these first settlers. In 1959 when the main tower in Old Main was reinforced, it was found that the instructions written on the beams were all in Spanish. On one rafter, it read *"Estamos a quince millas al sur de León."* León here is, of course, Lyons. By some peculiar coincidence in pronunciation, they thought the name was *León,* which in local Spanish would have been pronounced somewhat similar to Lyons. We have to remember that most of these people did not know English. The only system of phonetics which they had was Spanish. Spanish also was the "lingua franca" of most Indians, and you can be certain that this was the language generally used in Bent's Fort. Even in Kit Carson's home (he was married to Josefina Jaramillo), the language that was spoken was Spanish. Spanish remained, along with English and German, the official language of the state until 1900. Some of our early political figures, such as Casimiro Barela, had a very limited command of the English language. Much of early education in Colorado was bilingual. Interestingly enough, Colorado, the name of the State, although of recent vintage, is also Spanish.

José de Onís

1 Early Spanish Contacts With Colorado

Arthur L. Campa

Trading, mining, and agriculture were the basic interests that kept Spanish, French, and English settlers on the move in the Southwest when it was discovered and also during the succeeding periods of history in which these nations were involved. During the first two and one-half centuries that followed the settlement of New Mexico, there were no significant mineral discoveries made which would initiate large-scale population movements. The Spaniards of the seventeenth century had all the cultivable land in the upper Rio Grande needed for a relatively small number of colonists spread over the intermountain valleys in the early stages of expansion.

The Spanish conquistadores were not content, however, with establishing a colony and settling down. Don Juan de Oñate, the man who led the settlement vanguard into the northernmost province of the Spanish Empire in 1598, undertook the first exploration expedition scarcely a month after his colony had been established in San Juan. In the months that followed, he explored hundreds of miles west, east, and north, seeking information about the surrounding tribes and trying to locate mineral deposits. The conquest and settlement of the New World was an enterprise carried out by a vast military and political structure in which the army, the church, and the settlers took an active part.

The mining possibilities and the rich farming land of what is now Colorado did not escape the observation of the early Spanish explorers. They named the rivers, valleys, and mountains beyond Pike's Peak, known to them as El Capitán, and took careful note of the flora and fauna of the region. The Anglo-American frontiersmen who arrived two and one-half centuries later found a country from Kansas to California that had been crisscrossed by Spanish armies, by explorers, and by missionaries. The topographical landmarks had names which the newcomers translated into English whenever possible, even if they came up with such approximations as "Wolfano" for *Huérfano* and "Picketwire" for *Purgatorio*. The well-known Arkansas River that was to become the international boundary between Spain and the United States after the Adams-Onís treaty of 1819 was known as the *Napestle*, although Ulibarri christened it *Río Grande de San Francisco* when he crossed it in 1706. The Canadian was first *Rio Colorado*, the Red River was originally *Río Rojo*, the North Platte was known as *San Lorenzo*, and the South Platte as *Río de Jesús María*. The Platte farther east had the unaesthetic name of *Río Chato* for reasons known to the Spaniards alone. The *Purgatoire* of southern Colorado was known as *Las Ánimas* and the Saint Charles was *San Carlos*. Many of the principal mountain ranges such as *Sangre de Cristo* and *San Juan*, retained their original Spanish names, except the famous Pike's Peak, which was known to the Spaniard as *El Capitán* for more than two centuries before the advent of Zebulon Pike.

The expansion of Hispanic civilization into Colorado is a process which took place in three stages, beginning with the long period of reconnaissance and exploration from the sixteenth through the eighteenth century. The second period began with the Mexican land grants era, and with the first attempts by Taos families to settle in the Conejos River valley. The third stage of Hispanic expansion began after the American occupation, particularly when rapid industrialization took place in Colorado.

The first Spanish contacts in Colorado are not generally well known because most people assume that the founding of the town of San Luis in the south in 1852 constitutes the first entry of Hispanic people into the state. Historians and other well-informed individuals are well aware, however, of the events which took place since the middle of the sixteenth century. Professor Leo Grebler of the University of California believes that the lack of information about the Southwest arises "because so many Americans have a limited knowledge of their country's history, they are only dimly conscious of the early colonization of parts of the Southwest by people of Hispanic-Mexican origin. Or, if they know about it, they are inclined to shrug it off as a quaint accident of history without consequence."[1]

The story of the West from an eastern viewpoint naturally begins with the exploits of men like Lewis, Clark, Pike, and other forerunners of the American westward movement. This leaves a gap of more than two centuries between the modern Anglo-American period and the Spanish explorations of Vásquez de Coronado, Juan de Oñate, Diego de Vargas, Juan Bautista de Anza, and many others who reconnoitered and explored in this order much of what is now the state of Colorado. Many topographical features were named by these early explorers as they opened the trails which others followed centuries later. The Spaniards traveled north from outposts in the province of New Mexico, while the Anglo-Americans pushed from the midwest on trapping and fur-trading expeditions which eventually extended into the Spanish settlements. Since Anglo-Americans are more interested in the westward movement of their own frontiersmen, readers are more concerned with the exploits of these men than with the history that predates the American occupation of the Southwest. As a result, there is the impression that the American frontiersmen, known variously as Mountain Men, Traders, and Trappers, discovered an unknown land. Such expressions of primacy as "the first white man to cross the Rocky Mountains" and "the first white baby born in the west" overlook the long period of Spanish history of the Southwest.

Don Francisco Vasquez de Coronado was the first Spanish explorer to cross part of the territory from which Colorado was formed. When this conquistador and a detachment of his army marched along the Cimarrón in quest of the mythical Quivira in 1540, he was opening the way for many others like him who became more familiar with the eastern portion of the state in the years that followed. As Barnaby Thomas says: "His Odyssey to Quivira initiated on the plains a long procession of Spanish explorers. Their history furnishes the needed perspective with which to view the activity of the Anglo-American—i.e., the last phase of western plains exploration."[2]

The dream of fabulously rich cities and the treasures of Quivira that led Coronado's expedition over the Southwest was a disappointment which produced a lull in northern exploration for four decades. The Spanish frontier moved north from Mexico, however, as new mining sites like Zacatecas, Durango, and Parral were discovered. By 1580, the northern settlements had reached the headwaters of the Conchos River and opened a much shorter approach to the New Mexico region than the one Coronado used in 1540. One of the first aspirants to plan an expedition into the "unknown North" was a Franciscan missionary named Agustín Rodríguez. He obtained permission in Mexico City to form a party with which to explore the land of the Pueblos mentioned by Indian captives taken in punitive campaigns. Fray Rodríguez and two other Franciscans were escorted by a squad of soldiers and their commanders, Francisco Sánchez Chamuscado. The small party journeyed down the Conchos into the Río Grande and then followed this historic stream north as far as the Manzano Mountains of central New Mexico, east of the present city of Albuquerque. Their enthusiastic report of the country they had visited was an incentive to larger expeditions which penetrated deeper into the new land and reached closer to what is now Colorado. The explorers of each succeeding attempt used the experience of preceding expeditions as a springboard to further exploration.

The next explorer into the Southwest was Antonio de Espejo, a rich citizen of Mexico, who in 1582 also followed the Conchos trail with 12 soldiers; one of these, Miguel Sánchez Valenciano, brought along his wife and three young sons. After some difficulties arising from conflicting interests, three friars joined the expedition. Part of Espejo's mission was to ascertain the fate of the three other friars who had accompanied Sánchez Chamuscado the year before. At Puaray, he confirmed what everyone had already surmised, that the priests had been murdered by the Indians. Espejo was particularly interested in mines. The information he received from the natives pointed west; had there been some indication that there were mining deposits to the north, it is quite likely that what is now Colorado would have been visited much earlier by Spanish explorers. As it turned out, Espejo went as far north as the pueblo of Jemez and also probed in the vicinity of Santa Fe.

"A short cut to glory," as one historian puts it, was taken by Gaspar Castaño de Sosa in 1590 with an expedition of 170 people, including women and children. He traveled up the Pecos River and went as far as Taos, New Mexico, where he was arrested and brought back to the Spanish settlements. The expedition that followed this interrupted attempt started as an official raid against rebellious Indians in 1594, but the leaders, Francisco Leyba de Bonilla and Antonio Gutiérrez de Humaña, moved by reports of northeastern wealth, decided to do some explorations of their own, northeast of New Mexico. They reached the Arkansas and probably continued as far as the Platte. A quarrel between the two leaders led to the death of Captain Leyba at the hands of Humaña. There was no journal kept of this expedition since it was unauthorized, and more important, because of the tragic end of the entire party, with the exception of an Indian named Jusepe who fled and was held captive by the Apaches for a year. He escaped and made his way to one of the Pecos pueblos where Oñate found him in 1599.[3]

Humaña had gone beyond New Mexico into Kansas along the Arkansas, but whether he touched upon what is now Colorado soil is a matter of conjecture. The tragic ending of this expedition has given rise to the idea that since these Spaniards died without benefit of clergy, they were souls lost in Purgatory, a theological error which produced the name of the river in southern Colorado, *Las Animas Perdidas de Purgatorio*. Whether Leyba Bonilla and Humaña crossed this river or not, the folklore which surrounds it did crisscross it and produced not only the name of *Purgatorio* for the stream, but also *Las Animas* for a county and a city in Colorado. If we consider that Colorado was, until 1861, a part of the Kansas territory, it can be safely asserted that some of these expeditions did cross the state at that point in time.

Don Juan de Oñate, settler and Governor of the Province of New Mexico, was another of the early Spaniards who touched upon lands of which Colorado was a part during the first decade of its existence. In 1601, Don Juan led an expedition consisting of "more than seventy men . . . all very well equipped, more than seven hundred horses and mules, six mule carts, and two carts drawn by oxen conveying four pieces of artillery, and with servants to carry the necessary baggage . . ."[4] according to the "true account of the expedition. . . ." The army crossed the Pecos River and the Canadian farther east, following a northeastern direction until they reached the Arkansas. This seemed to be the usual travel route used by early explorers who still were guided by thoughts of Quivira. Oñate also passed through the land out of which Colorado was carved centuries later by following a route closer to the southeast corner of the state.

The first expedition to penetrate what is now Colorado was led by Juan de Archuleta in 1664, when he was sent to retrieve a group of malcontent Taos Indians who had run away to El Cuartelejo in eastern Colorado. Archuleta took with him 20 soldiers and a force of Indian auxiliaries, and he brought the Taos Indians back. This brief statement is the only description given of a perilous trip over mountain and plain where the hostile Apache and Comanche roamed, and which probably took about six weeks to accomplish. In all probability, the Archuleta party went north from Santa Fe by way of Taos, entered the plains by way of Trinidad or Walsenburg, and crossed the Arkansas near the present site of Pueblo. This can be adduced from other expeditions and from a study of the terrain. From there, Archuleta and his party probably turned east to the Cuartelejo in the Apache country and found the Taos Indians he had been sent to retrieve. From then on, Colorado's streams, mountains, and peaks became familiar sites for the Spaniards to explore.

By the middle of the seventeenth century, the Spanish settlers of northern New Mexico had become well acquainted with the territory north of Taos and southern Colorado. When Diego de Vargas led an expedition into what is now Costilla county in 1694, he spoke of rivers and mountains by names which were familiar to him and his army. Spanish expedition leaders entering unknown country, usually named the topographical features as they crossed them, but the fact that Vargas did not bother to name the rivers, mountains, and peaks which he used as landmarks for his route clearly indicates how familiar he must have been with the terrain.

After the reconquest of 1692, the Spaniards in Santa Fe were hedged in by surrounding hostile Indians who had thoughts of attacking the garrison and destroying the colony like they had done in 1680. Two years after the reconquest, the supplies the colonists had brought from the south and those which they had gleaned from abandoned granaries were at a dangerously low level, with no immediate relief in sight. Diego de Vargas, in conference with some experienced natives of the land, decided to venture out in search of food among the abandoned Tano and Tewa pueblos. In his roundabout journey, trying to avoid contact with the hostiles who surrounded him, he went by way of the "Yuttas" (Utes), a friendly nation where he could come out on the

Chama River and find buffalo. He placed the train between a vanguard of 40 soldiers and a rear guard of 30 more well-armed veterans. His route carried him north to Arroyo Hondo, past San Juan where he crossed the Rio Grande and followed the Chama to Caliente Creek and San Antonio Creek successively. He was attacked by a combined party of Taos and Picuries, but they were no match for the army. They camped along the Culebra River in present-day Costilla County, where the Utes mistook them for Tewas and attacked. The mistake was rectified, and the Utes explained that they had attacked Vargas because the Tewas and the Picuries went into Ute country disguised as Spaniards and even carried a bugle. On the way back, the Vargas expedition found a large herd of buffalo that supplied them well with much-needed meat. They also hunted elk and other game before returning to Santa Fe on July 23, 1694, after having been gone for 17 days and traveling about 350 miles.[5] Don Diego de Vargas Zapata Luján Ponce de Léon, Governor and Captain General of New Mexico journeyed to southern Colorado 82 years before the United States came into being.

Governor Don Francisco Cuervo y Valdez of the province of New Mexico received word from Don Lorenzo, chief of the Picuries who had fled to El Cuartelejo in 1696, stating his people's desire to return to Picurís. The Spanish Governor sent Juan de Ulibarri, a seasoned veteran, with 40 soldiers and 100 Indian allies to retrieve the fugitives in 1706. Unlike his predecessors, he didn't go to El Cuartelejo by way of the Canadian, but traveled north to Taos, hence to the location of today's city of Trinidad, crossed the Purgatoire, which he named the *Santa Ana* River, and reached the Arkansas after naming every stream and river along the way. He crossed the Arkansas, christened *Río Grande de San Francisco,* about 15 miles from the site of present-day Pueblo. He was so impressed by the valley that he made an entry in his journal describing it: "The plain on our side is a strand of a long league of level land and extremely fertile as is shown by the many plums, cherries, and wild grapes which there are on it.... It bathes the best and broadest valley discovered in New Spain...."[6] Twenty days after leaving Santa Fe, Ulibarri reached his goal on August 2, 1706. The Apaches were not hesitant in returning the Picuries, and within ten more days, they were ready to return.

Before beginning the long journey south at a time of the year when they were certain to run into early winter snows, "General Juan de Ulibarri, sergeant-major of this kingdom," as he called himself officially, decided to take formal possession of the land which he named "the broad new province of San Luis." His journal entry reads in part:

> The Reverend Father Fray Dominguez de Aranz... intoned the *Te Deum Laudamus*.... After these holy ceremonies were over, the royal Ensign Don Francisco de Valdez drew his sword, and I, [Ulibarri] after making note of the events of the day and hour on which we arrived, said in a clear, intelligible voice: "Knights, Companions and Friends: Let the broad new province of San Luis and the great settlement of Santo Domingo of El Cuartelejo be pacified by the arms of us who are the vassals of our monarch, king and natural lord, Don Phillip V—may he live forever." The royal Ensign said: "Is there anyone to contradict?" All responded, "No." Then he said, "Long live the king! Long live the king! Long live the king!" and cutting the air in all four directions with his sword the Ensign signaled for the discharge of guns. After throwing up our hats and making other signs of rejoicing, the ceremony came to an end.[7]

With this colorful ceremony, in the year of 1706, the region which is now Colorado became part of the Spanish Empire in America, 70 years before the new republic of the United States was born. Both the name of San Luis, now transferred to southwestern Colorado, and the Ulibarri family name have come down to the present day as a continuance of the state's early Hispanic origin.

There were three reasons why the Spaniards of the seventeenth and eighteenth centuries made long expeditions into Colorado. One was to punish Indian raiders or to bring back fugitives and captives from El Cuartelejo; the second was to scout for indications of French incursions into Spanish territory; the third reason was to search for possible mines. They looked upon the French traders as intruders who were trying to occupy the territory of Spain by inciting the Pawnees and the Comanches, who entered the Spanish domains for the first time in 1704, to attack the Spanish settlements.

Early Spanish Contacts with Colorado

In carrying out the above objectives, the Spaniards used three routes into Colorado. When they went to El Cuartelejo after fugitives or to repulse the incursion of the French, they headed north from Santa Fe and then east to the Culebra Mountains. They turned northeast to the Purgatoire and hence to the eastern plains. When they were prospecting for minerals, they usually went north to the La Plata Mountains, sometimes as far as present-day Gunnison and into the Great Basin past the present state line. Thirdly, they used a more direct route north through Taos to the present San Luis valley, as Vargas did in 1694.

The expedition of Governor Don Antonio Valverde Cosío in 1719 against the Comanches was a much larger force than the one taken by Ulibarri 13 years earlier, but it was directed toward the same Cuartelejo where the Comanches usually attacked those Apache tribes like the Jicarillas who were friendly to the Spaniards. Valverde started from the presidio of Santa Fe on September 15, 1719, with 60 presidials. In Taos, he opened ranks for volunteers to join the expedition and increased his force by 45 settlers and 465 Indian allies. He enlisted 196 more Indians from the Jicarilla Apaches along the Cimarrón, bringing his command to about 800 men, including regulars, militia, and Indian allies. He also had a combined total of more than 1,000 horses, not including pack animals. With this strong force, Valverde marched north, crossed the Purgatoire, renamed it *Las Animas,* and by this name the river was known for more than 70 years. It appears on Escalante's map that was undoubtedly prepared by his cartographer, Bernardo de Miera y Pacheco in 1778; the name *Las Animas* is also used by Juan López in his map of 1795.

Valverde did not follow the difficult trail of Ulibarri, because he had a large enough force to repulse any attack by the Comanches and the Utes. He moved northward through the location of present-day Dillon and Trinidad, crossed the Huérfano River, and proceeded to a point below the Arkansas southeast of Pueblo. For several days, Valverde followed cold Comanche trails and campfires until he met the messengers from El Cuartelejo, announcing the coming of the Apaches. The latter were eager to talk to him about protection from the hostile Comanches and Pawnees. After a long meeting several miles east of La Junta, he decided to start back before the winter set in. The Apaches told the governor about the alliance of the Pawnees and the Jumanos with the French, the armaments they used, and the imminent danger of being attacked.

Valverde's journal is an interesting and valuable document filled with human interest and with details of what they did en route, which reveal a great deal about Spanish culture and Indian life. He mentions having come to an Apache camp where the fields of corn and squashes were growing and how he cautioned his men not to tread on the field and damage the growing crops. When he met with Indians, he always shared his food with them, even to the point where he offered his own plate of mutton when Chief Carlana arrived at dinner time.

Valverde's diary is interspersed with anecdotes about meeting with bears, lions, and other fauna of the region. He was very well impressed by the abundance of game, fish, and plant-growth along the trail, although their experience with poison ivy and the men's reactions to its painful effects was not exactly pleasant. The governor's proclivity for naming every stream he crossed, even renaming those which already had been named, and the exclusive use he made of Saints' names is somewhat tiring. He also must have been a very religious man, to judge by the number of masses that were held along the way, even when pressed for time. Unfortunately, the part of the diary which tells of his return trip has been torn off, and so historians have to conjecture the route he followed. Valverde did mention that he did not return by the plains, which meant that he could return by the only alternate route—following the Arkansas to the Huérfano River and then crossing over the Sangre de Cristos to Taos. The inference is well taken by Barnaby Thomas, who assumed that the Governor returned by way of Taos and then south to Santa Fe.

The report of Valverde to the Viceroy in Mexico City that there were French establishments on the South Platte was very disquieting. He sent orders to establish a presidio at El Cuartelejo with a complement of 25 soldiers and some missionaries. The object of this fort was to hold back the advance of the French from the Platte to the Arkansas and possibly even to the Rio Grande. Governor Valverde preferred to establish an outpost on the Canadian in the rancherias of the friendly Jicarilla Apaches 100 miles from Taos. In the meanwhile, the Governor sent a reconnaissance expedition which would also be able to attack the French and their allies in case they met with them.

Pedro de Villasur left Santa Fe in July 1720 with a well-equipped army of 42 soldiers, 3 settlers, and 60 Indians. The now familiar route to Taos was followed by the expedition to the Cimarrón and northward to Trinidad and Walsenburg. They crossed the Arkansas below Pueblo and continued to El Cuartelejo. They did not tarry here because their object was to contact the French who were beyond Colorado in Nebraska. The army came to the South Platte and found no Frenchmen there, and so they crossed over to the North Platte and decided to look for the Pawnees who were allies of the French. Not far above the junction of the North and the South Platte, they found a large encampment of hostile Pawnees who rejected all overtures made by Villasur. The following morning, before sunrise, Villasur and his expedition were encircled by fierce Pawnees who poured a deadly fire into the Spanish camp and almost wiped out the expedition. The amount of gunfire, in addition to the Pawnee arrows, convinced those who escaped that there were Frenchmen in the attack. It was a setback to Spanish arms which at the time seemed almost fatal. The Spaniards had not only contacted Colorado again but had crossed it from south to northeast, albeit with disastrous results.

Governor Tomás Vélez Cachupín of New Mexico was greatly interested in exploiting the mineral resources of the province. Rumored mineral deposits in the region northwest of Santa Fe led him to send several expeditions into what is now southwestern Colorado. In 1765, he sent Juan María de Rivera into San Juan and Gunnison country with a prospecting party; encouraged by Rivera's reports, he sent two more parties, the last one in 1775. After several months of prospecting along the San Juan River and its tributaries, Rivera reported promising gold and silver discoveries. He crossed the La Plata Mountains to the Dolores River and penetrated north to the Gunnison River, where he carved the date and his name on a cottonwood at the mouth of the Uncompahgre.

Historians assume that not only Rivera but other Spaniards must have prospected throughout the southwest Colorado region, to judge by the names they gave to the mountains and streams, names that have come down to the present day. La Plata, which means "Silver" was given to both mountain and stream because silver was found there. Such river names as *Animas, Mancos, Florida, Los Pinos,* and the *San Juan* itself date back to the Spanish period of exploration around the time that Washington was fighting the British. These excursions also served to prepare men like Andrés Muñiz and Joaquín Laín, who served later as guides to the Escalante party in 1776.

The next explorer to penetrate into Colorado on the way to California was Silvestre Vélez de Escalante who came to New Mexico in 1768 and became interested in a joint project which Father Garcés had proposed when he was working in Arizona. Actually, the Escalante expedition grew out of the interest which the Jesuits had manifested in joining the province of New Mexico with California. Garcés had already accompanied Juan Bautista de Anza when they pioneered the first overland route to California from Tubac, Arizona.

The Escalante expedition consisted of the nominal head, Fray Francisco Atanasio Domínguez and eight men, including the map maker Don Bernardo de Miera y Pacheco, who was "to make a map of the land they might go through." Escalante's plan was to avoid crossing the chasm of the Grand Canyon by traveling through the friendly Ute territory. He left Santa Fe on July 29, 1776, and went directly to Chama; he crossed what is now the Colorado–New Mexico border on August 5, in the vicinity of the Navajo River. He followed the Navajo to the junction of the San Juan near Pagosa Junction describing this country as having "leafy forests of white poplars, low oaks, cherry trees, apple trees, citron (lemon) trees and cacti." He was in Colorado from August 5 to September 11, entering north of Dulce, New Mexico, and coming out below the Dinosaur National Monument on Highway 40. As was customary when Spaniards traveled over uncharted territory, Escalante named a few places along the way. Like his predecessor Ulibarri, he gave a complete description of the country he traversed and pointed out various locations where he felt settlements could be established and where farming could be successfully undertaken, observations which years later materialized. Coloradoans may derive great satisfaction from knowing that the scenic beauty of the state did not escape the observant eye of nature-loving Spaniards like Father Silvestre

Vélez de Escalante long before tourism became a significant economic factor in the state.

A man who deserves to be remembered in the history of Colorado is Don Juan Bautista de Anza, Governor of New Mexico from 1777 to 1788. He was a second generation *criollo* from a distinguished Spanish family in Sonora. Among other things, he pacified the Indians of that state and later founded the city of San Francisco. One of the first problems which he had to face in New Mexico was the constant forays of the Apaches, the Utes, and particularly the powerful Comanche nation, who attacked the weaker tribes and wiped out Indian pueblos and Spanish settlements alike when they needed horses and slaves for trading purposes.

When he became Governor of New Mexico, he was confronted with the Comanche problem, to which he gave the utmost priority. After training an army of 600 mounted soldiers, Governor Anza moved north through the San Luis Valley, defeated the rear guard of the Comanches, and engaged the main body of warriors south of Pueblo at the foot of Greenhorn Mountain. The Spanish army retrieved a considerable amount of property, more than 100 horses could carry, according to Anza, and completely routed the Comanches. Most of the important chiefs were taken prisoner and the leader, the vaunted Cuerno Verde, or Green Horn, whose depredations had been the scourge of the Southwest, perished in the encounter. As a reminder of de Anza's successful expedition, a town, a river, and a mountain peak in Colorado bear the name of his Comanche adversary whom he admired for his daring and valor, but the irony of fate is such that Anza's name has been reserved for motels instead! The confrontation of the Southwest's leading Indian chief and the Spanish commander was also reported by the popular muse in a historical play entitled *Los Comanches* where the encounter is reenacted to the present time and the final battle recorded in heroic verse. For almost two centuries, the play resulting from this battle, as well as three landmarks in Colorado, attest to the struggle of Indian and European for the hegemony of the Southwest.

Governor Anza understood the Indian problem in the Southwest better than most Spanish commanders who came in contact with the aborigines. He realized that the way to solve the problem was not simply by waging war, although he first had to gain their respect by conquest, a pattern common among the Indians. Once having done this, he set out to make peace not only between Indian and Spaniard but among the Indians who were constantly on the warpath against each other. First, he managed to bring the Utes and the Comanches to terms, and these two traditional enemies buried the hatchet. Knowing that the Comanches were the most powerful and most able fighters, he brought the principal chiefs to Santa Fe after the battle and had them received with great honors and a fiesta. A few years later, he brought together the Comanches in Pecos north of Santa Fe and entrusted the successor of Cuerno Verde with keeping the peace in the Southwest, an honor which Ecueracapa readily accepted. A trading fair followed during which a schedule of prices was set in order to protect the Indians who did not have a good sense of material values. The next step in order to remove the constant threat of the plains was to resettle this warring tribe by making agriculturists out of semi-nomads. Unlike his predecessors, Anza did not set out to punish his adversaries by executing them or by enslaving them. He was one of the few, perhaps the first, Spanish commander who tried to help the Indians and the settlers by insuring peace among them.

In order to resettle this warring nation, Anza set aside some land on the Arkansas, provided the Indians with seed to plant, plows, and all the necessary implements, as well as people who could teach them how to farm. Later, at the request of the Jupe Comanches, he sent 30 Spaniards from New Mexico to help them build houses for their new village of San Carlos. It was the first resettlement project in Colorado and, in a sense, the first unrestricted Indian reservation. Unfortunately, when Don Juan returned to his hacienda in Sonora, the Comanches also left the village, fearing that they could not enjoy the same guarantees under other Spanish leaders; they were probably right, for Colonel Anza was unique among the Spanish *conquistadores*. The fact that Juan Bautista de Anza was a second generation Spaniard, a *criollo* who was not planning to return to Spain where he could live in the splendor of his *conquistador* laurels, but an American who was willing to share the land and its resources with the original inhabitants, may have been the reason why he was successful in dealing with the Indians. If we add to these circumstances the fact that he was a man of great integrity and courage, his unusual leadership may be better understood. Colorado does well in claiming as part of her history an early American who left such a positive record for posterity to remember him by.

Soon after American independence was won, the Anglo-Americans began to "cast covetous eyes," as one writer puts it, toward the West. The incentives were many: riches in gold and silver extracted from mines by Spaniards, trapping for pelts along the virgin streams, trading with the citizens of far-off Santa Fe, and the acquisition of land were motivating drives in the minds of the Yankees. The land along the Mississippi had been ceded to Spain by the French in 1763, and so men living within the boundaries of the Louisiana territory were already in Spanish land. If they continued to move west into New Mexico and Texas, they would not be entering a different country. This changed after 1800 when Louisiana was ceded back to France.

The relatively easy journey to Santa Fe in 1773 by John Rozee Peyton, who was the first Anglo-American to enter the city from the east, would not have been so easy if it had been attempted 30 years later. One difficult barrier that stood in the way of trade and travel was the large number of Indian tribes that inhabited and roamed over the prairies between United States territory and the Spanish frontier. In the struggle for supremacy along this frontier, the Indian was often a pawn whose interests could be served by the quality and quantity of gifts bestowed on him by the French, the Anglo-Americans, and the Spaniards.

The official expeditions sent by the U.S. Government, such as those headed by Lewis and Clark and Zebulon Pike, indicated to the Spaniards the ultimate intentions of the newly formed republic. What they failed to grasp was the degree of aggressiveness of the Americans moving upon the western frontier. In an effort to sound the intentions of the French and of the Anglo-Americans, Spain sent expeditions north and east into Colorado and Texas. All military parties were ordered to enlist the cooperation of such tribes as the Comanches, the Pawnees, and the Kiowas. In order to accomplish this alliance, large quantities of presents and medals, the larger the better, were taken along to be distributed among the tribal chiefs. The Anglo-Americans and the French gave the Indians arms and ammunition as presents, tactfully strengthening their relations with tribes who were ambivalent about the Spaniards.

One of the pioneer pathfinders employed by the Spanish Governor in Santa Fe was a French interpreter and gunsmith named Pedro Vial whose first mission was the opening of a trail from San Antonio to Santa Fe in 1786. For two decades, Vial, who usually traveled alone, wrote his reports and diaries in poor French which had to be translated into Spanish, crossed over unchartered territory to Natchitoches, St. Louis, and the rest of the Spanish Southwest, including Colorado. He was at home with Utes, Comanches, Sioux, Pawnees, and particularly with all tribes with which he had to deal in carrying out his missions for the Spanish Government.

On October 14, 1805, Governor Joaquín del Real Alencáster of New Mexico sent Pedro Vial on an expedition to the Pawnees with a set of instructions detailing what he was to accomplish. The expedition was to spend the winter with the Pawnees and "to inform himself of the progress of the Anglo-Americans in Missouri...."[8] Vial was to learn all he could about the Lewis and Clark expedition and also to win the friendship of the Pawnees and other Indians of the region.

Vial's party left Santa Fe in October 1805 and traveled north by way of Taos, where he enlisted 50 more recruits. He continued in a northeasterly direction and crossed both the Vermejo River and the Colorado, which today is called the Canadian. The expedition penetrated into what is now the state of Colorado and followed Las Animas River, as the Purgatoire was called by the Spaniards, until they reached the junction with the Arkansas near the present location of the city of Las Animas. Had Vial been a Spaniard, he would have referred to the Arkansas by its Indian name of Napestle or by the longer Spanish appellation of Rio Grande de San Francisco.

They were met on the north side of the Arkansas by a band of more than 100 unidentified Indians who refused the expedition's peaceful overtures. The Indians attacked at midnight, pillaged their provisions and the implements they had brought for presents. After a series of running attacks, the Indians withdrew;

the Spanish party decided to return to Santa Fe because they were running low on ammunition. Several significant features about these Indians were mentioned by Vial. They were heavily dressed, they had no arrows, they were mounted in battle, and they all used firearms. Loomis and Nasatir conclude from these data that the affair had "all the earmarks of an American-instigated attack!"[9] The Vial party sustained only one casualty; one soldier was wounded in the leg. There seems to be a discrepancy in the report of the battle in that Vial spoke of the enemy having 100 men when they first met, but after the battle he said that "notwithstanding the fact that their force was three times the size of ours, [they] started to withdraw." This number of Indians would mean that they had 300 warriors to his 100 soldiers. Pedro Vial and his men were among the last to enter Colorado on official business of the Spanish Government. His associate, Juan Lucero of Santa Fe, continued successfully on many solo expeditions at the suggestion of Governor Alencáster who was well pleased with his performance.

In 1806, Lucero and an interpreter named Martin were sent to meet with the Comanches at the confluence of the Almagre (the Fountain River today) and the Arkansas. His mission was to win the cooperation of the Comanches and also to enquire about the activities of the Anglo-Americans who were moving into Spanish territory. He continued his travels into Indian country as an emissary of the Spanish Government and was probably the last person during the colonial period to make official contact with what is now Colorado.

The first period of Hispanic history in the state ends with the activities of Carabineer Lucero and Pedro Vial, the Frenchman who was in the service of the Spanish Crown for the last 20 years of his life. Together they opened new trails to Santa Fe, fought Indians defensively, and helped to open the way unintentionally for the commerce of the prairies that became eventually a connecting link between the settled Hispano-Mexicans of the Southwest and the incoming Anglo-Americans.

Notes

[1] L. Grebler, J. More, and R. Guzman, *The Mexican American People,* (New York: The Free Press, 1970), p. 6.
[2] Alfred Barnaby Thomas, *After Coronado* (Norman: University of Oklahoma Press, 1935), p. 5.
[3] Herbert Eugene Bolton, ed., *Spanish Explorations in the Southwest* (New York: Barnes and Noble, Inc., Reprinted, 1967), p. 20, fn.
[4] Bolton, *Spanish Explorations,* p. 251.
[5] J. Manuel Espinosa, "Journal of the Vargas Expedition to Colorado," *Colorado Magazine,* 16 (no. 3, May 1939), 81-89.
[6] Thomas, *After Coronado,* p. 18.
[7] *Ibid.,* p. 69.
[8] Noel M. Loomis, and Abraham Nasatir, *Pedro Vial and the Roads to Santa Fe,* (Norman: University of Oklahoma Press, 1967), p. 431.
[9] *Ibid.,* p. 436, fn. 25.
[10] Ralph Carr, "The Sangre de Cristo Grant," *The Brand Book,* Official organ of the Westerners, 3 (no. 7, July 1947), p. 5.

2 The Dominguez-Escalante Expedition of 1776

Leroy R. Hafen

Colorado is unique in having in 1976 both a bicentennial and a centennial celebration. She joins her sister states in commemorating the bicentennial of the Declaration of Independence of our country; alone she celebrates the centennial of her own statehood. The year also marks the bicentennial of a famous exploration venture into Colorado and adjoining states. This remarkable tour is generally known as the Escalante Expedition, but it should more properly be called the Dominguez-Escalante Expedition.

It was one of the great explorations in United States history. Comparable in extent and significance to the famous tours of Lewis and Clark and Zebulon Pike, it occurred some 30 years before these two expeditions. It was a journey of some 2,000 miles into new territory, most of which had never before been seen by white men. It revealed the western area of Colorado, nearly all of Utah, and large sections of Arizona and New Mexico. We do well to celebrate the bicentennial of such an important achievement.

Some of the southern and eastern sections of Colorado territory had been previously penetrated, but none of the explorations had been so far ranging or revealed so much of our own area as did the one led by the Spanish padres in 1776.

Spain was indeed the great pioneer in opening the Americas, North and South. She not only discovered America, but expanded from the West Indies and Mexico southward throughout South America, and northward into the present-day United States. This occurred within 50 years of Columbus' first voyage to the New World. The great Coronado expedition of 1540 was lured into the mythical land to the North, and it entered the southeastern tip of Colorado in 1541.

At the end of the sixteenth century, Spain occupied New Mexico, and soon her daring sons were exploring Colorado's domain. Ulibarri proclaimed possession of southeastern Colorado land in 1706; Villasur crossed Colorado's eastern plains to the Platte River in 1720. Even in the generally unknown land of western Colorado, there were minor explorations by Rivera and by traders to the Utes by 1765. But not until 1776 was the big survey undertaken.

Special conditions set the stage and lured hardy souls. In 1598, Spain occupied New Mexico, which for over 150 years was the northernmost province of Spain's empire. Spain had also gradually pushed up the Pacific Coast of North America. Spain had also expanded across the Pacific and conquered the Phillipine Islands in 1565. She established a trade route from these islands to Mexico, a route which ran with the Japan Current and the prevailing winds northeastward to the 1,000-mile string of Aleutian Islands and to the coast of Alaska. Then the trading ships—the Manila galleons—followed the west coast of North America southeastward to Mexico. This very long voyage was beset with the terrible scourge of scurvy, which decimated the crews of the galleons. There was need for a port of call and refreshment on the California coast.

In the meantime, the Russians, in pursuit of furs, had pushed across Siberia, along the Aleutians, and to Russian America— Alaska. Spain was alarmed for the security of her title to New Spain, which she had explored and claimed as far north as the Oregon country. In response to the two pressing needs, an outpost for the Manila galleons on the California coast and a block to the Russian threat to Spanish territory, Spain exerted herself and founded outposts in California, beginning with the first mission at San Diego in 1769.

Spain had difficulties in establishing her California missions. The Indians were unfriendly, agriculture was slow in developing, and supplies were brought with great difficulty in the small boats over stormy seas from Mexico. It was suggested that it might be easier to obtain supplies by land from Arizona-Sonora or from the old and well-established province of New Mexico. In addition, the Church leaders saw, in the unknown land enroute, a field rich for the harvest of converting Indians to Christianity.

Accordingly, the proposal for opening a route from New Mexico to California was authorized and launched.

Two Franciscan friars were chosen to lead the venture—Atanasio Dominguez and Silvestre Vélez de Escalante. Father Dominguez was the superior in ecclesiastical rank and the titular head of the expedition.

The second in command was Silvestre Vélez de Escalante. Historians writing in English have mistakenly assumed that the last term in certain Spanish names is the surname, and have uniformly called the man Escalante.[1] A similar error has been made in calling the exploratory tour the "Escalante Expedition." The journey was under joint leadership, and should not be called after the name of the junior partner. The diary was written in the first person, using the personal pronoun "we." It has been assumed by some that Escalante was the principal diarist, but of this there is no certainty, as both signed the original document, and the name of Dominguez appears first.

There seems to be some justification for the preeminence that Escalante has received heretofore from historical writers. He was the first of the two expedition leaders to reach New Mexico, coming in 1774. Being sent at once to Zuni, in this far-western outpost of New Mexico, he soon learned about the Zunis and their neighbors, as well as the geography of the region. Early in 1775, the Governor of New Mexico wrote to him asking for information regarding possible communication westward to California. To obtain further data, Escalante rode westward on horseback and reached the Hopi villages in late June of 1775. There, from a visiting Cosnina Indian he learned of the Cosnina village in Havasupai Canyon, the course of the Colorado River, and something about other Indians of the region. The hostility of the Hopis and of Indians west of them convinced him that a journey in that direction to California would be impracticable. This information he reported to his ecclesiastical superiors and to the Governor in a letter of October 28, 1775.[2]

Father Dominguez, Mexican-born friar, was sent by his church superiors to New Mexico; he arrived at Santa Fe in March 1775. He was given a threefold assignment: to inspect the missions of New Mexico, survey the archives of the province, and seek a route from New Mexico to California.[3] He immediately began work on his assignments, surveying the Santa Fe Archives and completing his inspection of the missions. His report was sent to Mexico City, filed in the archives, and promptly forgotten. It was discovered 150 years later by Professor F. V. Scholes, who hailed Father Dominguez as one of the most important historians of eighteenth century New Mexico.[4] This is, of course, in addition to his role as an explorer.

By April 1776, Dominguez was ready to push the project for opening a trail from New Mexico to California. He sent to Escalante, then at the Indian village of Zuni, an order to come to Santa Fe to assist in the undertaking.[5] The information already gathered by Escalante in the Zuni region would be of great value, and so he came readily, eager to aid the project.

Silvestre Vélez de Escalante, born in Spain in 1750, had become a Franciscan at age 17; he came to New Mexico in 1774. Almost immediately sent to Zuni, he had quickly learned about the people and the region, as already related.

Upon meeting in Santa Fe, the two friars found that in knowledge and abilities they complemented each other. Dominguez was 36; Escalante, 26. Both men were eager for adventure, and they lost no time in preparing for the expedition.

Before the preparations were completed, they received a letter from Father Francisco Garcés. This far-ranging Franciscan had made explorations from Sonora to California in 1774–1775; early in 1776, he traveled up the Colorado River to the Mohave villages and thence eastward to the Hopis in northeastern Arizona. From this point, he wrote a letter to the mission leader at Zuni, sending it thence by an Acoma Indian. Escalante had already been recalled to Santa Fe, but his successor at Zuni forwarded the letter to the religious leaders at the New Mexico capital and also a fuller report from interviews with the messenger who carried the Garcés letter. These gave Dominguez and Escalante full descriptions of the hostile treatment Garcés had received at the hands of the Hopis and a description of physical difficulties on the route Garcés had followed eastward to the Hopi village.[6] This reenforced the information Escalante had himself obtained from the Hopis and convinced Dominguez and Escalante that a more practicable route to Monterey, California, would be north of the more hospitable land of the friendly Ute Indians. Traders with the Utes had already broken trail for some distance northwestward from Santa Fe, and so the first miles would offer no serious difficulties.

While the line between ecclesiastical and governmental authority was rather thin in eighteenth-century New Mexico, it can be said that the famous expedition of 1776 was primarily an ecclesiastical venture, being directed and led by churchmen. It received administrative aid from the Governor of New Mexico, however. Supporting the joint Franciscan leaders were eight civilians, among whom were Captain Miera, engineer and mapmaker of the expedition, and several men who had previously gone as traders over a part of the intended route. The company was equipped with mounts, pack animals carrying supplies and a few cattle as provisions on the hoof.

The expedition set out from Santa Fe on July 29, 1776, in the same month and year when great events were transpiring in the city of Philadelphia on the East Coast. The first day of travel (nine leagues, about 23 miles) took the little exploring party through several Pueblo Indian villages and to Santa Clara, near the site where Oñate had made the first white settlement in New Mexico in 1598. The second day, another nine leagues brought them to Abiquiu, farthest settlement on the New Mexico frontier.[7]

After a solemn Mass and final adieus the company traveled up the general course of the Chama River and continued a northwest course that brought them on August 5th to the present border of Colorado and a little below the junction of the San Juan and Navajo Rivers. Here Miera, with his astrolabe, took the first astronomical observations of the trip, and doubtless the first ever taken in Colorado. His measurement of 37° 51' was nearly a degree beyond the true latitude.

On August 7th, the padres reached Rio de la Piedra Parada (River of the Standing Rock)[8] and recorded in their diary: "Here is a large meadow which we called San Antonio. It has very good land for crops, with opportunities for irrigation and everything else necessary for a settlement—firewood, stone, timber and pasturage, all close at hand."⁹ Continuing on to the Pinos River, they found this region, below present Ignacio, also good for a settlement.

After crossing the Florida and the Animas (about four miles below Durango), they reached the La Plata River, and wrote: "It rises in the same west end of the Sierra de la Plata and flows through the canyon in which they say there are veins and outcroppings of metal. But although years ago several persons came from New Mexico to examine them by order of the Governor . . . and carried away ore, it was not learned with certainty what metal it was. The opinion formed previously by some persons from the accounts of various Indians and of some citizens of this kingdom that they were silver mines, caused the mountain to be called Sierra de la Plata [silver]."

Near the site of Mancos, the party was delayed by rains and by the illness of Father Dominguez. They traveled north of the plateau of Mesa Verde and apparently were unaware of the remarkable prehistoric ruins there that were later to make the region famous.

Upon reaching the principal bend where the Dolores River turns northward, the party rested a day; the padres wrote: "On an elevation on the south bank of the river in ancient times there was a small settlement of the same form as those of the Indians of New Mexico, as is shown by the ruins which we purposely examined."

The canyon cut by the Dolores River in its northward course soon induced the party to detour to the west. After traveling northwestward on August 14 for about 17 miles, they entered a craggy canyon which led them northward. Following it for five miles, they came again to the Dolores River, near the mouth of Narraguinnep Creek and east of the town of Cahone. During the afternoon, the party was joined by two Indians, Felipe and Juan Domingo, who had fled from a Ute village. Juan had lived in Abiquiu and was a *genízaro,* that is, an Indian who had been purchased or captured from a hostile tribe and settled among the Spaniards.

The next day, the explorers climbed from the Dolores canyon onto the plateau at the west and took a northwestward route generally paralleling the course of the river. At night, they camped at *Agua Tapado* (Covered Pool), near the site of Egnar. The next morning, the Spaniards continued along a northwest route; in a broad canyon, they discovered a hidden pool of water—*Agua Escondida.* Miera, pushing ahead along the canyon, reached the Dolores, and he returned to the main camp by midnight.

On August 17, the party followed a broad trail through this winding canyon and by mid-afternoon reached the Dolores River for the third time. Here they found recent signs of the Utes. They thought that perhaps these Indians could direct the whites to some practicable route northward if they could find the red men's camp. The main party moved slowly down the bed of the river two or three miles the next day, while scouts explored the plateau above the canyon.

Failing to find a practicable route, the party continued five miles down the river to Gypsum Canyon, on August 19. To go farther along the river bed seemed impossible. Explorations of the plateau on both sides of the canyon brought discouragement, for they found the land was not only rugged, but also dry. Any water holes along the route would probably be empty. The diarists wrote: "We conferred with the companions who had traveled through this region as to what direction we might take to avoid these obstacles, and everyone had a different opinion. So . . . we put our trust in God and our will in that of His Most Holy Majesty. And, having implored the intercession of our Most Holy Patrons in order that God might direct us in the way that would be most conducive to His Holy Service, we cast lots between the two roads and drew the one leading to the Sabuaganas."

Accordingly, on August 20 they turned from the Dolores River at Gypsum Canyon and traveled eastward. They were making an abrupt change in the course of their route. Thus far, their trail had led uniformly on a northwest course some 300 miles from Santa Fe. Now they forsook their intended route and turned to the east to seek an Indian guide.

They traveled northeast to the San Miguel River and then followed its general course eastward. On the twenty-third day, they met a Tabehuache Ute. The diary relates:

> We gave the Indian something to eat and to smoke, and afterward through an interpreter we asked him various questions concerning the land ahead, the rivers, and their courses. We likewise asked him the whereabouts of the Tabehuacnes, Muhuaches, and Sabuaganas. . . . We asked him if he would guide us to the rancheria of a Saguagana chief said by our interpreter and others to be very friendly toward the Spaniards and to know a great deal about the country. He consented on condition that we should wait for him until the afternoon of the next day. . . .
>
> August 24. Before twelve o'clock the Yuta reached the place where we were awaiting him, accompanied by his family, two other women and five children. . . . They thought we had come to trade, and therefore they had brought tanned deerskins and other articles for barter. Among other things, they brought dried berries of the black manzanita. . . . We gave food to all of them, and the wife of our guide presented us with a little dried venison and two plates of dried manzanita berries, which we paid for with flour. After midday we gave the Yuta what he requested for guiding us; that is to say, two hunting knives and sixteen strings of white glass beads.

After going eastward, they crossed the Uncompahgre Plateau and on August 26 "reached the banks and meadows of the Rio de San Francisco, by the Yutas called Ancapagri [Uncompahgre] (which according to the Indian interpreter means Laguna Colorado) because near its source there is a spring of red water, hot and bad tasting.[10] In the meadow of this river, which is large and very level, there is a very wide and well-beaten trail. We traveled downstream a league and a half to the northwest and camped near a large marsh with very abundant pasturage which we called La Cienega de San Francisco," a little south of present Montrose.

They followed down the Uncompahgre River on the 27th, complaining of the hot sun, and camped in a meadow in a shady grove of cottonwoods.

Farther downstream and about four leagues to the north of this meadow of San Agustin, this river joins another and larger one which is called by our people Rio de San Javier and by the Yutas, Rio del Tomichi [Gunnison]. In the year '61 Don Juan Maria de Rivera reached these two rivers below their junction, having crossed the same Sierra de Los Tabehuaches, on whose crest according to the description which he gives in his diary, is the place he called El Purgatorio. The meadow where he halted in order to ford the river, and in which he says he carved on a second growth cottonwood a cross, the characters which spell his name, and the year of his expedition, is also found at the same junction on the south bank, as we were assured by our interpreter Andrés Muñiz. The latter said that although at that time he had stopped three days' journey before reaching the river, he again came past here along its bank in 1776 with Pedro Mora and Gregorio Sandoval who had accompanied Don Juan Maria on that entire expedition. They said that they had gone clear to the river then and from it had begun their return. Those two were the only ones who crossed it, having been sent by the said Don Juan Maria to look for Yutas on the bank opposite the meadow where they were camped and from which they turned back. And so this was the river they then thought was the great Río del Tizón [Colorado].

Continuing northeastward, they reached and crossed the Gunnison and ascended its north fork. The first Utes encountered here tried to turn the Spaniards back, saying they would come into the country of the Cumanche Yamparicas who would kill them.

On the 30th, the interpreter Andrés Muñiz brought in five Sabuaganas and one Laguna; the latter was from the "Timpanagotzi, or Laguna Indians, to whose country we now planned to go," the diary recounts. With presents of a woolen cloak, hunting knife, and some white glass beads the Laguna promised to guide the explorers to his home country at Lake Timpanagotzi (Utah Lake, Utah).

On September 1, "about eighty Yutas all on good horses" came out from their village, apparently to impress the Spaniards, who then followed to the Indian village. Father Dominguez, with interpreter Muñiz, "entered the chief's tent, and having greeted him and embraced him and his sons, he begged him to assemble the people who were there. He did so, and when as many of either sex as could come had assembled, he told them of the Gospel through the interpreter . . . the Father proposed to the chief who at this time ruled the ranchería, that if on conferring with his people they should accept Christianity, we would come to instruct them and arrange for them a mode of living to prepare them for baptism." The Father exhorted them to have no more than one wife. He "bought from them a little dried buffalo meat, giving them glass beads for it."

Despite the Sabuaganas' further urging that the Spaniards turn back, the latter insisted on continuing. They induced the Laguna to go as their guide, and he was joined by another Laguna boy. The padres' party now moved to the north, then traveled northwestward over difficult terrain and finally on September 5 reached the Colorado River, some distance above present De Beque.

According to the diary:

> We arrived at a river which our people call San Rafael and which the Yutas call Río Colorado. We crossed it and halted on its north bank in a meadow with good pasturage and a fair-sized grove of cottonwoods. On this side, there is a chain of high mesas, whose upper half is of white earth and the lower half evenly streaked with yellow, white, and not very dark colored red earth. This river carries more water than the Río del Norte. It rises, according to what they told us, in a great lake which is toward the northeast near the Sierra de la Grulla. Its course along here is to the west-southwest, and it enters the Río de los Dolores. At the ford it is split into two channels. The water reached above the shoulder blades of the animals, and some of them which crossed above the ford swam in places.

After ascending and crossing the Roan Plateau, they reached on September 8 the head of Douglas Creek. The diary relates:

> Half way down this canyon toward the south there is a very high cliff on which we saw crudely painted three shields or

chimales and the blade of a lance. Farther down on the north side we saw another painting which crudely represented two men fighting. For this reason we called this valley Canon Pintada. It is the only way by which one can go from the summit mentioned to the nearest river, because the rest of the intervening country is very broken and stony. On the same side of this canyon near the exit a vein of metal can be seen, but we did not know the kind or quality, although one companion took one of the stones which roll down from the vein, and when he showed it to us Don Bernardo Miera said it was one of those which the miners call *tepustete,* and that it was an indication of gold ore. On this matter we assert nothing.

At the mouth of Douglas Creek, near present Rangely, they reached the White River, which the Spaniards called the San Clemente. After pushing northwestward from the river for about three leagues, they came to a plain marked by "trails of the buffalo which come down to winter in this region." The next day, excitement mounted as the fresh trail was discovered and a buffalo was seen. Men were dispatched "on the swiftest horses and having chased it more than three leagues they killed it, and at half past seven at night returned with a large supply of meat, much more than comes from a large bull of the common variety. In order to prevent the heat from spoiling it for us, and at the same time to refresh the animals, we did not travel on the 12th, but camped at this place, which we named Arroyo del Cíbola [buffalo]."

They had just crossed, on September 11, the Colorado-Utah state line of today. Our present purpose does not call for a detailed report of the farther course of the great Dominguez-Vélez de Escalante expedition. But a brief account of the journey may be of interest.

A short day's travel on the 13th brought the party to Green River, which they called Río de San Buenaventura (Good Fortune River). They crossed a little above present Jenson, Utah, pushed westward and ascended the Uinta River. They crossed the Wasatch Mountains, descended Spanish Fork Canyon (named for them), and entered Utah Valley. Here they visited and preached to the Laguna Indians beside Utah Lake, near Provo, Utah.

After pushing southward, the explorers encountered, near present Minersville in central Utah, heavy snow storms, which induced them to consider giving up further travel westward into the barren and unknown country.

The proposal to turn back to New Mexico was favored by the padres, but was vigorously opposed by Captain Miera and other civilian members of the party. It was a momentous decision to make, and only a resort to prayers and to reliance on chance or Divine intervention by casting lots broke the deadlock and brought a decision to turn back to Santa Fe.

A hindsight view enables us to look at the modern map with its great desert stretches and mountain ranges to be crossed. We can also see the difficulties that were to be encountered by Jedediah Smith when 50 years after the Spanish padres' venture he succeeded in opening a route by way of the Virgin and Colorado Rivers and the Mojave Desert to California in 1826. The next year, he opened a shorter but more difficult one across middle Nevada. Peter Skene Ogden discovered the Humboldt River in 1828; six years later, Joseph Walker opened a path to California along the Humboldt River route. Hindsight also shows the terrible tragedies that emigrant parties suffered, however—the Donners in 1846 and the Death Valley parties in 1849, when they, like the Spanish padres, attempted to reach California.

Altogether, it appears clear today that the Spanish explorers of 1776 did well to turn back from the Minersville decision point. The padres did not suffer a terrible fate. They lived to tell their story.

In returning to New Mexico, they chose a shorter route to the south. After reaching the Virgin River of southern Utah, they turned eastward across northern Arizona, skirted the Kaibab Plateau and finally were able to swim to the Colorado River at the Crossing of the Fathers (named for them) above present Glen Canyon Dam. From there, they traveled south to the Hopi towns, eastward to Zuni, and finally reached Santa Fe on January 2, 1777. They had completed a 2,000-mile journey in about five months.

The story is in their diary. It is an important record of travel in western America 200 years ago. Hardly a turn in their trail is unrecorded, with distances, directions, and topography carefully given. Streams, creeks and arroyos, mountains and plains, shrubbery and trees are described in detail, and special reports are given of areas of land where streams and soil were suitable for the founding of settlements. But, contact with wild Indians was limited—none was encountered during the first 30 miles of travel from Santa Fe. Only one major village of Utes, on the Gunnison River, appears to have been contacted in Colorado.

The diary is also notable for its omissions. There is no report of hunting deer, rabbits, or other game, except for the final killing of one buffalo. A large collection of beaver dams is described, but there is no mention of trapping or killing beaver. The main fish mentioned are a few killed with arrows by their Indian guide. How many beef cattle did they take along? What difficulties occurred in driving them or in butchering them? The preparation of food, enjoying meals or going hungry, and becoming tired or footsore go unreported. Perhaps the austere life to which the padres were accustomed had inured them to concern over creature comforts.

How different in these respects is this diary when compared to those kept by fur trappers or emigrants who traveled the early West after them. However, an overall comparison of the padres' diary with those written by other travelers gives it a high place.

The purpose of a diary helps to explain its character. The padres were not making a pleasure tour or writing a diary to lure or to entertain possible future travelers. They set out to examine an unknown land, to test the possibilities of travel through it, the practicality of founding settlements enroute, and the feasibility of converting the Indian inhabitants to Christianity.

In making a general appraisal of the Dominguez-Escalante expedition, it must be admitted that it was not a complete success. They did not open a trail all the way to California, but they did traverse a very large part of the distance, and they revealed for the first time very substantial areas of the American West. We are greatly indebted to them; their service to history and geography in America was immeasurable.

Notes

[1] Instead, this last term applies to the place of birth of the man or his father, rather than being the proper name. This error has persisted so long in the literature that it seems inadvisable to change it now. The same practice in regard to Francisco Vásquez de Coronado and to Garcez Lopez de Cárdenas, notable historical figures, seems to justify the policy.
[2] Herbert E. Bolton, *Pageant in the Wilderness: the Story of the Escalante Expedition to the Interior Basin, 1776* (Salt Lake City: Utah Historical Society, 1950),p. 2. See also Eleanor B. Adams, "Fray Silvestre and the Obstinate Hopis," in *New Mexico Historical Review*, 38 (April 1963): 97-138. A translation of his journal reporting the trip to the Hopis is on pages 119-138.
[3] These developments are related by Dr. Ted Warner in "The Significance of the Dominguez-Velez de Escalante Expedition" in Charles Redd Monographs in Western History, No. 5, edited by Thomas G. Alexander, *Essays on the American West, 1973-1974.* (Provo, Utah: Brigham Young University, 1975), p. 63-80.
[4] This report is found in Eleanor B. Adams and Fray Angelico Chavez, translators and editors, *The Missions of New Mexico, 1776: A Description by Fray Francisco Atanasio Dominguez* (Albuquerque, New Mexico, 1956).
[5] Ted Warner, "The Significance of the Dominquez-Velez de Escalante Expedition," p. 68.
[6] These letters are published in Adams and Chavez, eds., *Missions of New Mexico,* p. 238-85.
[7] When I visited the pueblo in 1951, it was changed but little from its condition in 1776.
[8] The mountain top projection that gave its name to the river is now known as Chimney Rock. In the vicinity, the State Historical Society of Colorado excavated important archeological ruins some years ago.
[9] Bolton, *Pageant in the Wilderness,* p. 138. This and subsequent quotations from the diary are taken from the Bolton translation.
[10] This would be the spring and pond a little north of the town of Ouray, Colorado.

3   The Adams-Onís Treaty of 1819

José de Onís

The Transcontinental Treaty, better known as the Adams-Onís Treaty or the Florida Treaty of 1819, was the first international agreement signed by the United States embracing an entire continent from the Atlantic to the Pacific. This agreement involved the longest border concerned in any negotiation since the founding of the North American republic, and as stated by Philip Coolidge Brooks in his excellent work, *The Adams-Onís Treaty of 1819,* it marked the end of the first wave of territorial expansion with her first treaty title to land on the Pacific Northwest.

In some respects, the treaty was favorable to Spain. It ceded the two Floridas to the United States, but in exchange it recognized Texas as a Spanish territory, which had been in dispute since the Louisiana Purchase in 1803. And what was more important, it established a definite frontier between the United States and Mexico. Prior to this time these territories had been considered as the Spanish northern borderlands and their boundaries had never been clearly established. For the first time, there was a clear-cut division affecting the territory made up of what is the present-day state of Colorado.

Unlike the later treaty of Guadalupe Hidalgo, which came after a disastrous defeat, the Transcontinental Treaty came out of a Spanish position of moderate strength. The Spanish ambassador, Don Luis de Onís, was a seasoned diplomat, well qualified for the task. The United States had not yet recuperated from the War of 1812 with England. The Mexican liberals and their allies, the North American volunteers, were temporarily stopped at the Battle of Medina in 1813, clearing the Internal Provinces of any subversive action for the time being. Onís had hoped that by giving the colonies a well-defined border line on the north it would discourage the restless adventurers who were infiltrating from the States and would relieve the tensions created by the numerous disputes over the question of boundaries.

The Internal Provinces were an immense territory about as large as the rest of Mexico itself. Its northernmost province, New Mexico, in those days embraced more than it does now. Its capital was Santa Fe, and its main radius of action, from Saguache on southward to El Paso, was the entire valley of the Rio Grande. There also was some activity in the eastern foothills and in the plains as far north as present-day Pueblo. This section was by far the most progressive of the entire territory. The Spaniards had been here since the sixteenth century and were by now well established, but its northernmost fringes were little known or explored. On the western slopes of the Rocky Mountains the Escalante trail crossed much of the Colorado and Utah territory, and intercourse with the Utes and other northern Indian tribes was frequent. On the northeastern plains, the Santa Fe trail to Saint Louis had been in existence since Pedro Vial's trip of 1792. More recently, there had been several expeditions into what is today the State of Colorado: Pedro Vial's expedition to the land of the Pawnees in 1805 and Juan Lucero's expedition to the Kiowas in the same year. Vial had been sent to find the source of the Arkansas River, but he succeeded in getting only as far as its junction with the Río de las Animas, from where he returned to Taos after Indians had stolen his supplies.

The line of demarcation as established by the 1819 Treaty still left two-thirds of what is today the State of Colorado within the Spanish Territory. It remained thus, first Spanish and then Mexican, until 1848, when under the Treaty of Guadalupe Hidalgo, the present-day frontiers of the United States were definitely established. The 1819 boundaries started on the Gulf of Mexico, at the mouth of the River Sabine in the sea, continuing north along the western bank of that river to the 32nd degree of latitude; then a line due north to the Red River, along it to the longitude 100, and then due north to the Arkansas River, to its source in the west; it followed the eastern slopes of the Rockies to the 42nd latitude, and from there the line was drawn directly west, following the present northern border lines of the states of Utah, Nevada, and California to the Pacific.

The location of the course of the Arkansas was not clear. For this reason, it was stated in the Treaty that if the source of the Arkansas River should be found to fall north or south of latitutde 42, "then the line shall run from the said Source, due South or North, as the case may be, till it meets the said Parallel of Latitude 42, and then along the said Parallel to the South Sea." A commissioner and a surveyor were to meet at Nachitoches, before the termination of one year from the date of the ratification of the treaty, to ascertain the latitude of the source of the said River Arkansas and to determine the exact whereabouts of the line of latitude 42 to the Pacific.

Much haggling took place over whether the boundary was to be on the north or south bank of Arkansas or should follow the center. Samuel F. A. Bemis in his book, *John Quincy Adams and the Founding of the American Foreign Policy,* stated that as they approached the end of the negotiations, only one-half the width of the boundary rivers separated the two contestants for a continent. The disagreement between Adams and Onís had become personal. "The Cabinet was excited, trembling for success of the negotiation. The President was nervous, alarmed, eager to meet Spain in midstream." At a reception given by President Monroe on the evening of February 18, he shook hands most cordially with Onís. "I will do anything you want," stated the President. "I have had a personal esteem for you ever since the first day I dealt with you. Have a glass of wine with me."

These complimentary expressions of politeness in answer to a remark made to President Monroe by the Spanish Foreign Minister were interpreted as an agreement to make the boundary the south bank of the river. Onís did not lose any time before writing home that all was reconciled, but not without the resentment of Secretary Adams, who, according to Bemis, "could not forget the shame of having his ultimatum destroyed in all its points." Adams resented the fact that Onís had gone over his head to the President, which he considered an unconventional procedure. He did not press the point, however, when it finally came up in the last Cabinet meeting before the signing of the Treaty. Don Luis de Onís, on the other hand, felt that his position had been vindicated and he now could be more magnanimous about the whole affair; therefore, out of his own volition, he graciously agreed, at the last moment, to the south bank of the river as a boundary. The final version of the agreement read as follows: "All the Islands in the Sabine and the said Red and Arkansas Rivers, throughout the course thus described, to belong to the United States; but the use of the Waters and the navigation of the Sabine to the Sea, and of the said Rivers, Roxo and Arkansas, throughout the extent of the said boundary, on their respective banks, shall be common to the respective inhabitants of both Nations."

Onís' intent was that the boundary would follow the natural geographic boundaries formed by the River Arkansas and the foothills of the Rockies. He believed that the United States represented a real threat to the entire Hispanic World and he wanted the boundaries between the two countries to be defensible. In his two volume *Memoir* on the negotiations between Spain and the United States which led to the Treaty of 1819, Onís states that: "Americans now believe themselves superior to all the nations of Europe, and that it is their manifest destiny to extend their domination immediately to the Isthmus of Panama, and later to all the regions of the New World." He did not want to lose the advantage of establishing the limits to the west of the Mississippi. He was against creating neutral ground along the border, which he believed would only provide sanctuary for lawless adventurers. In a letter from Washington, dated February 3, 1819, to his son Mauricio Carlos, he states:

> Yo me he quedado admirado de ver lo presentes que tiene [el Marqués de Casa Irujo] hasta los mas miserables riachuelos, pero aun está en una cosa equivocado y es en que cree que será mejor que suscribir a una línea desventajosa, dexarla pendiente. Aunque sea dar hasta el Istmo de Panama, es preferible a dexar de fixar una sola pulgada, y esto es lo que aquí se desea para ir tomando todo lo que se les antoje. Nada de país baldio o despoblado que no pertenesca a nadie, y nada que no se señale terminantemente, para evitar disputas en lo sucesivo.
>
> Ahora, si se hace el tratado y no se empieza a poblar y a guarnecer las fronteras, nada se adelanta, pues los piratas fijaran allí su residencia ya sea en Galveston, La Trinidad, Pasa Caballo o Matagorda. Las tropas de La Florida deben enviarse inmediatamente a aquellos puntos, y procurar a

ellos una población distribuyendo tierras, que son soberbias sobre todo en el río de Trinidad.

Many vested interests of the Spanish-speaking inhabitants of the territory were taken into account.

The Adams-Onís Treaty provided for the free exercise of all religions.

The inhabitants of the Territories ceded to the United States by the Treaty were to be incorporated into the Union of the United States, as soon as it was consistent with the principles of the Federal Constitution, and "admitted to the enjoyment of all the privileges, rights and immunities of the Citizens of the United States."

All the land grants made prior to the twenty-fourth of January, 1818, by the King or by his representatives, were to be validated "to the same extent that the same grants would be valid if the Territory had remained under the Dominion of His Catholic Majesty." Onís had suggested that any land grants which might be ruled out by this provision could be replaced by lands in Texas or on the south bank of the Arkansas, which remained assured to the Crown, and which were of infinitely better quality, and in a better climate.

There were three types of land grants to be honored: communal land grants or *ejidos,* belonging to a community or town; personal land grants, *mercedes,* which the King or his representatives bestowed on some individual in compensation for services rendered or simply just to favor him; and contract land grants, charts awarded to an individual or company that assumed the responsibility of colonizing and defending a given territory.

To protect the new frontier, Don Luis de Onís recommended awarding land grants to an individual or a land company which agreed to populate the region with Catholic colonists who would become Spanish citizens. Proclamations advertising for agriculturists and other bona fide artisans were circulated in Switzerland and other Catholic countries. The land was to be given free, exempt from taxes. The new citizens were to enjoy freedom of commerce, inside and outside of the Spanish provinces. The municipal administrators were to be elected by popular vote. Conditions of climate and soil were described as ideal. There were, according to these brochures, "from eight to nine feet of top soil."

It was said that numerous North American families were waiting for the treaty to be ratified so that they might move into Spanish territory. One of these was Moses Austin, who had already enjoyed living in Missouri when that region was a Spanish Territory. There were, no doubt, many Frenchmen and Anglo-Saxons who had fared well under the Spanish rule. In March, 1804, therefore, when the Spanish flag was lowered from the staff in Saint Louis and the new American administration was installed, some of its more aristocratic citizens must have looked nostalgically toward the Spanish provinces of New Mexico and Texas. Among them was the family of Charles de Lássus, Lieutenant Governor of Louisiana during the Spanish regime; he was the uncle of Ceran Saint Vrain, who years later immigrated to Taos, New Mexico, and who was to contribute so much to the development of northern Colorado during the early years of the nineteenth century. He is remembered today as the founder of Fort St. Vrain; the North and South St. Vrain Rivers just north of Boulder were also named after him.

Another group at this time said to be interested in immigrating to the Spanish provinces was made up of the Napoleonic exiles in America. It consisted of about a hundred men under the command of Generals Lallemand and Rigaud. Their motives were not always clear, but they professed to be Royalists, faithful to the Spanish Crown. At first, it was difficult for Onís to believe that men who had so long pursued a military career could resign themselves to a peaceful existence. He could not make up his mind who represented the greatest danger, "the French adventurers or the grasping Americans." For a time, he held out the possibility of their employment in the Spanish royal service "if they would be willing to live peacefully and defend the Spanish dominions in America." The French venture, however, never did materialize, primarily because of the well-founded suspicions of Apodaca, the Viceroy of Mexico.

In the region of the Arkansas River, trappers also were invited to come into the region with the condition that they teach their trade to the native population. Here the soil was not as promising as it was in Oklahoma or Texas, but grazing was excellent, and some New Mexicans did answer the call to the new frontier. The Bartolome Baca grant, which included parts of northern New Mexico and southern Colorado was reconfirmed during this period.

Many of these trappers, whether they came from Illinois or Kentucky, had already come in contact with Spanish culture and had partially accommodated themselves to Spanish ways. In Missouri, the fur trade had flourished under the Spanish system of monopolies, and it continued to prosper after restrictions were removed. The Spanish had had little success in controlling the Osage Indians until Rene Auguste Choteau and his relatives were awarded exclusive trading privileges and built a post among them. From here, the Spaniard Manuel Lisa, a legendary figure who did more than anyone else to explore the region of the upper Missouri River, made several attempts to establish contacts with New Mexico. In 1804, Lisa and his partners in the Missouri Fur Company sent Jean Baptiste Lalande to Santa Fe with a load of merchandise. It seems that Lalande sold the goods but failed to return with the profits. In 1807, Lisa, in conjunction with a Portuguese named James Clamorgan, sent still another expedition to New Mexico. Clamorgan for a time had been very much interested in building a fort on the Platte River, and once made a petition to this effect.

The Spaniards officially had been in Missouri since the Treaty of Paris of 1763 to 1800, when Louisiana was secretly returned to Napoleon, and then unofficially until 1803, when the French sold it to the United States. All told, they were there 34 years—an entire generation that was to see the town of Saint Louis change from a small frontier village to a respectable city. During this time, Spain employed many Frenchmen to help administer the vast territory she had acquired. They in turn became imbued in the ways of Spanish culture, often acquiring Spanish given names, as in the case of Pedro Vial, who originally was called Jean Vial. Many of these immigrated to Santa Fe and later returned to northern Colorado as Mountain Men.

Chronologically, Onís appears on the American scene when Missouri no longer belonged to Spain but when many of its

Spanish antecedents were still very much in existence. Caught between the Spanish provinces of Missouri and New Mexico, Colorado was to become the heartland of what some historians have called the "Adobe Empire."

Don Luis de Onís' task had been an arduous one. After what must have seemed to him endless clever debates and much quibbling over details, the Treaty was finally signed at eleven o'clock in the morning of February 22, 1819.

It was with Onís that John Quincy Adams was to conduct the most important negotiation of his career. "On Onís," states Bemis, "fell the duty of watching over the complicated and arduous relationships of the Republic of the North with Spain's revolted provinces in the New World, and fighting with the Secretary of State a rear-guard diplomatic campaign for defense in North America of the dissolving Spanish Empire, responsibilities to task the ablest head and bow the broadest shoulders."

Indeed, part of his task in preparing the agreement had been to prevent the United States from intervening in the struggle for independence which was starting to unfold in Mexico and in South America. This, of course, included the Internal Provinces, the Spanish Territory most immediate to the United States. Here there were two prominent individuals whose names appear repeatedly in Onis' correspondence: José Bernardo Gutiérrez de Lara and José Alvarez de Toledo. The first of these two came to New Mexico to enlist support for Father Miguel Hidalgo's revolt; and later after Hidalgo's death in Chihuahua, in 1811, remained to become one of the leaders of the revolt in Texas. A man of considerable spiritual resources, he made a trip to Washington, where he visited President Madison. Onís, who was keeping tabs on all of Gutiérrez' moves, reported to the Spanish Viceroy in Mexico that Gutiérrez, after a meeting with Secretary Monroe, was dismayed when he realized that they wanted to use him for their own plans and that American aid might prove to be as dangerous as Spain itself. It seems that the adjustment of the Louisiana boundary, made to include the entire Province of Texas, was made a prerequisite by Monroe for military aid.

The other, José Alvarez de Toledo, Marshall of the Northern Mexican Revolutionary Army, was a more complicated personage and one who was to plague Don Luis for the rest of his existence. He had first come to the United States, claiming to represent the Spanish American delegates to the Cortes of Cádiz, to promote the independence of Cuba and the other Caribbean islands, but was persuaded instead by Washington to go to the Internal Provinces and become the leader of the revolt there. Subsequently he was appointed by Morelos, Marshall of the Northern Mexican Revolutionary Army. He finally was defeated by Arredondo and the Royalists' forces on August 18, 1813, at the battle of Medina. This was six years before the signing of the Transcontinental Treaty, but it placed Spain in a favorable position as far as the Internal Provinces were concerned.

After the independence of Mexico in 1821, many of the same frontier policies established by Onís were continued. The great Mexican historian, Carlos Pereyra, called Luis de Onís "un americanista genial." After this, Mexican land grants were also awarded to individuals of French and Anglo-Saxon origins who were Catholics and naturalized Mexican citizens. Some of these grants were in the State of Colorado, as is described in following chapters. But Onís knew that, in the long run, the terms of the Treaty would not stop North American expansion. The boundaries in the Southwest were approved by Mexico in her treaty of January 12, 1828, but they were not ratified until 1831. In the meantime, President Jackson had hoped to acquire Texas for the Union. No successful surveys were made for many years, as was stipulated in the Treaty. As far as Colorado is concerned, large parts of the territory remained abandoned until gold was discovered in 1859. It is interesting to note, however, that many of the state lines in the South and Southwest in the United States are those that were established by the Transcontinental Treaty of 1819. Colorado is the exception, a fact which might be explained because Colorado was created arbitrarily out of the New Mexican and Kansas Territories.

In his last days, when he was the Spanish Ambassador to England, Don Luis writes nostalgically to his son Mauricio, "I know I will receive no recognition for the part I have played in the Treaty of 1819, because I have been labeled a Jacobite and a liberal by my conservative enemies, but if some day they want to compensate me for what I have done they can just call me Don Luis de Onís of the Sabine and the Arkansas."

Selected Bibliography

Bemis, Samuel Flagg. *John Quincy Adams and the Foundation of American Foreign Policy.* New York: Alfred A. Knopf, 1949.

Brooks, Philip Coolidge. *Diplomacy and the Borderlands: The Adams-Onís Treaty of 1819.* Berkeley: University of California Press, 1939.

Onís Papers. The family archives, including records and letters not only of Luis de Onís, but also of his son Mauricio Carlos de Onís, who also was a diplomat. A good example of the letters written by Luis de Onís is one from Philadelphia, Feb. 14, 1812; published in Blanco y Azpurúa, *Documentos* III, 608. Onís' letters were published at different times in: *Gaceta de Buenos Aires,* 1810-1821; *Mercurio Chileno,* 1811-1813; *El Argos,* 1821-1823. Fray Melchor Martínez published the "Avisos de Don Luis de Onís" in his *Revolución de Chile,* p. 42. Mier discusses these letters in *Memoria político-instructiva,* pp. 121-122.

Luis de Onís' memoir first appeared in Spanish under the title *Memoria sobre las negociaciones entre España y los Estados Unidos de América, que dieron motivo al tratado de 1819. Con una noticia sobre la estadística del pais. Acompaña un apéndice que contiene documentos importantes sobre el asunto,* Madrid, 1820. It was translated into English in Baltimore, 1821, *Memoir upon the Negotiations between Spain and the United States of America, which led to the treaty of 1819* by Luis de Onís. Translated with notes by Tobias Watkins. The following year, the *Memoir* was refuted by H. S. Forsythe, Minister of the United States to Spain in a pamphlet entitled *Observaciones sobre la Memoria del Señor Onís relatives a la negociación con los Estados Unidos* (translated by Father Thomas Gough). In 1826, Ward published the *Memoria* in Mexico, and it was with the purpose of counteracting its effects that Poinsett wrote the *Exposición de la conducta política de los Estados Unidos,* México, 1827.

Pereyre, Carlos. "Un americanista genial (Luis de Onís)." In *Unión Hispano-Americana* III (1919), No. 38: 2-3.

4 Spanish and Mexican Land Grants in the Southwest*

Harold H. Dunham

Some authorities on pioneering settlements in North America seem to believe that Spanish and Mexican land grants are either not very important or that there is nothing new to be said about them. For example, the projected 18-volume series on the American frontier now in the course of publication has not provided for a separate treatment of the grants. Yet I am convinced that they justify further study and more complete treatment than they have yet received. There is a need for a fresh and comprehensive, if not also an up-to-date, account of land grants in New Mexico and certain other states. In addition, a thorough analysis of similarities and differences in grant systems and methods throughout the Southwest could prove valuable. Although the land grants of Florida, Louisiana, and Missouri lie beyond the scope of our present topic, they should be included in any larger analysis of grants. In short, the subject offers various opportunities for the dedicated and interested scholar.

My review of certain highlights of the land-grant story of the Southwest is divided into four parts. The first sketches the Spanish policies in New Mexico until 1821. The second describes developments in Texas from the early eighteenth century to the end of the Mexican period. The third considers the story of California from 1769 to the United States confirmation of Spanish and Mexican grants. The fourth reviews perhaps the most clouded segment of all, namely, land-grant activities in New Mexico from 1821 through the first half-century of United States jurisdiction. Occasionally, I will transgress these chronological limits.

It is a well-known fact that Don Juan de Oñate, first Governor of New Mexico, led his settlement party into the upper Rio Grande valley in 1598. By that time, New Spain had established a

*Lecture delivered at the University of Colorado, February 22, 1971.

system of government and methods of land distribution that were ready for implanting in the heart of the Pueblo Indian country. Earlier in the century, the Viceroys, Audiencias, and Governors of New Spain had exercised their authority in granting lands under the powers implicit in their offices. By 1578, they had obtained specific powers, under a royal cédula, to make private grants and settlement grants, the latter complete with public squares, liberties (ejidoes), reservations (propios), pastures, and commons. The cédula enjoined the officials of New Spain to take particular care in protecting the persons and property of Indians. Whenever land grants were to be given to Spaniards, "whether for tillage, pasture or other purposes," respect must be paid to Indian rights. Full treatment of how well this injunction was obeyed in New Mexico may be found in H. O. Brayer's *Pueblo Indian Land Grants of the Rio Abajo, New Mexico* (1938).

I would like to mention, however, a special feature of Spain's system of land control that Oñate introduced into New Mexico to the detriment of the Indians. This feature was the encomienda system, under which a prominent Spaniard was granted authority over a large section of land in order to care for the Indians thereon and teach them the Catholic religion. In return, this encomendero could require tribute from the Indians to assist him in furnishing men and horses to the Governor when military protection of the area was necessary. After Oñate, the Viceroy ordered the creation of 35 encomiendas for the defense of the Kingdom of New Mexico. Although the order was carried out with far-reaching effects, particularly because of abuses, the encomienda system died out in the eighteenth century, and so can be dropped from further consideration here.

Spanish settlements in New Mexico progressed slowly but steadily after Oñate, with the exception of the temporary setback caused by the Pueblo Revolt of 1680. The growth was measured by population figures for 1821, which showed about 30,000 *gente de razon* (that is Spaniards, mestizos, and Christian Indians) in New Mexico. This number of citizens meant that there had been an extension in the size and number of towns (pueblos), and villas, as well as in farming, ranching, and mining enterprises. To be sure, there were periodic modifications of procedure or authority for making land grants, as shown in the *Recopilacion de Leyes de los Reynos de las Indias* and by the establishment of the Internal Provinces under a Commandante General in 1776. Yet the fundamental methods of obtaining land grants, as R. E. Twitchell has shown, remained fairly constant for New Mexican citizens. That is to say, there were private grants to individuals and families, and to contractors who would facilitate settlements of whatever kind, and also there were town (pueblo) grants.

At this point, I might call attention to two incidental but significant items. First, unlike the system adopted for Texas later, New Mexico does not seem to have experienced the contractual or empresario type grants that marked out a large region within which settlers might obtain title to land and the empresario receive title to an amount of land proportional to the number of settlers being brought in. Furthermore, there is no certain way to always distinguish between settlement (pueblo) grants and individual grants. As an illustration of this latter difficulty, note the incident related by the twentieth-century lawyer-historian, William A. Keheler. He describes the case of an intended grant purchaser who employed two experienced land-grant lawyers, quite separately, to evaluate the same set of title papers. One of the lawyers assured his client that the grant was of the town (pueblo) type, and the other lawyer was equally positive that it was a grant to an individual. I will explain more fully later why such a contradiction could arise, while stating now that it was possible largely because of the production of partially or wholly spurious title papers.

The precise number of land grants approved by Spanish governors in New Mexico, which continued to be occupied into the post-Mexican period, is not easy to determine. According to the list of grants submitted to the U.S. Surveyor General of New Mexico by 1887, there were 103 private and pueblo-settlement grants for the period to 1821 (exclusive of Indian Pueblo grants). Nevertheless, all Spanish grants that had been approved during more than two centuries were not presented to the Surveyor General; some that were presented seem to have lapsed long before, yet had been resurrected from among old title papers in order to obtain their confirmation by the United States; furthermore, some Spanish title papers had become lost and the lands affected had been regranted to descendants of the original claimants by Mexican officials.

An example of a regrant is found in the case of Socorro. In 1817 and 1818, the Spanish Governor had approved a land grant to the town, but the title papers had subsequently been lost. About a quarter-century later, town officials petitioned the Mexican Governor, Manuel Armijo, for a new title, and on November 30, 1845, he seemingly complied. When this title was submitted to the U.S. Surveyor General in 1878 for confirmation, there was serious doubt as to the authenticity of Armijo's signature, but the Surveyor General approved the grant and ordered that a survey be made. The survey resulted in establishing boundaries which embraced 843,259 acres of land, although the identification of the boundary marks was so difficult that one witness who testified in the matter claimed that the east-west line for the grant measured approximately 100 miles, rather than the fifty-five accepted for the survey.

The U.S. Congress failed to act on the Socorro grant, and so later the town leaders petitioned the Court of Private Land Claims, which was established in 1891, for confirmation of their claim. This court recognized that a settlement had existed at Socorro for nearly two centuries, except for a brief interval, but in August 1892, it rejected the boundaries established by the Surveyor General and awarded the town four square leagues of land (17,371 acres). The land was to be held in trust by descendants of the original 70 settlers who had established the town. Thus a Spanish grant for which no title papers survived became a Mexican grant, but one which was confirmed only for an amount of land authorized under a general Spanish law for town grants.

Rather more curious, as an outgrowth of the Spanish period, is the fact that the villa of Santa Fe could produce no title papers after the United States acquired possession of New Mexico. There was no doubt that the villa had been established a decade before the English Pilgrims settled in Massachusetts Bay, or that by 1846 Santa Fe could claim about 5,000 inhabitants. In 1874 when the city's leaders applied to the U.S. Surveyor General for approval of their claim to 17,000 acres of land, they frankly stated "your petitioners do not know from record or otherwise what land, if any, was so granted to their ancestors, or the quantity thereof. . . ."

It required only three days for the Surveyor General to approve the claim for four square leagues. Yet Congress hesitated to confirm the grant, partly because there were eighteen other Spanish grants having boundaries which overlapped those of the Santa Fe grant, and so the claim was submitted to the Court of Private Land Claims and was confirmed by it in 1900. Government attorneys took exception to this decision, however, and therefore appealed it to the U.S. Supreme Court. This body adopted a stricter view of Spanish law than that taken by the Court of Private Land Claims, and held that Santa Fe was not entitled to claim any land grant. Such an alarming status for the residents of the Territory's capital was quickly rectified when Congress passed a measure, on April 9, 1900, granting the city, with certain necessary exceptions, an amount of land one league in extent, measured from a central monument toward the four cardinal points of the compass. The next year, the General Land Office issued a patent to the Santa Fe city fathers, covering 17,361 acres of land.

While Spanish governors and land policies created difficulties over land titles for subsequent United States officials, it should not be forgotten that many of those governors confronted problems arising from land claims in their own day. Out of the well-documented examples that might be selected, two must suffice. The first concerns the Baltasar Baca grant which originated in 1768 when Baca and his two sons petitioned the governor for a *grazing permit* on land located near the Zuñi road, a league and a half beyond Encinal. After the permit was approved, the Baca family settled on the land, a step which had not been authorized, and it was discovered that the land was claimed by the Laguna Indians. It was a difficult matter to resolve this conflict.

A second example is found in the controversy between two branches of the Durán y Chávez family at Atrisco, near Albuquerque, during the latter part of the eighteenth century. A recent study of this controversy "exposes some unscrupulous adventurers," and highlights problems arising from "subdivisions of land, nebulous boundaries, questionable titles, [and] costly litigation. . . ."

Now let us turn our attention to Texas and then California for résumés of Spanish land policies in each. Present-day Texas, not differing too greatly in extent from Spanish Texas, embraces approximately 171,000,000 acres of land. Effective Spanish settlement of this vast region was not begun until 1716, more than 100 years after the founding of Santa Fe, New Mexico. The buildup of population was slow, so that by the end of the period of Spanish control, the number of residents did not greatly exceed 4,000, and perhaps 1,000 of these were soldiers. These people were concentrated in the area of the villa of San Antonio, the pueblo of Nacogdoches, and the presidio of La Bahía. Of course, there were other settlements, such as those at Goliad and Laredo, as well as some near the various Spanish missions. These Texas missions, however, had practically ceased operations for Christianizing and civilizing Texas Indians before the eighteenth century ended.

According to R. N. Richardson, the governors of Texas were likely to be army officers, who, after the establishment of New Spain's Internal Provinces in 1776, were responsible to its Commandante General. Occupants of this latter office tended to follow restrictive immigration policies until 1820. Hence, Texas under Spain, unlike New Mexico, experienced only a limited amount of land distribution for town settlements and for ranching and farming to that time.

Then in 1820, the Spanish Cortes adopted a liberal policy for its dominions, in the form of a law which permitted the immigration of foreigners who would respect the constitution and laws of the nation. This reorientation of policy set a pattern which Mexico, after gaining its independence in 1821, was to follow with a great impact on settlement and land policies in Texas. It was under the Spanish law of 1820 that Moses Austin, the erstwhile Connecticut Yankee and later business failure in Missouri, was enticed to visit San Antonio in order to obtain permission for establishing a colony of 300 families. He succeeded in his quest, although he died before he could take advantage of it. However, his son, Stephen Austin, took charge and began to promote settlement on the Brazos and Colorado Rivers. Stephen encountered delays in obtaining new approval for his father's grant, following the Mexican Revolution. Nevertheless, by 1823, Mexican authorities confirmed the former Spanish grant to him.

It should be understood that Austin was an empresario or contractor whose grant was conditional, that is, he would induce heads of families to settle on land within his grant boundaries. The land titles each settler received, for which the limit was a sitio, or one square league (4,428 acres), was given the settler by a Mexican official. Austin himself was to receive title to 65,000 acres for each 200 families he induced to settle on the grant, or a proportionate amount if the number of settlers was larger or smaller than 200. For example, by 1824, Mexican officials had issued 272 titles to Austin settlers, and Austin had earned and was given 22 square leagues of land (or 97,416 acres). Note that the title to all land within his grant boundaries not taken up by settlers or earned by Austin remained in the government. Of course, he had been given a time limit for bringing in settlers.

Austin expanded his colonizing efforts—in fact, he received three more empresario grants, but they were negotiated under the general Colonization Law of Mexico of 1824 and the Coahuila-Texas state colonization law of 1825. The Colonization Law of 1824 laid down certain broad stipulations and left detailed provisions to the states. It permitted granting lands to foreigners, although there was to be preference shown to Mexican citizens, and there were special provisions for soldiers. It set a limit of 11 square leagues for each individual, and it permitted contractors to bring in families to settle on land at their own expense.

The state law of 1825 allowed heads of families to acquire a sitio of land for $30, plus survey costs; payments could be made in installments over a six-year period; empresario grants were to accord with the national law, with a limit of 23,000 acres to empresarios for each 100 families settled; and no empresario could contract to bring in more than 800 families. News of the adopton of this law brought a swarm of speculators to the state capital at Saltillo, and almost immediately the Governor signed contracts calling for the settlement of 2,400 families in Texas. Within the next four years, he awarded contracts involving a total of 7,000 families. Texas seemed to be plastered with empresario grants, but most of them proved to be only modestly successful in promoting settlement. As a matter of record, Austin induced as many immigrants to settle on his four grants as all the other approximately 25 empresarios obtained for their grants. By 1833,

Mexican officials had issued 1,055 land titles to settlers on Austin's grants, and others were issued later.

One of the state empresario grants had been issued to Hayden Edwards in the Nacogdoches area. He overreached himself by treating the settlers already residing within his grant boundaries in such high-handed fashion as to cause the prompt cancellation of his contract. Three other such grants, signed respectively by D. G. Burnet, Joseph Vehlein, and Lorenzo de Zavala, were used for a highly speculative venture. The contractors pooled their resources and, with the aid of capital obtained from the eastern United States, formed the Galveston Bay and Texas Land Company. The company sold land scrip in Europe for 7,500,000 acres at a cost of from one cent to ten cents an acre, sublet huge amounts of land to subordinate contractors, and advertised their lands widely. Of course, the scrip gave no claim to land in Texas.

Another contractor was Dr. John Charles Beales, an Englishman who had settled in Saltillo and married a Mexican girl. He obtained a grant in western Texas that originally had been assigned to S. J. Wilson, though Wilson had lost his rights because he failed to fulfill any part of his contract. Beales imported colonists in 1833 and 1835, yet he utterly failed to provide for their welfare, in what has been described as a case of criminal negligence, so that the colonists became dispersed in fear and want, subject to the hazards of Indian attacks. When the land of this grant came under U.S. jurisdiction, the claimants sought to have the Government recognize their right to 60,000,000 acres that extended into New Mexico and Colorado.

Two Irishmen, who had become residents of Matamoras, received a grant and established an Irish colony at San Patricio, on Hybernia. It was located west of San Antonio. The colony received only 84 families and could scarcely be considered a success. Farther to the west, that is, beyond the Nueces River, there were many individual Mexican grants, held by Mexican citizens who were forced to flee at the time of the Texas Revolution. It was one of these grants, the Rincón de Santa Gertrudis claim, that Richard King purchased for $300 in 1853 and began the development of his famous King ranch. He placed a standing order with his lawyers to buy adjacent land as it became available, and so he gradually acquired the derechos or rights of the original owners, although he occasionally had to repurchase land that he had bought at one time, because it had been subdivided during several generations. By the time he died in 1885, King held all or part of 15 old land grants, in his 614,140-acre estate.

The population of Texas had grown from about 4,000 in 1821 to 24,700 in 1834. Nearly 5,000 of these residents were Mexicans, 16,000 were Anglos and Europeans, and 4,000 were slaves. From 1716 to 1836, Spain and Mexico had disposed of 26,280,000 acres, or about 15 percent of the land of present Texas. After 1836, the Republic of Texas and later the state of Texas formulated their own policies of land disposal, considerably influenced by the system of the previous sovereign authorities.

Moving now to the region of California, which the Spanish began to settle in 1769, we find that the frontier institutions of the Mission, the presidio, the pueblo, and the rancho helped produce widespread though sparse occupation along the Pacific Coast. There, the 21 Missions established by the 1820s made a notable contribution to economic growth, while seeking to Christianize and civilize the primitive coastal Indians. Even though the Missions obtained extensive claims to land, they received no land titles, for they were expected to prepare the Indians for ranching and farming so that they, the Indians, could become landowners. Under Mexican jurisdiction, Mission land claims were converted to private ownership, beginning in 1834, after the Missions were disestablished.

The more lasting forms of land development sprang from the presidios, pueblos, and ranchos. Ultimately, two pueblos and five presidios were established within the region extending from San Diego to San Francisco Bay. Each of these seven centers was allowed four square leagues of land, although after the United State acquired possession of the province, neither San Francisco nor Los Angeles, like Santa Fe, New Mexico, could prove title to its claimed number of leagues. Nevertheless, it was the desire for the use of land outside of a presidio claim that gave rise to the first ranchos. The first request to be allowed to exploit vacant crown lands arose in the region of Los Angeles in 1784, when three soldiers of San Diego presented their petition for land to the Governor of California.

It might be instructive to trace the record of one of these claims, the Alamitos grant, from its origin into the latter part of the nineteenth century. Under the regulations established by Viceroy Antonio María Bucareli and the California governor of 1779, a soldier by the name of Manuel Nieto petitioned Governor Pedro Fages for the right to graze his cattle and mares on land along the San Gabriel River. The Governor gave provisional approval to Nieto's petition and then sought confirmation for his decision from the Commandante General of the Internal Provinces. A year later, the governor was informed that he might make such concessions, under the stipulation that Nieto (and others who had applied) would be limited to the use of three square leagues of land. Thus originated the Alamitos grant, which curiously enough was later found to encompass 33 leagues of land, not the three which had been specified.

Nieto completed his tour of military duty in 1795 and lived on his land until his death in 1804. His four children inherited the rancho and held it as undivided property. In 1822, after the Mexican Revolution, they obtained confirmation of the title to their claim, but 12 years later, they requested Governor José Figueroa to divide the estate among them. Perhaps they believed it wise to ensure their title under the Mexican Colonization Law of 1824 and the Regulations of 1828. Whatever their reason, in 1834 Governor Figueroa complied with their request, and so one of the sons, Juan José Nieto, was assigned a tract of six square leagues that became known as the Nietos grant. We will not endeavor to trace the disposition of the other portions of the Alamitos grant.

In the following year, Governor Figueroa purchased the Nietos grant, or rancho, for $500. He then obtained more livestock for the tract and sold it in 1842 for $6,000. The purchaser was Able Stearns, a former New Englander who had moved to Mexico, became a Mexican citizen, and then entered the merchandizing field in Los Angeles. At the time of his land purchase, Stearns was reputed to be one of the wealthiest men in Alta California. Incidentally, in 1841 he had married the 14-year-old daughter of his friend Juan Bandini. Following the Mexican War, Stearns obtained confirmation of his grant of 28,000 acres from the Board of Land Commissioners which had been established by the U.S. Congress in 1851 to review all Spanish and Mexican land grants in California. Adverse financial conditions struck Stearns in the early 1860s, however, and so he mortgaged his Nietos grant for $20,000, but he was soon forced to sell it under a court order. Further descent of title can be omitted here.

During the period of Spanish possession of California, its various governors approved somewhere between 45 and 90 grants or concessions. The total number is uncertain, as it was in New Mexico, partly because of later Mexican grants that divided tracts like the Alamitos grant of 1784 among the descendants of original grantees. Furthermore, original grantees or their descendants might sell portions of their grants through the time of Mexican jurisdiction, thus creating multiple claims before the U.S. Board of Land Commissioners. In any case, the population of California in 1822 was approximately 3,500, exclusive of Indians. These citizens occupied the Missions, pueblos, presidios, and ranchos established or acquired under Spanish law.

In turning to the Mexican period of California's history, it is unnecessary to repeat the account of the provisions of the Colonization Law of 1824, although several of the sections of the Regulations of 1828 should be mentioned. These Regulations stipulated that the governors (gefe politicos) of the territories could grant vacant lands, under the law of 1824, to Mexicans or foreigners, to contractors, to families, or to private persons. It prescribed the method to be followed in petitioning for land and required that the prior consent of the territorial delegation be given for grants to private persons or families, unless the supreme government received appropriate notice. Grants to contractors were not considered definitely valid until approved by the supreme government after it had received the necessary documents from the governor and the territorial deputation. Each applicant would be given a signed document from the governor as evidence of title, when all the necessary steps had been taken, and a record of each grant should be entered in a book kept especially for that purpose. The governor could determine a reasonable time for a settler to cultivate or occupy his lands, if his grant was to remain valid. It should be noted that there were separate provisions under Mexican law, continuing those of Spain, for obtaining rights to mineral land. A discoverer of minerals had to receive approval of his title from the supreme government, after obtaining the approval of territorial officials. And his claim might rightfully rest within the bounds of a settlement grant, for the latter type which carried surface rights only.

R. G. Cowan maintains that there was no great rush of applicants to take up vacant land under the Colonization Law and the 1828 regulations, although many claimants of Spanish concessions applied for grants to insure their holdings, as noted above in the Nieto grant story. Gradually, however, the number of approvals for new ranchos increased until, for the period 1840-1846 alone, there were 366. Lacking definite statistics for the amount of land granted under Spanish jurisdiction, we nevertheless have a total for both the Spanish and Mexican periods of 13,000,000 acres in California. There would seem to be considerable significance in the fact that of this total, 2,845,000 acres were granted to foreigners.

Some California grants did overlap with or become duplicates of others, but on the whole, it appears that considerable care was taken in carrying out the various steps necessary in apportioning land to perhaps 1,000 claimants. This statement is not meant to ignore the bogus land grants that came before the U.S. Board of Land Commissioners in the 1850s. In any case, since the largest grant recorded in California contained only 116,858 acres (the San Fernando grant, one which was sold by the Governor under special circumstances and therefore not given), the land-grant procedures in that coastal state are in striking contrast to those of New Mexico, where grants above 500,000 acres abound, in defiance of Mexican law. One further aspect of California grants is of special interest, and that is that after the secularization of Mission lands began in 1834, Indians who had been former parishioners or retainers did acquire land titles through government action. A case in point would be El Escorpión rancho of one and one-half square leagues which Governor Pío Pico granted in 1845 to three Indians from lands formerly belonging to the San Fernando Mission.

The treaty of Guadalupe-Hidalgo, which terminated the U.S.-Mexican War, stipulated that Mexican citizens, whether they chose to remain as such or to become United States citizens, would have their titles to property in the ceded area of the present Southwest duly recognized and "be acknowledged before American tribunals." After considerable debate as to the appropriate method of confirming land titles in California, the U.S. Congress passed a Land Act in March 1851, creating the Board of Land Commissioners, referred to above, which began to hold hearings in San Francisco in January 1852. The work of this Board, during the five years of its operation, in reviewing the 813 claims submitted to it, has been considered by historians to have been basically fair to claimants. On the other hand, the experts, with the exception of Paul W. Gates, have held that the provisions of the law which created the Board were unwise.

The Board confirmed 521 titles and rejected 273, while 19 were discontinued for lack of satisfactory proof. A large number of cases, either of those that were confirmed or that were rejected, were appealed to the U.S. District Court. Of the 273 rejected by the Board, 132 were so appealed and 98 won reversal, in some instances by further appeal to the U.S. Supreme Court. It should be obvious that claimants faced numerous difficulties in presenting their titles for confirmation: lawyers' fees, time and expense in appearing before the Board (especially for those whose claims lay in southern California), disputes regarding overlapping or indefinite boundaries, contests of claims by squatters who had joined the gold rush, legalistic rulings by the Board, and perhaps even delays in obtaining a patent after all other obstacles had been overcome. Expenses and delays are said to have impoverished all but a few of the claimants, and too frequently a grant had to be sold to meet the costs of the proceedings. Thus, R. G. Cleland could conclude that the system "worked gross and inexcusable injustice."

At the same time, the Board of Land Commissioners, the courts, and the government attorneys confronted an almost impossible task of preventing ingenious and reprehensible attempt at fraud, and they were not always successful. The most notorious case in which they *were* successful grew out of the claims of J. Y. Limantour, a Frenchman who had become a merchant in Monterey. He petitioned the Board for confirmation of his eight claims to a total of 600,000 acres of land. His explanation for the number and extent of the claims was that they had been given him in return for goods and loans he had furnished the Government of California. The Board did confirm two of the claims, although it rejected the other six.

The two confirmed Limantour grants were appealed by government attorneys to the courts in 1857. One of the grants covered four square leagues of land (17,200 acres) in the heart of San Francisco. At that time, the land was estimated to be worth between $10,000,000 and $12,000,000. Testimony in support of Limantour's titles was obtained from a former Mexican cabinet minister (Bocanegra, Minister of Exterior Relations), an ex-governor (Manuel Micheltorena), and even the President of Mexico (Mariano Arista). Yet despite all the favorable evidence and testimony, U.S. attorneys proved to the satisfaction of the Supreme Court that Limantour's title papers were fraudulent and stamped with a bogus seal. In rejecting the claims, the court termed them "without parallel in the juridical history of the country. . . ."

Two other cases of Mexican grants that were presented to the California Land Board deserve mention. One, the Castillero case, concerned the New Almadén quicksilver mining claim near the mission of Santa Clara, and the other, the Mariposa estate of John Charles Fremont. The Castillero case had its origins when Andrés Castillero discovered evidence of quicksilver on the rancho of José Reyes Berreyesa and then applied to Governor Pío Pico for possession of the mine. Although the power to vest property in mines rested in the Supreme Government of Mexico, Governor Pío Pico gave Castillero possession of the mine, together with 3,000 varas of land measured in every direction from its mouth. The owner promptly sold his claim in 1846 to an English group that formed a mining company, which by 1858 had extracted nearly $8,000,000 worth of quicksilver from the mine.

Meanwhile, the Board of Land Commissioners had approved the claim, but the government attorneys had appealed the case to the courts. It reached the U.S. Supreme Court in 1863, and there it came under further elaborate argument, for the government believed that certain of the title papers were false, fraudulent, antedated, and forged. In support of this belief, the Attorney General's office introduced into evidence letters that had been written during and after 1847 by an agent of the mining company in San Francisco to correspondents in Tepic, Mexico. In one letter, the agent requested the procurement of certain essential title documents and specified how they were to be worded. Such evidence convinced a majority of the Court that the claim was fabricated and therefore void. Nevertheless, three justices offered a dissenting opinion.

The Mariposa Estate came into the possession of John Charles Fremont in 1847, while he was acting as Governor of California. He purchased the claim from Juan Alvarado, a former governor, who had obtained it as a rancho of 11 square leagues through the approval of his successor, Governor Micheltorena. Indian threats and disturbances were said to have prevented Alvarado from being placed in actual possession of the land, which was to be located along the Merced River near Coulterville. After purchasing the grant, Fremont had returned east to face court martial for his defiance of General S. W. Kearny during the Mexican War. Before he could return to California, the Mariposa grant was confirmed by the Board of Land Commissioners, even though it was an inchoate grant.

The government appealed the confirmation in September 1853 to the District Court, which reversed the Board and rejected the claim. The defendants then appealed their case to the U.S. Supreme Court, where the U.S. Attorney General argued in behalf of upholding the lower court. He summarized his objections to confirmation by stating that "there had been no survey; no plan; no occupation; no site even; no confirmation by the proper [Mexican] authorities; no performance of any of the conditions precedent or subsequent annexed to the grant. . . . Such is the extraordinary pretension of paper title only." In the face of these impressive objections, the Court held, however, in 1855, through a decision written by Chief Justice Roger B. Taney, that the grant was valid and should be confirmed. Such liberality, if not irresponsibility (in my opinion) of interpretation set a precedent which held out promise to other claimants with questionable titles both in California and New Mexico.

The final section of our topic concentrates on New Mexican land grants for the period from 1821 through the efforts for grant confirmation by the U.S. Government. The Spanish system of making land grants did not change much in New Mexico in the Mexican era. Of course, the Colonization Law of 1824 and the Regulations of 1828, which have been described in connection with California, set certain new official prescriptions, but since the governors of New Mexico operated rather independently, far from central authority in Mexico City, they were the central figures in making individual and settlement grants. This is not to overlook the role of the territorial assembly, which probably was guided by the governor in its decision in land-grant matters, as well as other affairs.

The population of New Mexico for the 35-year period of 1821-1846, increased from 30,000 to perhaps 80,000. With that increase came a growth in the number and population of towns (either as the result of town grants or of town settlements on various types of grants), and an extension of the number of private grants to individuals and families. An approximately accurate figure for the total number of Mexican grants that were issued by New Mexican governors is 210.

It is more difficult to present satisfactory statistics for the amount of land claimed under Spanish and Mexican grants out of New Mexico's present 77,866,240 acres. On the one hand, it is possible to show that Congress confirmed grants which in 1887 contained 9,074,380 acres; yet this figure was substantially reduced from the acreage claimed by grant title holders, as, for example, in the reduction of the 4,000,000-acre Vigil and St. Vrain grant to 97,000 acres. To the 9,000,000-acre total just mentioned could be added the total acreage confirmed by the Court of Private Land Claims, which amounted to 1,934,986. On the other hand, not counting the 12,000,000-acre fraudulent Peralta grant, only a small part of which lay in New Mexico (and the rest covered Arizona land), there were claims calling for approximately 22,185,884 acres. Obviously, there are some duplications of claims involved in this total and some overlap with claims already confirmed by Congress. Nevertheless, it is clear that there is a vast discrepancy between the amount of land claimed in New Mexico and the amount confirmed by Congress and the courts.

It should also be clear that the average amount of land claimed by each grantee was huge. Taking only the figures for grants confirmed by Congress to 1887, the average size of a grant was 189,000 acres. The question naturally arises, how could there be such enormous grants in New Mexico, as compared to California? And a related question is how could the land laws of

Spain and Mexico have been so grievously flouted? Only simplified answers can be suggested here.

The first fact to be noted is the great distance between Mexico City and Santa Fe and the consequent relative independence of the New Mexican governors, as previously mentioned. A certain amount of independence also stemmed from the devastating Indian raids which New Mexican authorities frequently faced, in contrast to conditions in California. Second was the periodic destruction of official documents in New Mexico, during the Pueblo Revolt of 1680, the Chimayo Revolt in 1837, the Taos Rebellion of 1847, and various other losses caused by or during the U.S. military occupation of the Department in 1846-1847. Third is the almost dictatorial power exercised by the last New Mexican governor under Mexican rule, Manuel Armijo. Fourth is the fact that Governor Armijo became personally interested as a part owner, sub rosa, in several of the very large land grants he approved to other claimants.

Fifth is the system the U.S. Government established for New Mexico, in contrast to that in California, for confirming land titles. This system permitted a land claimant to submit to U.S. officials evidence of his title, without requiring corroborative evidence from official New Mexican archives. Furthermore, the system first placed the task of inspecting and recommending the validity of land titles in the hands of the Surveyor General, a man burdened with other responsibilities and one not necessarily trained in the law or in knowledge of Spanish and Mexican land laws and customs. Land claimants were not required to submit their evidence of title within any time limit, as they were in California, but they were protected in their right to continue to use the land they claimed, even though they may have held bogus title papers. A final step in the initial system for confirmation of titles in New Mexico was the requirement that Congress review and take such action as it saw fit on all recommendations of the Surveyor General. This step in the procedure broke down when Congressional leaders came to recognize how ill-equipped they were to do justice in the questions of title, particularly after they discovered that many of their earlier confirmation acts created injustice for the people of New Mexico. Yet it was more than 35 years after such a farcical and inequitable system was adopted before Congress provided a remedy by establishing the Court of

Private Land Claims for New Mexico. The Court was to confirm all valid titles, provide supervision over survey approval, and be guided by the 11-square-league limit which Mexican law set for individual claimants. More than a dozen years were required for the Court to complete its difficult and arduous assignment.

In addition to the factors that have been enumerated to explain the great number of New Mexican grants which exceeded the limits set by Mexican law, it is necessary to call attention to the land ring that arose in the latter days of Mexican administration. The ring was composed of both Mexican citizens and Anglo residents in the Department, and it was soon supplemented, if not replaced, by the predominantly Anglo Santa Fe Ring of rather notorious reputation. This Ring dominated the political life of the Territory and land-grant activities in an unwholesome fashion. The last factor to be mentioned, supported in its nefarious operations by several of the aforementioned items, was the skill and assiduity of penmen who could draft on order partially or completely fraudulent land title papers. No one has yet studied their accomplishments adequately. In the light of such an unfortunate combination of imperfect systems and human frailties, is it any wonder that there have been inequities in the New Mexican land-grant story?

It would be instructive to review the record of a few more New Mexican land grants, and to note in passing that not all such grants were indictable. The case of the Jornada del Muerto grant may or may not fit into this latter category. It was claimed by Juan Bautista Vigil, the last secretary of the New Mexican Government before the United States military occupation of New Mexico, and the official who surrendered the Department to General S. W. Kearny after Governor Armijo had deserted his post. There have been reports that Vigil later carried away from Santa Fe sacks full of land-grant papers extracted from the official archives there.

In any event, Vigil and a few associates had applied to Governor Armijo for possession of a tract of land in the dread Jornada del Muerto on December 28, 1845. The petitioners bound themselves to construct two wells for the relief and aid of travelers who crossed this waterless desert and to establish two factories for the use of the government and the protection of the region from Indian forays. Governor Armijo hesitated to approve this petition because of its novel character, although he did submit it to the Departmental Assembly for consideration. On January 10, 1846, the latter body approved the grant, which was later claimed to cover 2,000,000 acres.

Apparently there was no act of possession and little, if anything, was done to carry out the promised construction work. Yet after the United States acquired New Mexico, Vigil and his associates applied to the Surveyor General for confirmation of the grant. The latter official refused to approve it, and so the claimants applied directly to Congress for confirmation. Congress avoided taking a direct stand by authorizing the claimants to bring suit in the Territorial courts in order to have their rights determined judicially. They therefore filed a suit in the Supreme Court of the Territory and won confirmation of their title. Government attorneys then appealed this decision to the U.S. Supreme Court. In December 1871, the Supreme Court explained that the only laws in force in Mexico for granting land were those of the Colonization Law of 1824 and the Regulations of 1828, and that Governor Armijo had failed to follow the steps required by these laws for the Jornada del Muerto grant. Furthermore, the number of acres claimed "was enormously in excess of the maximum quantity grantable under the law." Therefore, the Court reversed the decision of the Territorial court and rejected the claim.

A final case study concerns the San Miguel del Bado grant, although I originally intended to conclude with an account of the Tierra Amarilla grant. The reason for the change was that the latter grant has recently been discussed in the *Albuquerque Journal* and in Richard Gardner's *¡Grito!* (1970), and so it might be better to use the records of a less well-known grant to bring out certain aspects of the involved question of common lands.

The San Miguel grant originated in 1794 from a petition signed by Lorenzo Marquez, for himself and in the name of 51 other men, including 13 Indians. They sought to obtain a tract of land on the Pecos River, the boundaries of which were identified by certain natural objects. When these objects were later used as the basis for a United States survey, they were shown to enclose 315,300 acres of land. On November 25, 1794, Governor

Fernando Chacón approved the petition and directed the principal alcalde of Santa Fe, Antonio José Ortiz, to place the grantees in possession of their tract. Before taking the prospective settlers to the grant site, Alcalde Ortiz informed them "that the tract aforesaid has to be in common, not only in regard to themselves, but also to all the settlers who may join them in the future." He also charged them: "That the construction of their plaza, as well as the opening of acequias and all other work that may be deemed proper for the common welfare, shall be performed by the community with that union which in their government they must preserve." Then the Alcalde accompanied them to their lands, gave them general possession within stated boundaries, and notified them that "the pastures and watering places" were "in common."

Nine years later, another alcalde distributed lots equitably among 58 families that had been cultivating land on the grant. He also marked out the boundaries, but said nothing about common lands. However, he did mention that out of the large portion of land that remained undistributed there was an ample amount "for the inhabitants of this town [San Miguel] who may require more land to cultivate, which shall be... [distributed] by the consent of the justice of said town who is charged with the care and trust of this matter...." None of the 58 heads of families was to sell or dispose of his lands for the next ten years. This entire arrangement was approved by Governor Fernando Chacón.

Later alcaldes made distribution of land to new settlers, with the approval of the town's ayuntamiento, and by the time the United States took over New Mexico, there were at least 4,000 or 5,000 people residing within the grant boundaries, many of them in seven other towns that had been established there. Spokesmen for the grant applied to the Survey or General of New Mexico in 1857 for approval of their grant, and even though he did approve it, Congress took no action to confirm the grant.

After the Court of Private Land Claims was established, other San Miguel spokesmen petitioned it for confirmation of the title to "all the present settlers and residents upon the said grant...." U.S. attorneys questioned the right of the petitioners to receive all of the land within the grant boundaries, for they maintained that said petitioners were entitled to receive only that which "was actually appropriated, occupied and cultivated in severalty prior to 1846." In other words, unassigned and common lands should not be confirmed to the occupants. The Court of Private Land Claims, however, rejected the U.S. attorneys' arguments and confirmed the entire grant to the petitioners.

The case was then appealed to the U.S. Supreme Court; it found that under Spanish law, common lands were reserved to the Crown. Even though the Board of Land Commissioners in California had not been placed under limitations by Congress with respect to a strict interpretation of Spanish law, the Court of Private Land Claims for New Mexico was required to be strict. Therefore, in 1896, the Supreme Court ruled in this case of *United States v. Sandoval,* that only lands that had been distributed to settlers could pass with the grant title, and common lands remained in the possession of the government. This meant that the Court of Private Land Claims was not only obligated to accept this ruling for the San Miguel Case, but to apply it in all similar cases.

It should be noted that in confirming the claim of the town of San Fernando de Taos, the Court of Private Land Claims offered many reasons why it would have favored recognizing the town's right to possession of its common lands, but it acknowledged the necessity for following the precedent established by the Sandoval case. A further aspect of the disputed question over rights of grant settlers to common lands arose from grants which Congress itself confirmed, as in the instance of the Tierra Amarilla grant, but I will again refer you to the *Albuquerque Journal* analysis of that grant's history, where the treatment of its common lands is considered.

In conclusion, let me call attention not only to the similar but also the distinctive features of the land-grant record in Texas, California, and New Mexico. A larger study emphasizing comparison and contrasts of the three areas seems abundantly warranted, although I would suggest that such a study cannot readily be prepared until more attention is paid to the basic aspects of grants in New Mexico.

5 Mexican Land Grants in Colorado

Charles S. Vigil

In Colorado, land grants or *mercedes* came from Mexican governors on the same path laid out by Spanish kings in Texas and California and elsewhere in what is now the United States of America. New Mexico territory extended into Colorado, and even in late years it was always understood that the Arkansas River was the northern boundary of the territory.

At least six land grants extend into what is present-day Colorado. An outline of these grants and the stories connected with them is filled with endless intrigues and plots.

I. *The Tierra Amarilla Grant* made to Manuel Martínez and his eight sons and associates by the territorial deputation of New Mexico on July 20, 1832, was confirmed by an act of the United States Congress on June 21, 1860.

II. *The Beaubien and Miranda Grant* has popularly been called *The Maxwell Land Grant* because it was taken over by Maxwell who married one of the Beaubien daughters. This grant was given to Guadalupe Miranda and Carlos Beaubien by Governor Don Manuel Armijo of New Mexico on January 11, 1848, and was confirmed by the United States Congress on June 21, 1860. It passed by inheritance to Lucian B. Maxwell, son-in-law of Carlos Beaubien.

III. *The Sangre de Cristo Grant* was given to Stephen Louis Lee and Narciso Beaubien by Governor Armijo December 30, 1843. Both grantees were killed in the Taos uprising in 1847. This grant later passed to Carlos Beaubien by inheritance from his son, and he immediately purchased the other half from the heirs of Lee Beaubien. This grant was confirmed by the United States Congress on June 21, 1860.

IV. *The Conejos* was also a rather large grant in southern Colorado; the papers making the original grant in 1833 are lost. José María Martínez, Antonio Martínez, Julián Gallegos, and Celedón Valdez were granted a renewal by Prefect R. Archuleta February 21, 1842. The *Court of Land Claims* set up by the United States, however, refused to confirm this grant in 1900. Lafayette Head, founder of the town of Conejos, and others colonized on this grant.

V. *The Vigil and St. Vrain Grant*, largest of the land grants, totaled more than 4 million acres. This grant was made to Cornelio Vigil and Ceran St. Vrain (founder of Bent's Fort), by Governor Armijo on December 9, 1843. The United States Congress on June 21, 1860, confirmed 11 square leagues to each of the *original grantees*, totaling *97,390 and 95,100 acres*. Among claimants at this late date were the descendants of Charles Bent, Kit Carson, Uncle Richens (Dick) Wooten, and Zan Hicklin (who married Bent's daughter, Estaban), who received part of this grant and settled on Green Horn Creek below Pueblo.

VI. *The Nolan Grant* to Gervacio Nolan was made by Governor Armijo on December 1, 1843, but only 11 square leagues were confirmed by the United States Congress in July of 1870.

VII. *The Luis María Baca Grant* was given as a substitute for a New Mexico grant by the United States Congress on June 21, 1860. This same grant was selected in 1883.

It has been said that land grants go back to the days when the Pope decreed that Spain was entitled to possess all lands not occupied by any Christian power, lying west of a meridian drawn 100 leagues west of the Azores and the Cape Verde Islands. Spain and Portugal by the Treaty of the Alcocobas had agreed to abide by these Papal Bulls and by the Treaty of Tordesillas, of June 7, 1494. These two countries agreed that the line of demarcation be changed to 370 leagues west of the Azores. Following this practice, the first conqueror of this region, Juan de Oñate, under his contract with the Viceroy, claimed the right to extend *encomiendas* and *repartimientos* which, in a way, may be considered land grants.

New Spain, of which Colorado was a part, was divided into divisions called provinces, and the King's authority was required for any alienation of Crown lands. Later in the nineteenth century, the United States bound itself by treaty to acknowledge and protect all bona fide titles granted by previous governments, thus perpetuating the land-grant system.

The Treaty of Guadalupe Hidalgo eventually gave full rights of all property to the grantees. There were, however, some reservations on the part of the United States Government that should be considered. President Polk said that the objection to the tenth article of the original treaty was not that it protected legitimate titles which under our laws would have been equally protected without it, but that it unjustly attempted to resuscitate grants which had become a mere nullity by allowing the grantees the same period after ratification to which they had originally been entitled after the date of the grants for the purpose of performing the conditions for which they had been made. Should the Mexican Government persist in retaining this article, then all prospects of immediate peace would be ended.

On May 26, 1848, a supplemental agreement, referred to as Protocol, was presented. This was to the effect that the deletion of Article X in no manner affected the repeated pledge to respect legitimate titles but only to oppose grants which were extinct or grants not in full force and effect at the time of the cession. The Mexican commissioners accepted, and the Treaty of Peace was ratified.

A large number of land grants in New Mexico and Colorado were made during the quarter century of Mexican rule, and apparently the Mexican Government merely followed the pattern set by Spain. The asking party filed his petition before the Governor, who referred it to the proper Alcalde, or in some instances, the Territorial Deputation, and when it came back, if favorable, the Governor approved the same to the authorities in Mexico City where presumably record was duly made thereof.

When the Anglos arrived, after 1848, one of the main problems that had to be solved was that of the land grants. In July 22, 1854, Congress created the office of Surveyor General. The Surveyor General was to ascertain the character and extent of all claims to land under the laws and usages of Spain and Mexico. He was authorized to proceed, with right of legal process, to inquire into and report to the Congress his recommendation of such grants as he approved.

William Pelham, the first Surveyor named, applied to Governor Merriwether for delivery to him of all the archives of the Spanish and Mexican Governments. The request was refused on the excuse that the Governor had no authority to incur the expense of collecting all of the voluminous uncatalogued papers which had been collecting dust in the Old Palace of the government since occupation. Others had been disposed of as useless waste paper, and a number of priceless documents had been lost unintentionally.

A Court of Private Land Claims was authorized. The Court as organized was composed of a Chief Justice, Joseph R. Reed of Iowa; and Associate Justices, Thomas C. Fuller of North Carolina, Wilbur F. Stone of Colorado, William C. Murray of Tennessee, and Harry G. Sluss of Kansas.

Before the Court had completed its work, Chief Justice Reed died and was replaced by F. J. Osborne of North Carolina. Three of the Justices were Republicans, two were Democrats. The United States Attorney was Matt G. Reynolds, the Deputy Clerk was Irineo Chávez, and the interpreter was Eusebio Chacón, from Trinidad, Colorado.

This unusual court was convened in Denver, Colorado, on July 1, 1899. The work was difficult and slow. In determining the validity of the grant titles claimed, it was operating as to procedure under laws of the United States, but its decisions were in the main based upon interpretation of the laws of foreign nations, Spain and Mexico. The oral testimony given was almost entirely in a foreign language and understood by the court only through translations.

The Court concluded its work and adjourned "sine die" on June 30, 1904. In the years of its existence, claims were presented covering approximately 35,000,000 acres of land. Those finally approved and confirmed were 2,051,526 acres, and the fact that claims were rejected in the tremendous amount of 33,500,000 acres is clear evidence of the voluminous work involved.

The earliest grant in the archives was given September 18, 1692, to Alfonso Faél de Aguilar, Royal Ensign and Companion in Arms of the re-conqueror, Don Diego de Vargas.

Spanish land grants in this region were generally smaller than the Mexican ones. Grants which were given in reward for military service were known as *Caballerías,* being the amount of land a horseman could encircle in a day. A grant of this type is *The Alameda Grant,* given on January 2, 1710, by Governor Chacón to Francisco Montes Vigil y Oca. This grant was for 63,746 acres. When Vigil transfered the grant to Captain Juan González several years later for 1,000 cows, the approval of the Governor was required. The Alameda Grant was the subject of much litigation, involving an appeal to the Supreme Court of the United States and was finally approved but partitioned.

Grants often were made to encourage settlements. The title passed to the empresarios and those who joined them in establishing a settlement, whether the lands were occupied or not. One *repartimiento* of this type already mentioned, the Tierra Amarillo Grant, in the County of Río Arriba, Territory of New Mexico and Colorado was made in 1832 on the petition of Manuel Martínez.

In the next generation, Francisco Martínez, who was then living on the property and who was a son of Manuel Martínez, deceased in 1844, petitioned the Surveyor General of the Territory of New Mexico for the confirmation of said grant by Congress, representing himself as the heir of Manuel Martínez. The Surveyor General of New Mexico rendered his opinion on September 10, 1856, in which he found that Francisco Martínez was the then present claimant of the said grant and tract of land and that indeed the testimony showed that the original grantee and the present claimant, Francisco Martínez, had been in the peaceable and quiet possession of the land for a period of 22 years. The Surveyor General confirmed that the grant was originally made to Manuel Martínez, of which Francisco Martínez was the then claimant and that the same was deemed by his office to be a good and valid grant. He thereupon recommended that the

Congress of the United States approve the same and cause a patent to be issued therefore by the proper department and that the land embraced within the boundaries of the grant be surveyed.

He also found that the tract of land was situated in the County of Rio Arriba, Territory of New Mexico, and was called "Tierra Amarilla." It was bounded on the north by the Navajo River; on the south by the Nutrias River; on the east by the mountain range, and on the west by the mouth of the Luguna de los Caballos. The grant was confirmed by an act of Congress, approved June 21, 1860, "as recommended by" the Surveyor General of the Territory of New Mexico.

On February 21, 1881, the President of the United States, under and by virtue of said act of confirmation, caused a patent to be issued for said tract of land which contained 594,515.55 acres and was located in the Territory of New Mexico and State of Colorado in favor of Francisco Martínez, his heirs and assigns, as the confirmees thereof. Manuel Martínez, the original grantee of said grant and tract of land, had died in the year 1844, having had various children and descendants:

José Manuel Martínez, a son who died in the year 1828, with only one child and descendant surviving, Maria Manuela Martínez, married to Tomás Lucero.

María de la Luz Martínez, a daughter who died in the year 1826 and left surviving her only one child, who died prior to 1838 without issue.

Julián Martínez, who died about 12 or 13 years prior to December 8, 1885. He resided in Taos, New Mexico.

María Dolores Martínez, who died more than 12 years before December 8, 1885. She was married to José Manuel Chaves, who died about 40 years before December 8, 1885. They left only two children as descendants, who were still living on December 8, 1885.

Vincente Martínez, a son, who died about 20 years prior to December 8, 1885, at Taos, New Mexico, and left several children as descendants surviving him at that place.

Eusebio Martínez, a son, who died in the year 1841 or 1842 and was married to María Josefa Chaves. They had only one child, who died young and without issue prior to the death of its father.

Francisco Martínez, a son, who died in the year 1874 leaving, surviving him, his widow, María Encarnación García and ten children, all of whom were living on December 8, 1885.

Sixto Martínez, a son, who lived in California, where he died about the year 1870; he left children and descendants residing there.

José Antonio Martínez, who died between 1882 and 1885.

Prudencio Martínez, a son, who died in the year 1831 at the age of 11, and without issue.

María de Jesús Martínez, a daughter, who was the wife of José María Chaves, the person who made the affidavit.

María Antonia Martínez, who died about the year 1865 and was the wife of José María Martínez, who died about the same time as his wife, or prior thereto. They had only one child and descendant, whose name was José Manuel Martínez, who was still living December 8, 1885.

A patent issued by the United States Government dated February 21, 1881, for the tract of land called the Tierra Amarilla Grant, known as private land no. 3, containing 594,515.55 acres of land in the Territory of New Mexico and State of Colorado, recites the decision of the Surveyor General of New Mexico, recommending Congress to confirm the grant. The act of Congress, dated June 21, 1860, also confirms the grant and field notes of the survey, and states the same was thereby given and granted to Francisco Martínez, his heirs and assigns, and that the patent should only operate as a quit claim or relinquishment of the title of the United States.

María Manuela Martínez and Tomás Lucero, her husband, deeded the whole land grant on a bargain and sale deed of right, title and interest of grantors in the Tierra Amarilla Grant to

Thomas B. Catron on September 6, 1876. It was acknowledged September 6, 1876 and recorded April 18, 1877.

Although the Tierra Amarilla lies primarily in a small valley in New Mexico's northern mountains, approximately 40,000 acres of this land grant are in Colorado. The story of this land grant is very similar to the history of all of the land grants.

Persons residing in the territory ceded by Mexico thus were given the choice of becoming American citizens or remaining Mexican citizens. Those who stayed in the territory elected to become citizens and Americans by free choice, although retaining full right to their Spanish names, customs, religions, and traditions and real and personal property; they were therefore Spanish-named Americans.

All *encomiendas* or grants have common points of interest and comparison. The settlers and grantees were Spanish and Mexican citizens and retained a constant attitude of independence and individualism. Some foreigners became citizens of Spain and Mexico to become eligible for land grants.

The history of the grants is filled with legal and local battles from the time that the land was given to the settlers. Titles acquired under Spanish and Mexican land grants were determined according to the laws of the granting sovereign country. However, when a nation acquires territory, by cession or otherwise, the subject holds their lands under the constitution and laws of their own government. This is the rule our courts and Congress followed.

Much the same can be said for the Maxwell Land Grant. French-Canadian Carlos Beaubien settled in Taos in 1823, married the daughter of a prominent New Mexico rancher, became a Mexican citizen, and set himself up as a merchant, Indian trader, land-holder and politician. In 1841, together with Guadalupe Miranda, Beaubien petitioned the Mexican Governor for a grant of land east of Taos and embracing the site of the present town of Cimarrón. Mexican law nominally limited the size of individual land grants to 11 square leagues. It was comparatively easy, however, to evade this limitation by forming a partnership and thus obtain 22 square leagues of land.

The Beaubien-Miranda Grant, subsequently known as the Maxwell Land Grant, was approved in 1841.

Another important *merced* was granted when Governor Armijo approved the petition for the Sangre de Cristo. On January 12, 1844, Louis Lee and Narciso Beaubien were officially placed in possession of the land by Justice of the Peace José Miguel Sánchez. It consisted of almost one million acres. The ownership of the grant, however, took a strange turn. In the insurrection of 1847 in Taos, both Louis Lee and Narciso Beaubien were killed. As a result, Carlos Beaubien, Narciso's father, inherited one-half of the grant. He acquired the other half shortly afterward.

In order to pay the debts of the deceased sheriff, Joseph Pley received permission from the court to sell Lee's half-interest in the million-acre *Sangre de Cristo Grant*. It was no coincidence that Beaubien purchased this interest from Pley for $100, thus becoming sole owner of the grant on May 4, 1848.

Don Carlos, in 1853, in an apparent effort to protect his estate from loss in the court by the imposition of property taxes and the inability of his heirs to meet the levy, vested title to three-sixths of the grant in his noted "mountain man" son-in-law, Lucian Bonaparte Maxwell, and in Joseph Pley and James H. Quinn.

In accordance with the procedure established by Congress in order to protect the Spanish and Mexican landholders by treaty of Guadalupe Hidalgo, Don Carlos (Beaubien) filed a petition in 1856 with the Surveyor General of New Mexico seeking congressional confirmation of the Sangre de Cristo Grant.

Most *encomiendas* had settlers—or squatters—on them. An example was the Maxwell Grant. Yet when grant titles were established, private holdings within private land grants were confirmed in the grantees, their heirs and assigns, as to both the occupied and the unoccupied lands.

The Río de Las Animas Perdidas en Purgatorio ran through Colorado and was the northern boundary of the Maxwell Grant paralleling for 15 or 20 miles the northern boundary of New Mexico, though it was about 12 miles north of the Colorado boundary line. The Elkins and Marmon Survey had run along the edge of the river for many miles and had then crossed to its north bank, dipping still deeper into Colorado, thus creating the extent of 300,000 acres of Maxwell Grant in Colorado.

The Department of Justice, investigating the Maxwell Grant, secured considerable testimony at Trinidad, Colorado, and in August of 1882, filed charges in the Eighth Circuit Court of Colorado. The government claimed that officials of the company had practiced fraud on the land department so as to secure 300,000 acres in Colorado that were never included in the outboundaries of the grant. It attacked particularly the north and east boundary lines. During the following year, the government amended its bill to include the proposition that under Mexican law only 97,000 acres could have been granted. The Maxwell Company denied both charges; in 1884, Federal Judge Brewer gave a preliminary decision that contained some points favorable to both sides. He pointed out that the Treaty of Guadalupe Hidalgo was concluded between Mexico and the United States on February 2, 1848, and it provided for the protection, by the United States, of all property rights of inhabitants within the area formerly belonging to Mexico. He also pointed out that even though the treaty protected all existing rights of property, it neither created new rights nor defined them.

Also included in the discussions was that the United States never made claim that it was the owner of lands with Mexican titles, but only that title passed at the time of the cession to the claimant under Mexican laws. The treaty of Guadalupe Hidalgo provided for the protection of the claimants in their property acquired and held under the former laws. The patent is a record of the United States Government's action upon the title of the claimant as it existed upon the United States acquisition of the country. The inhabitants retained all rights and were entitled to protection in them.

So it was that Charles Hippolyte Trotier, Sieur de Beaubien, a French Canadian adventurer, became Carlos Beaubien, the Taos trader. He piled high the shelves of his adobe store and bade the world to enter, to buy, to bargain, and to trade.

Beaubien never lost sight of the goal which had drawn him across the prairie. The man who started life in a French-Canadian birthplace at Three Rivers, Quebec, later became a citizen of old Spain and then of the Republic of Mexico, and ended up his nationalistic career as a citizen of this country and a judge of a Territorial District Court of the United States. He found himself one bright day the absolute owner in one unbroken tract of 1,380,000 acres of land, known as the Sangre de Cristo Grant, as well as 1,714,000 acres in another chunk of rock, sand, and sagebrush—incidentally loaded with still untold quantities of gold, silver, coal, and fine timber and pasture—which immediately adjoined it on the southeast.

The second acreage, originally called the Beaubien and Miranda, and later, the Maxwell Grant, includes a large portion of what are now Colfax, Taos, and Union Counties, New Mexico, and Las Animas County, Colorado.

Carlos Beaubien acquired the title to the Sangre de Cristo Grant which contained more than 1,600 square miles of the most valuable agricultural, grazing and mineral lands in southern Colorado and northern New Mexico, together with enormous landscapes of the grandest mountain scenery the Rocky Mountain region affords, for an outlay of exactly $100.

Yet another character in the land-grant story was English. William Blackmore traveled overseas from England and the continent in quest of money (which he found) with which to buy a half-million acres at one dollar an acre, as well as the funds with which to construct a railway line around the Mule Shoe along the base of La Veta Mountain and over the pass into the San Luis Valley at a time when not another foot of railroad was being built in the United States because of the panic of the '70s. Congress was to enact legislation to validate the titles which had been established prior to the Mexican War by the losing combatant. Into the halls of our Congress for many subsequent years, controversies were to be injected that involved proposed resolutions calling for the exposure of alleged land frauds and the punishment of private individuals and public officials, who, it was asserted, had actually stolen millions of acres of land.

Since the patent to the Sangre de Cristo Grant, by its express terms, however, purports to be only a quit claim deed; since that instrument was not signed by Rutherford B. Hayes in his official capacity as President until 20 years after the Congress had passed a law authorizing its execution; and, since numerous persons claimed interests which antedated the action of Congress by many years, the background of that instrument became important.

A policy of making great concessions of lands to settlers who were Mexican citizens but born in a foreign country became prevalent across the entire northern frontier of New Mexico. The grants of land later known as the Tierra Amarilla, the Maxwell, the Mora, the St. Vrain, the Nolan, and the Montoya and Antón Chico were made for the purpose of aiding and carrying out this policy. Petitions for lands lying within the districts covered by these immense concessions were made at times by persons of American birth. The Mexican Government had a well-organized system of espionage, and the presence of strangers on the Arkansas, at Bent's Fort, and in other localities was immediately reported to the Governor at Santa Fe.

The showing made by young Beaubien and Sheriff Lee must have satisfied the requirements of the Mexican laws, in the opinion of the territorial chief executive, because three days later on December 30, 1842, Governor Armijo made the following marginal notation on the first page of the petition: "Referred to the prefect in order that if the land petitioned for not be otherwise disposed of, he caused the possession referred to by petitioners to be given." This was attested by Donaciano Vigil, acting Secretary of the Territory, on January 7, 1844, in a ceremony of the Livery of Seisin (known to feudal England), and in the presence of witnesses, Lee and Narciso Beaubien were placed in actual possession of the land by the Justice of the Peace, who receipted for a fee of $30.00 on the back of his report. He certified that they traveled around the exterior boundaries, as was required by law.

What is roughly the northwest quarter of the grant was sold to a company with land booming as its objective. The northwest quarter constitutes the Trinchera ranch; it eventually was acquired by the late Ruth Hanna McCormick Simms, to whose estate it belonged.

Concluding this brief outline, certainly volumes have been filled with charges that the whole grant system was the result of fraud. Professor Harold Dunham wrote his doctoral thesis entitled "Government Handout," on this premise. Needless to say, Spanish-surnamed Americans have not benefited from the grants given to their forefathers. Perhaps the future will tell a different tale.

6 Miguel Alona: The Hero of Cochetopa Pass

Ann Federici Martin

Colorado's history is filled with struggle and pain and heroic efforts by many people. The fact that this state is one of the most mountainous in the Union means that much of the struggle, pain, and heroic effort had to do with conquering the mountains.

Many stories have been told about the expeditions that took place during the early days in Colorado. Many of the scouts who guided these expeditions became famous. Miguel Alona was not a scout, and his name is remembered by only few people. He participated in an eventful expedition in late 1857 that tested the knowledge and skill of many hardy pioneers and mountain men. The man who saved the expedition was an unknown—Miguel Alona.

The expedition was led by Captain R. B. Marcy of the 5th U.S. Infantry. The group was encamped at Fort Bridger, Utah Territory, in late November of 1857. Captain Marcy received orders to cross the mountains by the most direct route into New Mexico to procure supplies. The object of this march was set forth in the following extract from a report of the Secretary of War made in 1858:

> The destruction of our trains by the Mormons [in 1857] and the disasters which necessarily flowed from it, drove General Johnston to the necessity of sending a detachment of men to New Mexico for supplies essential to enable him to prosecute his march with all practicable dispatch.
>
> This expedition was intrusted to Captain R. B. Marcy, of the 5th Infantry. . . . It may be safely affirmed that, in the whole catalogue of hazardous expeditions scattered so thickly through the history of our border warfare, filled as many of them are with appalling tales of privation, hardship, and

suffering, not one surpasses this, and in some particulars it has been hardly equaled by any.

It was no surprise that General Johnston selected Marcy to carry out the expedition.

"Captain," Johnston said when Marcy came before him, "I am sending you in charge of a winter expedition to Fort Union, New Mexico. You will arrange there to have supplies sent to us to keep us through the winter and to get us ready to go after the Mormons in the spring, as soon as the snow thaws and we can get through the mountains between here and Salt Lake City."

"Yes sir," Captain Marcy said.

"Take a large group, in case you have trouble. Above all, take a guide that knows the country. You will have to cross Cochetopa Pass [The Pass of the Buffaloes near Gunnison], for there is no other way through the mountains. If you miss the pass, you will be in trouble."

"Yes sir," Captain Marcy said. "Have you any idea how long the trip will take?"

"I've talked to mountain men. They agree it should take no more than 25 days. There will be more snow in the pass, but it should not be deeper than two feet at this time. But every day you delay will increase the chance of heavy snows. Let me know what you think you will need as soon as you can make plans."

"Yes sir!" Captain Marcy left the room, his mind already at work. Who would be the best guide he could possibly take? A name came to him at once, that of a well-known mountain man—Jim Baker. He immediately sent for Baker.

Many tales have been told about this famous old scout and his contributions to the settling of Colorado and about the countless wagon trains he guided over the unmarked trails leading westward. He had guided numerous United States Army units across the mighty rim of the Rocky Mountains on expeditions to Utah, New Mexico, and California.

Miguel Alona: The Hero of Cochetopa Pass 81

When Baker stood before him, Marcy was impressed. The old mountain man carried a small, short-handled axe under his left arm pit; as they sat and talked, he absent-mindedly took the axe out and began to sharpen it with a small pocket whetstone.

He was very handsome, in spite of a few small scars caused when a repeating rifle had blown up in his face some years earlier. His mien was thoughtful and serious.

"I reckon I can find the way," Jim Baker said, "but things are going to look mighty strange with all this snow on them. If'n we can get some Indian guides to show us the pass when we get into the mountains, it would be a good idea."

"Right," Marcy said. "Let's get ready and be on the way as fast as we can."

When the expedition got under way, Captain Marcy gazed at the late November scene, and his mind flashed ahead to the journey across the Rockies. Marcy was no tenderfoot, having seen 20 years of dangerous service on the frontier, and he insisted upon taking along rations for 30 days, even though the journey was expected to last only 25.

The expedition consisted of the Captain, 40 enlisted men, 25 mountaineers, and the 66 mules and other animals belonging to them.

Among the mountaineers, there was a quiet little man who seldom spoke. He was a hard worker and followed orders, but he did not make friends easily, possibly because he spoke very little English. He had a strong Spanish accent. No one knew much about him—where he had come from or why he had decided to sign up for this expedition. Some said he just wanted to get back to Taos, New Mexico, where he had lived at one time. His name was Miguel Alona, but the men called him "Mikey."

When all was ready, they set out from Fort Bridger, taking a southwestward course to the Green River. At the far eastern bend of the Green River, they entered the sheltered valley of Brown's Hole.

After following the canyon that climbed for miles, the party came out near the Roan Plateau, which separates the waters of the Green and Colorado Rivers.

Ten miles of trudging over this bleak stretch of white countryside brought them to the great cliffs that end the plateau and break off almost straight down 2,000 feet to the Colorado River below.

Marcy decided to camp on the edge of the bluff. Snow was cleared from patches of gray ground, and eager hands gathered dry wood from the ground near scrubby bushes. Soon fires were crackling and spitting and throwing shadows of dancing troopers against the tightly stretched tents. Mules were unloaded and grazed on the half-covered bushes and buried grass.

This was the moment when Marcy had to call upon Jim Baker and his knowledge of the country and the hidden trails that led across it. For miles along this escarpment, there was but a single trail capable of descent by pack animals. Could Baker find it in the strange white landscape? He was gone a long time, scouting. Captain Marcy worried, for he knew familiar signs were unrecognizable under the white mantle. Marcy noticed that Miguel Alona walked back and forth and seemed to be concerned with Baker's return. Baker's search continued for hours, but at last he returned; with a gruff voice, he said, "Took a while, but I found it." Marcy breathed a sigh of relief, and Alona retired into the background of the camp.

When pale morning light lit the snow-covered Rockies, the camp was astir. As the light grew into day, worried men peered over the cliff into the deep canyon where the river flowed. Brown earth and bare rocks could be seen on the bottom land, and happy cries of surprise ran through the camp at the absence of snow in the canyon.

The narrow path leading down to the river was steep and slippery. Although the mules were sure-footed, once in a while one would slip and go tumbling down the incline, rolling a mad race with the articles which flew out of his pack. Sometimes a tree or projecting rock brought him to a stop, and sometimes the shouting men were able to pull the mule back onto the trail and repair the damage as best they could. Sometimes mule and pack were lost forever.

When they reached the valley floor, the mules were turned loose to graze, and the men enjoyed a brief rest from the frost of the snow fields on the high plateau.

The 8th of December found Marcy and his men in the valley of the Gunnison River, at the site of what is now Delta, Colorado, near the ruins of another fur-trading post, Fort Robidoux, founded in the 1830s by a famous trader from St. Louis.

Bands of ragged Ute Indians who lived mostly on rabbits and other small animals flocked about the troops, trying to steal anything they could.

When Marcy asked their chief if they could furnish a guide to lead the troops over the mountains, the Indians replied, "Not ready to die," and repeating this over and over they hugged themselves and shivered as though suffering from a cold chill. They shook their heads vigorously and pointed toward the mountains and a look of fear came into their eyes. "Bad spirits, bad spirits. You all die."

Marcy tried to persuade the chief to accompany them as a guide to the summit of the mountains and offered him the value of three horses, but the chief refused, saying that he was not yet ready to die and that, unless the troops turned back or stopped and passed the winter with them, they would perish. Marcy's interpreter asked him how much snow he supposed they would find in the mountains. The chief replied that he was not positive as to the exact depth, but that he had crossed over the same route they proposed to travel when the leaves were commencing to fall, and that he had then found about one foot upon the summit; that there had been a great deal of rain in the valley since that time, which he presumed had its equivalent in snow upon the mountains, and he was of the opinion that Marcy might encounter from four to five feet, and perhaps even more than that. He concluded by saying, "You may think I do not tell the truth, but if you will only cast your eyes toward the mountains you can see for yourselves that the snow is there."

It was now that Marcy began to realize the seriousness of the march. His Commander, Albert S. Johnston, had made it clear that they must get to Fort Union as soon as possible. They could not wait for spring and the melting snows. They had to find the all-important pass, "The Pass of the Buffaloes." It could mean the lives of many men. It could mean the success or failure of the "Mormon War" the following spring.

In spite of the warnings by the Indians, Marcy and his men were determined to push on. They knew that their comrades at Fort Bridger were waiting for supplies. If all went well, six days of travel would bring the party to "The Pass of the Buffaloes." This pass is located where one would least expect to find a low pass in the continental divide. The best passes across the Rockies in this latitude would appear to be at the headwaters of the Gunnison and Uncompahgre Rivers from the west, and the Arkansas and the Rio Grande from the east. These promising streams, however, lead on and on to the icy, barren wastes above timberline, where the backbone of the continent is reached, and a branch of the Gunnison leads to the comparatively low Cochetopa Pass.

On the 11th day of December, despite the gloomy and discouraging prospects held out to Marcy by the Indian chief, they packed up the mules and commenced the ascent of the western slope of the Rocky Mountains. They had proceeded but a few miles when the snow began to impede their progress very seriously. The snow became deeper and deeper with a crust on the surface which cut the legs of the mules and the order of march had to be changed.

"We can't go on like this. Something has to be done," Marcy told his scout, Jim Baker. Jim suggested that instead of having the animals break trail, the men should be ordered in front and should proceed in single file, trampling down a path. This was done; however, it was very hard work for the few of the leading men and in order to equalize the labor as much as possible, Marcy directed that every man, as he came in front, should retain that position a certain length of time, after which he was permitted to turn out of the track and allow all the others to pass him, taking his place at the rear. By these alternations, the work was very much lightened, and, after the party had all passed, a good track was left for the animals. It was at this time that Marcy again noticed Miguel Alona. He saw that Miguel had good endurance; when it was Miguel's turn to lead the party, he could exceed the ordinary yardage before becoming exhausted. He always seemed to be in good spirits and never became weary or discouraged; his example had a cheering effect upon his comrades.

Despite these tremendous efforts, the poor mules began to weaken. Bitter needles from the evergreens formed their only food, and on this unwholesome forage the famished brutes grew thin and weak and began to die.

"We just have to lighten the loads on these critters," Jim insisted, "if we want to make the crossing." Accordingly, all surplus baggage was cached, but still the mules continued to die. On one day, five were lost, and on the following morning, eight others lay stark and rigid on the mountainside.

The snow increased day after day as they ascended, until it was four feet deep. It was so dry and light that the men, walking in an upright position, would sink to their waists and could not move. One of the men made a pair of snow shoes and attempted to walk upon them, but he sank so deep in the soft snow that it was impossible to use them.

During all of this time, not a word of complaint had been heard from the only woman in the party, the Indian wife of Tim Goodale. She had been patient and helped with the cooking and in any other way possible. She had a pet colt that followed the mare that she rode, and the colt seemed to give her a great deal of pleasure. She mothered it and petted it during the evening when the march of the day was halted. The colt sometimes nestled down near her and her husband in their hollowed-out spot in the deep snow at night.

The next morning, as he looked around him, Marcy told his scout, "What worries me more than anything else now is that our food supplies are getting low. It's bad enough that our daily pace has been cut down, but this also means that we have to make our food last longer than we expected." All the beef cattle had already been eaten and the bread supply was limited. To conserve the strength of men and animals, Marcy now ordered all baggage discarded except food, arms and ammunition, and one blanket for each man.

Rations were exhausted before the summit of the divide was reached. The only food now available to the hungry men was the meat of the famished animals. It was evident that the animal which could best be spared was the pet colt belonging to Tim Goodale's Indian wife. It was not without bitter tears that she finally agreed that her pet should be eaten. The meat of the colt was tender, and it tasted delicious to the starving men.

During the 12 days that followed, the men lived on the meat of starved and exhausted horses and mules. As the salt supply ran out they discovered that gunpowder sprinkled on the meat took the place of both salt and pepper. The lean meat and the thin soup made from it did not satisfy for long the cravings of the appetite. Within a short time after a meal, the men seemed as hungry as before they had eaten. Twelve of the men now had such badly frozen feet that they were unable to walk, and Marcy was obliged to let them use some of the serviceable animals to carry them. One of the privations most keenly felt was the lack of tobacco.

In constructing the nightly bivouac, each set of two or three men dug a hole seven or eight feet square down to the ground. A bed of soft pine twigs was laid and over this a blanket was spread. On the windward side, two forked sticks were stuck in the snow and against these a windbreak of pine boughs was built. With a fire burning in the snow pit, the night was passed with a fair degree of warmth.

It was during the day that the soldiers suffered most from the cold. Their clothes were insufficient and were wearing out from the hard march. Men repaired their shoes with green mule skin, and when this wore out, wrapped their feet in blankets or pieces of their coat tails. The dazzling reflection from the snow brought on cases of snow blindness, but the men soon discovered that the remedy for this lay in blacking their faces with powder or charcoal.

The following is an extract from Marcy's journal, written on the evening of the 1st of January, 1857:

This morning dawned upon us with gloomy auspices, far from promising to us a happy New Year. We have been engaged since daylight this morning in wallowing along through snow at least five feet deep, and have only succeeded, by the severest toil, in making about two miles during the entire day. From our bivouac to-night we can see the fires of last night, and in the darkness they do not appear over a rifle-shot distant. The leading men have been obliged to crawl upon their hands and knees to prevent sinking to their necks, and could only go a few yards at a time before they were compelled, in a state of complete exhaustion, to throw themselves down and let others take their places.

For several days, Miguel Alona marched in the vicinity of Marcy and Baker; in the evenings, he drew near their campfire and listened closely to their remarks. Marcy and Baker had been troubled with a fear that gnawed at their hearts, but they hardly spoke of it, even to each other. Somehow speaking of the fear made it seem more real and more terrible, and they certainly did not mention it to any of the other men. The fact was that they now had grave doubts as to whether they were following the course that would lead to "The Pass of the Buffaloes!"

With the summer landmarks obscured by snow, Jim Baker was not certain of his course. Finally, he confessed to his leader, "I'm just plain lost. I'm lost. I'm lost! I can't seem to think straight. Everything looks so goldfarned unfamiliar to me anymore." He was in the depth of despair and shame. There was nothing Marcy could say—but fear lay in his heart.

Notes of despair began to be heard in the camp. Captain Marcy grew melancholy and could not sleep. More and more, Miguel Alona seemed to want to be near his captain; he appeared to be deep in thought and many times seemed on the verge of saying something. All the men knew that only nine years before, the great General Fremont had attempted to penetrate these mountains from New Mexico and had encountered so much snow that all his animals perished and he was forced to turn back, with the loss of several men before the party was extricated from their perilous position. No wonder it was with many fears that Marcy looked out over the long stretches of white Colorado mountains and realized that a major part of the battle to settle this state would be the conquering of its mountains.

For another miserable day, they followed an uncertain course. That night, it was a dejected group of men that grouped around the fires to eat the evening meal. No one was hungry, and very few words were said. The pallor of death hung about the camp. It was the first time that anyone had noticed that the Indian woman wept.

Suddenly, Miguel Alona stepped out into the firelight. He was a pitiful sight to look upon. He was tired and bedraggled, and his feet were tied in rags; his eyes were sunken in his head, and the light of the fire caught in them and they shone with a crazed glow.

"Señor Capitan," he said, "if you will forgive me, I must talk to you. I am almost sure that we turned from the right route three days ago." A hush fell among the group. Only the quiet weeping of the Indian woman could be heard.

Captain Marcy questioned Miguel Alona, and before the evening was over, he was convinced that this man did know the country. Miguel pointed toward a depression in the mountains at right angles to the course they had taken, some 30 miles distant. He said that was the Cochetopa Pass. Marcy asked him how it happened that he knew the country. Miguel replied that he had been there before and that he knew it well. Captain Marcy promised him a handsome present if he would guide the party safely to New Mexico, but added, "If at any time I find you leading us in the wrong direction, I'll have you hung to the nearest tree."

Miguel looked out upon the stretches of snow and walked about the camp, looking in all directions. When he returned to the fire, he said, "Very well, I'll risk my neck on it, Capitan."

Several of the men laughed and the sound of their laughter seemed to lift the spirits of the entire group. It had been many days since anyone had laughed. Marcy shook Miguel Alona's hand. "Very well, Miguel, from now on you are my guide. Good night."

The next morning, there was no sign of road or trail and the snowy mountains rose peak upon peak before them. The uncertainty of their position was now crystal clear, as was knowledge of the fact that if they failed to strike the Cochetopa Pass, they must all perish. Not a living thing was in sight except the ragged, pinch-faced men and the famished, tottering mules.

Miguel lead the exhausted men and animals, step by step, along the western slope of the mountains as rapidly as the snow and their exhausted condition would permit. The men began to believe that they had placed their destiny in the hands of a madman but at the end of ten days, the pass was finally sighted in the white distance. Ragged caps whirled in the air, raspy voices shouted, and Miguel grinned triumphantly.

Seventy-five miles of snow-covered valley still separated them from the nearest help, Fort Massachusetts, but the road ahead was known. Two men on the strongest remaining mules were sent ahead to bring back supplies, as they were now reduced to a state bordering on starvation. One of the men was Mikey Alona and the men gave him a cheering send-off.

It was 11 horribly long days later before a rescue party from Fort Massachusetts came into sight. The joy manifested upon the union with the rescue group was a combination of laughter, dancing, and screaming—and tears. Men had no qualms about crying like little children.

Captain Marcy was overcome with joy and thanksgiving. He had not slept half an hour at a time for more than 20 days and nights and was reduced from 170 to 131 pounds in weight. Over and over, the thought crossed his mind that the mere accident of Miguel's being a part of the group, without any doubt, had saved the lives of all of them, since without him they could never have found the pass and would surely have perished in the mountains.

Two days later at Fort Massachusetts (in present-day southern Colorado), more supplies were obtained, and easy marches brought the party to the New Mexican settlements.

At Taos, the hero of the journey, Miguel Alona, was given a reward of $500.00 for his services. That night, Miguel disappeared and was not seen for two days. Later when he was questioned he said, "The money is gone, I am a beggar again. But, oh what a wonderful two nights I have had, Dios Mio!" Some of the men said he had lost his money in a game of monte bank.

Tim Goodale's Indian wife, who had measured up so admirably to the severe test of the journey, was presented by Captain Marcy with a new pony, to replace her pet colt.

The great scout Jim Baker, who had suffered a severe shock to his confidence, told Captain Marcy, "I'm through with those danged mountains in Colorado." He had decided that he would give up the wilderness life and settle down in Taos. He had purchased a new outfit of clothes, and the men hardly knew the old mountain scout. Baker had to pay the price of civilization, however. When the Captain complimented him on his new attire, the mountain man replied, "Confound these yere store boots, Cap'n, they choke my feet like hell!"

It was the first time in 20 years that Jim Baker had worn anything but moccasins, and his feet were not prepared to "break in" a pair of ill-fitting boots.

However, once a mountain man, always a mountain man, and long before the command was ready for the return journey to Fort Bridger, Jim Baker had discarded his boots and resumed the softer gear of the mountains. His restlessness for the mountains gripped him and he was eager to be off on the trail again. His latest experience in the Rockies only proved that, like all humans, he could make a mistake.

Captain Marcy with his company proceeded to Fort Union, some miles east of Santa Fe, where supplies for Johnston's army were duly obtained.

But what happened to Miguel Alona, the Hispano hero of Cochetopa Pass? Does his name appear in the history books about the settling of the West and Colorado? Or is his name, like the name of many others, gone like the drifts of snow in the high mountains that melt in the heat of summer?

7 Hispanic Folklore in Colorado

Arthur L. Campa

The folk traditions of Colorado were until recently an unsevered continuity of the folk heritage of New Mexico. First, the present state of Colorado was for two and one-half centuries part of colonial New Mexico until the American occupation. Secondly, the people who first settled southwestern Colorado moved directly from the adjoining New Mexican villages in 1851 and established San Luís, the state's oldest town. A third factor which helped to maintain the cultural continuity of the San Luis Valley residents was the unchanged pastoral life which they led in the farming communities of southern Colorado.

The second region in Colorado occupied by New Mexican folk grew out of the freighting expeditions of Pedro Valdez and Felipe Baca who hauled flour from Mora, New Mexico, to sell in the Denver gold fields. As they passed through the Purgatoire Valley, they were very favorably impressed by the fertility of the land and the easy access to water. On the return trip to Mora, they took melons and vegetables with which to convince their friends and relatives that southern Colorado offered greater promise as farming land than the cold, isolated valley of Mora. In 1860, twelve families loaded their possessions into 20 wagons and drove over Ratón Pass into the present site of the city of Trinidad. They founded a number of *plazas,* as the fortified homes were then called, which eventually developed into such towns as San Miguel, Trinchera, San Francisco, Apodaca, Medina, and Trinidad itself.

The south-central portion of Colorado around Trinidad soon became the main travel artery north and south. The highway, and the railroad which followed in the seventies, gave additional mobility to the Hispanic population in the adjoining valleys of the Purgatoire and the Arkansas Rivers. Hispanos from Santa Fe and other New Mexican towns moved north beyond Ratón Pass and were joined from time to time by Mexican nationals whose names figure in the life of Trinidad around the turn of the century.

The San Luis Valley residents west of the Sangre de Cristo range were more isolated by the lack of important means of communication and were, therefore, less influenced for several generations by the folk traditions of Mexican nationals. There are former residents of the San Luis Valley living in Denver who claim that they never ate *tacos, enchiladas,* and other well-known Mexican dishes until they moved to Denver. The folklore of this older part of Colorado is still closely related to the folk heritage of northern New Mexico. The language spoken by the Hispanos of this region is no different from that spoken in New Mexico, and their folkways are also identical. Folklorists such as Aurelio M. Espinosa, Juan B. Rael, and Edwin B. Place usually refer geographically to their studies as being from "New Mexico and southern Colorado" because of the similarity of both regions.

As the state became industrialized, there was a marked movement of Hispano population from south-central and western Colorado, as well as from New Mexico, into the mining region of Walsenburg, the Pueblo steel mills, and the sugar-beet industry north of Denver. The pastoral culture of these residents underwent a very noticeable change as they were exposed to urban life in such cities as Pueblo, Denver, and, to a lesser degree, Fort Collins and Greeley. The village fiestas and the traditional folkways to which they were accustomed in the rural areas began to disappear under the impact of urban life. The young generation of Hispanos whose ancestors came from southern Colorado have become so acculturated to Anglo-American life that they know virtually nothing of Hispanic lore. The Spanish language, if used at all, has become the language of the hearth.

The arrival of large numbers of Mexican nationals and border Americans of Mexican descent during the first and second World Wars introduced a more current folk tradition from Mexico which displaced to a large extent the Spanish folkways of many Hispanic Coloradoans. Before very long, Mexican nationals and their descendants, who are now called either Mexican-Americans or Chicanos, outnumbered the Hispano Coloradoans; they Mexicanized the lore and folkways of Spanish speakers in the urban centers. The original settlements in the Southeast still preserve many vestiges of their traditional life, but the inevitable changes brought about by modern civilization, both American and Mexican, have altered much of the original pastoral culture.

Hispanic folklore in Colorado today consists of a twofold heritage; the old Hispanic traditions which the original settlers brought with them from New Mexico, and the more recent accretions introduced by Mexican nationals during the past 60 years. In the folk dance, for example, Mexican-Americans emphasize Mexican dances taught by visiting dancemasters of the *Ballet Folklórico* of Mexico City. The Hispano-Coloradoans lean more toward Spanish dances such as *jotas* and *flamencos* with a sprinkling of a few Mexican dances. The growth of Mexican traditions, particularly those emphasizing Aztec dancing and court pageantry, is not so much a folk outgrowth and development as a result of the recent activistic upsurge of the Chicanos and Mexican Americans.

Religious Folk Drama

One of the most popular forms of entertainment employed extensively by Hispanic people in the Southwest until recently is the traditional folk theater introduced by the missionaries as a means of presenting Christian theology to the Indians in Mexico City. Eventually, this folk drama that was written by the priests spread north into New Mexico and Colorado where it continued as a form of religious entertainment during church holidays. Numerous versions of these folk plays became disseminated throughout the Southwest wherever there were Spanish-speaking settlements. The Hispanic villages and towns which now are part of Colorado continued the folk-drama tradition and still present some of these plays at Christmas time.

The religious folk plays known as *autos, coloquios,* or *comedias* are based on biblical subjects. There are two groups referred to as "cycles"; they dramatize salient events in the Old and the New Testaments. The first cycle[1] includes *Adán y Eva* and *Caín y Abel,* which, as the titles indicate, are based on the fall of man and on the first crime, respectively. These two folk plays were performed in the early days of Trinidad and the San Luis Valley, but they have long been discontinued. Some of the old residents of Costilla County remember the plays but did not get to see them performed.

The second cycle has always been more popular and is still presented in Colorado.[2] The first play is an importation from Mexico called *La Aparición de la Virgen*. This dramatized account of the apparition of the Virgin to the Mexican Indian Juan Diego on Tepeyac Hill, where the shrine of Guadalupe now stands in Mexico City, is not closely enough related to Colorado so far north. The second play of the cycle is entitled *San José*, in which a husband for Mary is chosen. All men are requested to appear in Jerusalem holding a tall reed in one hand. The chosen one's reed will sprout flowers at the time of divine selection; Joseph's reed sprouts in his hand. This tradition has given the name to the ordinary hollyhock as *Varas de San José*, that is, "Reeds of Saint Joseph." This play was presented in years past in Pueblo, but it also has been discontinued.

The third selection is actually a singing skit today of what once was a short play called *Las Posadas*, or "Search for Lodging." Joseph and Mary called at nine houses in a singing procession with lighted candles. Satan precedes the callers and hides behind the door in order to impersonate the man of the house or the innkeeper. When the group searching for lodging sings:

> ¿Quién Dará posada a estos peregrinos
> Que vienen cansados de andar los caminos?
> Who will give lodging to these pilgrims
> Who are tired of traveling along the road?

The Devil answers from within:

> Posada no damos ni podemos dar
> Que pueden ser ladrones que vienen a robar.
> We do not give you lodging, for we cannot serve
> Those who may be thieves coming here to rob.

Symbolically, at the ninth door, the Nativity play of *Los Pastores* takes place. *Las Posadas* is one of the episodes of the Nativity which has continued in popularity throughout the Southwest to the present time. The character of the Devil and the dialogue between him and the innkeeper is deleted. The whole presentation consists of a candle procession with the traditional melody of *Las Posadas,* an interesting old Spanish melody in which the singers hold some of the syllables in coloratura fashion very adeptly.

La Pastorela or *Los Pastores* is the most widely diffused folk play throughout Colorado. When Edwin B. Place was Chairman of the Department of Modern Languages at the University of Colorado, he made a brief study of a "Group of Mystery Plays Found in a Spanish Speaking Region of Southern Colorado" in 1930 which included *Los Pastores* along with *El Niño Perdido* and *Las Posadas.*[3] He found that the version of *Los Pastores* from Costilla County was similar to the versions from San Rafael, New Mexico, and San Antonio, Texas, published in detail by M. R. Cole in 1903.

The Nativity play is presented in two acts. The shepherds are watching their flocks by night when the Angel appears to them announcing the birth of the Christ. They decide to go to Bethlehem, and while on their way, they are joined by a hermit. Satan joins them in disguise and manages to have the hermit run away with the wife of a lazy shepherd named Bartolo. After this mischief, he alerts the rest of the company, who bring the couple back and proceed to Bethlehem. Meanwhile, Satan is vanquished by the Angel Miguel and rushed off the stage. In the second act, the shepherds arrive at the manger and present their gifts to the newborn child.

Throughout the play, there is a good deal of humorous dialogue between the shepherds and lazy Bartolo, who is always asleep on his pallet. Every scene opens with a song called a *letra* which introduces each character. At the end of the presentation of gifts, all the shepherds join hands and sing a lullaby to the Child and then depart with a farewell song. The music of the *Pastorelas* is one of the principal features of this folk drama. Richard B. Stark of the Museum of Anthropology in Santa Fe has made an excellent study of these melodies and presented them in a book entitled *The Music of the Spanish Folk Plays in New Mexico.*[4]

The fifth play of this sequence is *Los Reyes Magos,* or "The Magi Kings." The sixth of January corresponds in Spanish to Christmas Eve, and this play celebrates the visit of the Magi as related in the Bible. The three kings, guided by the traditional star, stop at King Herod's court. Herod asks them to return on their way back in order to learn of the Messiah's whereabouts. They return by a different route in order to avoid the king, whereupon Herod orders the slaughter of the innocents. This scene is particularly gruesome. The directions call for entrails of sheep to be spilled on the stage to simulate the blood of the slaughtered children. The last scene depicts the flight to Egypt and the deception worked upon Herod by a group of rustics.

El Niño Perdido is the last play of the New Testament cycle. Joseph and Mary have lost track of Jesus, who has now grown to a boy of twelve. He wanders away from home and stops at the home of a wealthy man at dinner time, hoping to get an invitation to dine. Parts of this play have a strong flavor of the drama of Calderón, Spanish dramatist of the late Golden Age. The numerous conceits and salient *cultismos* seem to indicate that the author of this play was well versed in Spanish classical drama. There is dramatic foreshadowing in one of the speeches of the Christ Child as He walks by the palaces of Herod and of Pilate. He says:

Al tránsito de mi muerte
Cuando me estén azotando
Tres veces he de llegar
En una columna atado.

On the way to my death,
As I am being lashed,
Three times I shall arrive
Tied down to a column.

Finally the lost boy wanders into the temple where he holds discourse with the Jewish Rabbis and amazes them with His learning. His parents finally find Him after a long search and lengthy lamentations, but Jesus rebukes them, saying:

¿No sabéis que en los negocios
importantes de mi padre
me conviene más estar?

Know ye not that I must be
about my Father's business?

Much can be said about the relation of this folk drama to the Spanish compositions of the same nature going back to the middle of the twelfth century. Scholars such as Stanley L. Robe of the University of California, George C. Barker, Ralph S. Boggs, Juan B. Rael, M. R. Cole, and others have made studies of the same plays found in Mexico as well as in the Southwest. The usual procedure is to find a *Director* who has presented a play and to secure a manuscript from him. In 1929, I found in Alamosa, Colorado, an 85-year-old director named Juan Andrés Bernal who knew the entire play of *El Niño Perdido* by heart. He went over some of the incomplete or garbled manuscripts which I had collected and restored scenes and speeches which had been left out.

These plays were presented in village halls, in the front room or *sala* of someone who had a large enough house, or in the open when weather permitted. The costuming was quite simple, and the acting entirely amateurish. Each actor recited his lines perfunctorily, except the Devil or *Satanás* who took great delight in ranting and threatening the Angel. Comedy was emphasized whenever possible and was carried out by ad-libbing and improvising by actors who usually wove in some of the village gossip in their remarks. Unfortunately, most of this folk drama has given way to television, the movies, and other forms of modern entertainment.

Secular Folk Drama

It was customary for Mexican players to travel north of the Río Grande and present programs along the way in cities and villages of New Mexico and southern Colorado. These summer stock types of troupes were a combination of trapeze artists, clowns, and singers, in addition to the actors who presented the plays. Many of the pieces they presented were one-act comedies or what in Spanish are called *sainetes*. In New Mexico and Colorado, a number of these one-act comedies were taken up by the people and became part of their own traditional repertoire. At times, longer romantic plays were introduced by the Mexican companies, and even a few of these were presented later by the folk when they were able to secure a copy of a play. Such skits as *Margarita Piojo,* "Margaret Louse" and *Chepe Polilla,* "Joe Weevil" were amusing comedy pieces which could be put on with a minimum of staging. Longer plays such as *Una Lluvia de Ingleses,* "A Shower of Englishmen," circulated among New Mexican folk and crossed over into Colorado whenever there was a producer who was willing to present them. In Trinidad and in the San Luis Valley, some of the smaller Mexican troupes appeared from time to time, but they emphasized more the trapeze artists called *maromeros,* clowns, singers, and *títeres* or marionettes. These performers usually brought along their own tents and remained in the region for several days.

The most spectacular presentation in Colorado is *Los Comanches,* a drama probably written by a member of the New Mexican militia or by an officer in the Spanish Army after the campaigns against the Comanche Indians in 1770 to 1779.[5] The original manuscript disappeared long ago, but a few incomplete copies have survived. Professor Aurelio Espinosa edited the first published copy in 1907; it was translated later by his brother, Gilberto Espinosa, an Albuquerque attorney and historian.[6] The most nearly complete copy known today states in the manuscript's only footnote that it was taken from *Cuadernos de comedias sacados en el año de 1864 por Miguel Sandoval.* In translation, it says that this play was taken from the comedy notebooks of Miguel Sandoval in 1864. Apparently, Mr. Sandoval had a number of these comedies copied in his notebooks, but nothing is said regarding the origin of the play. The owner of the copy that I located was a man from La Jara, Colorado, who had copied Sandoval's manuscript into a daybook interspersed with such entries as: "Today the bay mare had a black colt. Today, the 25th of April, 1906, the masked cow had a strawberry roan bull."

Los Comanches is the enactment of a pitched battle between the Spanish army under Don Carlos Fernández and the Comanche Indians who were led by the famous leader Cuerno Verde or Green Horn. The lines are drawn up in the open with a *castillo* as a backdrop for the Spanish army and the tepees of the Indians on the opposite side. Each actor advances to the center of the stage on his prancing horse and delivers his threats and boasting while the armies stand fast. The mighty chieftain Cuerno Verde opens the play with a heroic speech:

> *Desde el oriente al poniente,*
> *Desde el sur al norte frío,*
> *Suena el brillante clarín*
> *Y brilla el acero mío.*

> From the sunrise to the sunset,
> From the South to frigid North,
> Blare my mighty battle clarions
> And my steel brilliantly shines.

Don Carlos Fernández, the Spanish Commander, rides his horse to the center of the stage, flying the colors of colonial Spain; he answers the Chieftain:

> *Aguarda, detén, espera*
> *Que soy de tan noble brío* [*brillo*]
> *Que vengo sin que me llames*
> *A cuidar este castillo.*

> Bide your time, hold now and wait;
> For I'm of such noble mettle
> That I come without your call
> To protect this Spanish castle.[7]

The challenges are heard across the camp from both sides until Cuerno Verde gets restless for the battle to begin and orders a war dance. From the ranks of the Indian camp, there is a roar of war whoops. With the Spanish battle cry of "*¡Santiago!*" the opposing camps converge on the center arena for the battle. Sometimes the sham battle assumes strong semblances of reality. The Comanche part is usually played by Indians from the nearby pueblos, and sometimes as the "battle" becomes heated, both sides forget that they are actors.

The historical battle between the Spaniards under Don Juan Bautista de Anza, Governor of New Mexico in 1779, and the Comanche nation under Cuerno Verde took place below the present site of Pueblo at the foot of Greenhorn Mountain. Cuerno Verde was killed in this battle, and the Comanches were soundly defeated. Both the mountain and the village at the foot of it are named after the Comanche chieftain. Until recently, the inhabitants of the Purgatoire Valley used to present this outdoor historical drama. The author is unknown, but the internal evidence clearly indicates that he was well acquainted with the historical events and with all the participants of Indian and Spanish camps. The imagery and prosody also suggest a highly literate and cultured author. The nativistic romanticism which has lately influenced large portions of the modern Hispanic generation has caused interest in this historical play to wane because it highlights the victory of a Spanish conquistador. In actual fact, the Indians in Anza's day respected the Governor and had high regard for him because he tried to help the various tribes live in peace, including the Comanches themselves. The scourge of this powerful Indian nation was greatly lessened after the defeat of Cuerno Verde, but the battle left an interesting folk play for the Hispanos of Colorado and the Southwest.

Hispanic Folk Songs in Colorado

Singing has always been such an integral part of Spanish cultural tradition that the abundance of folk songs in the Southwest has been constantly increasing since the arrival of the colonists at the end of the sixteenth century. These early settlers brought songs which were current in their day, but most important, however, was the tradition of composing and singing. This was what kept alive the vast repertoire of old and new folk songs written by succeeding generations. Village troubadours composed a variety of verse that spoke of love, of suffering, of man's inhumanity to man, and of countless other themes of their everyday lives.

As the folk moved from place to place, from New Mexico to Colorado, the songs went with them and multiplied as time went on. It was a cultural organism infused with life given to it by people to whom music and song were an integral part of their enjoyment.

The oldest type of folksong in Colorado is the Spanish ballad or *romance*. These compositions tell of incestuous loves, of the eternal triangle, of kings' pages, unfaithful wives, and more often of shepherds and shepherdesses. The best known of the old ballads is *Delgadina,* the young princess who rejected the incestuous advances of her cruel father and suffered imprisonment in the castle's tower rather than submit to his indignity. When she called for a drink of water as she lay dying, the king had his servants take her some in a golden goblet, but when they arrived, she had expired. The ballad ends there, but in Colorado, they add two more verses, telling how Delgadina went to Heaven and her father was in the custody of *el Diablo Mayor.*

The ballad of Charlemagne's page, *Gerineldo,* has a happier denouement. The aggressive young princess suggests to Gerineldo that he visit her in her bedroom that evening, but the virtuous young man refuses, saying that she is merely teasing. She leaves her bedroom door ajar and is not disappointed. The following morning, the Emperor calls for his page, but he does not answer, whereupon the royal sire takes his sword and goes in search of his errant page only to find him in his daughter's bed. His first impulse is to strike him dead, but having reared the young man from childhood, the Emperor changes his mind and with a royal gesture leaves his sword between them. When the couple awakes and finds the sword, they realize that the father has paid them a visit. The ballad ends there. Hispanic tradition in the Southwest however, improves the lovers' morals by adding two more verses saying that they joined hands like man and wife.

Y allí se tomaron las manos como mujer y marido.

Bernal Francés was a French nobleman who was having an affair with a Spanish nobleman's wife. The ballad is entitled *La Esposa Infiel,* "The Unfaithful Wife." The husband finds out about the tryst and under cover of night replaces the lover in the garden and makes ardent love to his own wife who mistakes him for her French lover. The Spanish honor code calls for blood in this case, but the folk couldn't decide whose blood should be spilt. They compromise by ending the ballad three different ways: the lover Bernal is killed by the offended husband, or the unfaithful wife is killed, and as a third alternative, the husband kills the lover and then commits suicide in order that the philandering wife may suffer the loss of both for the rest of her life.

The Spanish indirect address so often used in folksongs is used in the ballads of *Agraciada Golondrina* "Graceful Swallow" and *La*

Calandria "The Lark." In the former, a missive to the lover's object of his affections in a distant land is given to a swallow who takes the message to the girl and returns on the third day with no written answer, only an oral message telling the young man to console himself with the cage because the bird has flown away, or

> *Le di la carta a tu dueña pero no te contestó: solamente me decía, y esta noticia te envió:—Consuélate con la jaula que ya el pájaro voló.*[8]

In the case of *La Calandria,* a lark imprisoned in a golden cage promises a sparrow to marry him if he sets her free, whereupon the bird tears the cage wires and frees her. The ungrateful lady bird takes to the air and ignores her promise. The gallant sparrow sits in the open cage to reflect on the fickleness of the female sex and philosophically advises his friends in the closing lines:

> *Les encargo a mis amigos*
> *antes de acabar de hablar;*
> *Unos son las que las sacan*
> *y otros las van a gozar.*

> I should like to warn my friends
> before I end this discourse;
> Some may come to rescue them,
> but others will enjoy them.

For some unknown reason, the ladies in most of the ballads seem to take the initiative and the young men appear shy and reluctant until they are won over. In the pastoral ballad of *La Dama y el Pastor,* "The Lady and the Shepherd," a wanton young lady tries to entice a fickle shepherd. To judge by his behavior, he could have been a buffon in the guise of a shepherd who ignores the artifice of love. Despite the lady's entreaties to spend a night or three with her, the shepherd insists that he must return to his flock in the mountains. On the way back, he changes his mind and returns to the lady who, having been scorned once, turns him down saying,

> *Llora tu soledad, que yo la lloré primero.*
> Weep in your solitude, for I was the first to weep.

From La Jara, Colorado, comes a charming ballad entitled *El Zagal,* "The Shepherd," also known in northern New Mexico. It opens with a classical ballad line:

Salí una mañana al campo, mi rebaño a apacentar;
I went to the fields one morning, my flock of sheep to tend;

The shepherd meets a shepherdess whom he had never seen before and asks her for a kiss. She promptly consents, providing he pays with gold. The wily shepherd tells her that his gold is in his camel's saddlebags, and his camel is far away in Fermán. She mischieviously counters by saying:

Los besos que traigo en mis labios, mis dientes están detrás;
la boca donde los guardo cerrada con llave está,
la llave tiene mi madre, mi madre está en Fermán.

My teeth are behind my lips where I keep my kisses, sir,
The mouth wherein I keep them is sealed with lock and key
My mother who holds the key is also down in Fermán.

There is a widely diffused ballad about a love-sick cowboy which is known throughout Mexico, the Southwest, and as far south as Argentina. The Colorado version is worded differently, but the main idea remains the same, although it has undergone some distortions. The title varies from *El Payo, El Charro, El Vaquero,* and *Nicolás.* In Colorado, it is also known as *El Vaquero Nicolás.*[9] It seems that a young cowboy is very sad, whereupon *Nicolás* answers him that if he doesn't want him to be sad, he should give him what he wants. The boss tells him to go ahead and ask, *Ve pidiendo, Nicolás.* The vaquero asks for money, a good horse, and saddle. The boss grants him this, but Nicolas is not satisfied yet. He finally asks for a girl he's in love with, but the boss tells him *Tiene dueño, Nicolás.* "She's got a man, Nicolás." The sad cowboy decides to shoot himself in one version of the song or to jump off a cliff in another one. The boss simply tells the love-sick swain, "Jump head first, Nicolás" or "Shoot straight, Nicolás." The well-known writer and traveler Charles F. Lummis found this ballad also in California.

Another ballad theme which in other parts of the western world appears also in prose is the exaggerated absurdity. The English author Foote had a unique absurdity written in prose:

> So she went into the garden to cut a cabbage-leaf to make an apple pie; at the same time a great she-bear, coming up the street, pops its head into the ship. 'What! No soap?' So he died, and she very imprudently married the barber.[10]

In Colorado, as in all of the Southwest, these absurdities written in eight-syllable verse were called *Mentiras,* "Lies," and they usually included a long list of impossible doings by the animal and insect world. For example, they speak of a crow that drags a pine tree over a canyon road or of a centipede and an ant that make tamales. In the ballad of *El Piojo y la Liendre,* a nit and a louse decide to get married, but they lack just about everything. The whole barnyard provides all the necessaries, but at the last moment they discover that they have no best man. The mouse volunteers for the role, but while the guests are passing the wine around, the cat breaks in and gobbles up the best man!

Suéltanse los gatos y sóplanse al padrino.

Colorado children played the usual games of the Hispanic world, such as *Naranja dulce limón partido, Dame un abrazo que yo te pido.* They were action and singing games; about 90 percent of them were of Spanish origin. A folklore class polled at the University of Colorado indicated that most of the 40 students knew the games but that they are played by children only in the small villages of southern Colorado. There is an attempt to reintroduce them in the public schools and in clubs today. Richard B. Stark,[11] Curator of the Museum of International Folk Art in Santa Fe, New Mexico, has just published an excellent collection of children's games with directions and music.

One type of song which has had a continuous popularity is the *corrido,* a variation of the traditional ballad. Instead of the usual 16-syllable line of the ballad, the *corrido* splits the line into two of eight syllables each and arranges it into quatrains. In Denver, there lived until recently a well-known composer by the name of Arculiano Barela. In 1914, he wrote a *corrido* telling of the "Ludlow Massacre" at the mines of southern Colorado when the labor unions were trying to get established in the mining industry. Mr. Barela was one of the miners whose *corrido* became known as *El Estraique de 1910*,[12] or "The Strike of 1910." Following the tradition of the *corrido* writers he began,

Que viva, que viva,
Y que viva la nación
Que aquí estamos peleando
Por una fuerte unión.

Long live, long live,
And long live the nation,
For we are fighting here
For a strong and lasting union.

Señor Barela sang this *corrido* for us in 1948 when he was in his seventies. A recorded copy was sent to the Folksong Archive of the Library of Congress. He composed another *corrido* based on the tragedy of a man called Rosendo Moya who was executed in Canyon City for having killed Joseph Sims in 1930. Most of the *corridos* deal with tragedy, violence, and death. They are seldom if ever concerned with love affairs. The *corrido* of *Rosendo Moya* opens typically by giving the date of the event:

El 27 de enero
este caso sucedió
Fue cuando Rosendo Moya
a Joseph Sims mató.

It was January 27
when this event took place
This was when Rosendo Moya
killed Mr. Joseph Sims.

There are many cowboy songs written in English about the cattle drives to Kansas, but they seldom mention the Mexican vaqueros who helped drive the steers. The folklorist Brownie McNeal, formerly of the King Ranch in Texas and now a college Professor, became interested in the subject of the vaquero in Texas and collected several *corridos* about the Chisolm Trail written in Spanish. McNeal, completely bilingual, recorded these *corridos* along with his other cowbody songs. In Colorado, the folk sing one of these *corridos* that tells the story of the trail to Kansas under the title of *El Vaquero*.

> *Cuando salimos pa' Kansas*
> *Con aquella novillada*
> *Ay! que trabajos pasamos*
> *Alla en aquella llanada!*

> When we drove out toward Kansas
> With that bunch of rangy steers
> Wow! What troubles we endured
> Driving through those endless plains!

The composer gives details of the dusty drive, the storms they drove the cattle through, the rivers they had to ford, and finally, when they have returned home, a mother doesn't see her son return and she asks for him, only to be told that her son was killed by a steer in a corral.

> *Su hijo lo mató un novillo*
> *En las trancas de un corral.*

There are other types of songs known in Colorado by the old settlers; these were entitled *Inditas, Cuandos,* and *Décimas,* but they are all written in the traditional eight-syllable line and usually in quatrains, except for the *Décima* which consists of 44 lines, beginning with an introductory quatrain, followed by four ten-line stanzas, each ending with one of the four lines of the introductory *copla*. There were many lyric songs of an amorous nature which were regularly sung until recently throughout Colorado. The titles below indicate the subject of each folksong.

Trigueña Hermosa, "Beautiful Brunette" speaks of a beautiful girl who has offered her heart to a young man. *Enséñame a Amar,* "Teach me to Love" is a singable melody in which the man asks the girl to teach him how to love but begs her not to teach him to forget, because that is something he'd rather not learn.

> *Enséñame a amar*
> *Enséñame a querer*
> *No me enseñes a olvidar*
> *Que eso no quiero aprendar.*

Another lover doesn't know what to do because he cannot forget the girl who left him. Wherever he goes he imagines he hears her voice.

> Amigo, no sé que hacer
> Con esa mujer que no la puedo olvidar.

Still in a romantic vein but mixed with tragedy or bewailing an unrequited love, the following selections are also part of the folksong repertoire of Colorado. A very lonely and sad lover decides that the only way to alleviate his sorrow is by going down silently to the tomb where he can look for his lost peace of mind.

> Bajaré silencioso a la tumba
> A buscar mi perdido sosiego.

A young married girl pines away and cries constantly because she is inexorably estranged although recently married.

> Yo soy la recién casada
> Que lloraba sin cesar
> De verme enajenada
> Sin poderlo remediar.

The old theme of the husband at the saloon is the unhappy lot of a wife whose drunken husband spends all day in the *taberna*.

> Mi marido es un borracho
> No se acuerda ya de mí,
> Se mantiene en las tabernas
> Sin apuro y sin cuidado.

Many songs of the romantic Mexican school have been brought to Colorado by the large influx of Mexican nationals over the past 60 years. *Carmen Carmela, Las Mañanitas, La Rielera,* and *Perjura* have become familiar to the Colorado Hispanic population by means of the radio, phonograph recordings, and lately by the Mexican programs on television.

Some of the sixteenth century songs from Spain have come to Denver in a very roundabout and interesting manner. Sephardic Jews from the Levant, particularly from Turkey and from the island of Rhodes, have brought the songs their ancestors learned in pre-Columbian days when they lived in Spain. In the one entitled *A la Una Yo Nasí,* the girl says that she was born at one, grew up at two, had a lover at three, and was married at four. The language of the Spanish Jews is called *ladino.* It is archaic and sometimes not easy to understand. The second song shows a Turkish influence in the refrain *Barmeenam!* which in Turkish means "Heaven forbid!" The first line of the song is "I have a foolish daughter, Barmeenam!" which in the *ladino* Spanish of the Sephardic Jew reads,

Una hija bova tengo, Barmeenam!

The urban centers of Colorado have a much richer folksong repertoire due to the influx of Mexican nationals over the past 60 years who have added their own *canciones* and *corridos* to the singing tradition of the state. The older villages of the San Luis Valley and the mountain towns have not had as strong a cultural contact with outsiders, hence they have for the most part only the old songs originally brought from New Mexico 125 years ago.

Folkways

As a culture moves away from its original source, there is a tendency to lose or change much of its content unless it is replenished by travel back to the source or by the arrival of individuals from the homeland. Hispanic folkways first came from Spain to Mexico, hence to New Mexico, and finally to Colorado. In this long transmission of almost five centuries, customs, traditions, and practices have become fractioned and sometimes garbled.

The children's games which Olibama López includes in her unpublished Master's thesis are good examples of folk traditions which have been altered in passing from New Mexico to the San Luis Valley. The game which she calls *Quiebro Bolitas de Oro* is a combination of parts from several games. The original game was called *Hilitos de Oro* in Spain and was used by Lope de Vega in his short play called *Daca mi mujer,* published in 1644. Twenty-three different versions of this ballet-game were published by 1946, from

New Mexico to Argentina, but the Colorado version is the only one that speaks of breaking balls of gold.

A New Mexican children's gamed called *La Gallinita Ciega,* "The Blind Little Hen," is changed in Colorado to *La Manita Ciega,* but the game is still similar to "Blind Man's Bluff."

The game which in Colorado is called *La Pelota,* "The Ball," is known in New Mexico as *El Chueco,* "The Crook," because they use a stick with a crook at one end similar to an ordinary golf club. It is more in the order of field hockey with two competing teams. The object of the game is to drive a small ball beyond established goal lines. Indians in the Southwest play a similar game, but it is not known whether the Indians or the Spanish inhabitants invented the game. Olibama López gives a good description of how the clubs are fashioned by heating them over hot coals and bending into proper shape. This same method was used by the Indians in shaping their bows and straightening arrow shafts.

Another game played in Colorado, well known throughout the Southwest, is *Pitarrilla.* In the San Luis Valley, they play a version of this game, which according to some informants is somewhat like Checkers. This game was the specialty of lonely sheepherders who played it on the sand by drawing three concentric rectangles with lines connecting the corners from the center out, and a straight line from each side to the inner rectangle. It is played like Checkers in that a player can jump another one, but it is also like Bingo, because when a player lines up three or five men in any direction he calls "Pitarrilla!" and wins the game.

Las Iglesias is a sort of baseball played with a soft homemade ball. In the days when boys wore leg stockings, they would unravel one or two made from *popotillo,* a mercerized yarn, and wind it into a ball which was then sewed to keep it in shape. The batter hit the ball with his hand and if a fielder caught it he tried to hit the runner with it before he reached a base, an *Iglesia,* that is, the asylum of the "church." He was "out" or *quemado* when hit. Players advanced as they do in baseball.

In Colorado, they also call this game *Cazulejas,* but in reality the game properly called *Cazolejas* derives its name from the *cazuela*-like holes dug in the ground, one for every player. The one "at bat" rolls the ball into the row of *cazuelas* and the one into whose *cazuela* the ball rolls must grab it and hit the "batter."

Men used to congregate on Sunday on some vacant part of the village to play *Tejas* or "Tiles," a game comparable to horseshoe pitching, except that they used flat, round stones about three to three and one-half inches in diameter with sloping edges. Instead of throwing at a peg, they threw at a hole just big enough for the stone to fall into. The game of *Tejas* is still played in a number of Colorado villages. There are also games of chance like *Cañute*, in which stock or grain was often bet instead of money in the old days.

The game gets its name from the cane sections with which it is played. The Spanish name for a knot to knot section of a bamboo cane is *cañuto,* but in Colorado and New Mexico they change the *o* to an *e*. The game in Colorado varies somewhat from the manner in which it is played in New Mexico, but it's essentially the same. Four *cañutes* named uno, dos, mulato, and *cinchado* are used by the two sides betting. The *escondedor* or "hider" places a small object (a penny, a nail) inside one of the *cañutes* and buries them in a sand pile with the name of the section showing. The object is for one side to guess which one has the concealed object. The leader of one of the betting sides touches the one on the right and then the one on the left before attempting to guess the right one. If one of the end cane sections has the object and is touched, the player loses a number of points agreed upon beforehand. A mistake passes the *cañute* to the opposite side.

In Colorado, the village troubadour improvises verses as the game is played or sometimes he sings an appropriate folksong. Olibama López cites this song from southern Colorado:

Cinchado si.
Cinchado no,
Cántele bonito
Que ya le herró [*erró*].

Cincado is it
Cinchado is not
Sing a pretty song
For he has missed.

One of the features of Hispanic folk life which the Anglo-American frontiersmen noticed when they arrived in the New Mexican settlements early in the nineteenth century was the number of dances and fiestas which were attended by the entire population. Even Zebulon Pike and his men were treated in Santa Fe to this type of diversion, the Lieutenant as a guest of Governor Alencáster and the soldiers as guests of the townspeople. They usually referred to their dance gatherings as *fandangos,* and many of the English-speaking visitors thought that this was the name of a particular dance.

In southern Colorado, each settlement had an annual fiesta in honor of the village's patron saint. There were also regular dances which old and young attended, the young to see and be seen and the old to supervise in the traditional manner. There was no lack of *músicos,* men who could play any instrument: a guitar, an accordion, a clarinet, or a violin. In the days of the early settlements, they played the traditional tunes for polkas, *espinados, cunas, taleanes,* and a variety of waltzes called *valses chiqueados, despacio, de paños,* and *de cadena,* as well as *chotis* and the stately *Varsoviana.* There were scores of other folk dances varying in popularity from town to town and village to village. The *Cuna* or "Cradle" dance was performed by four couples joining hands and going through a series of intricate girations, over and under movements, ending with all hands in the center in the form of a cradle. The music changed into a rocking movement and they rocked the cradle.

The waltzes combined figures and movements of other folk dances, some with a handkerchief, either holding ends by each couple or waving it to the rhythm of the music. The handkerchief is used in many Hispanic dances from Colorado to Chile where the *Cueca* is danced with a handkerchief held aloft by the man as in the graceful *Marinera* of Peru.

Of all of the folk dances in Colorado, *La Varsoviana* is the one most widely known throughout the state. Among Anglo-Americans, it is called "Put Your Little Foot." As the name of this dance indicates, it originated in *Varsovia* or *Warsaw* and from there it spread to Mexico and New York. The two variations of this folk dance met in the Southwest, where it was particularly popular a few years ago and is still danced in the small villages of New Mexico and Colorado.

In a land where settlers were pioneers, they relied almost entirely on custom to guide them. There was a customary way of courting a girl, of conducting a wedding, celebrating an engagement, and attending a funeral. From the time a child was conceived, the expectant mother relied strongly upon tradition to guide her. There were taboos and practices which could insure her health, as well as the welfare of her potential offspring. A key in her pocket would prevent harelip, and a deformity of any sort could be prevented by avoiding *susto* or *espanto,* that is, self-induced fright or one caused by an outside agent. Most important of all, a woman with child should never be denied an *antojo,* a sudden craving for a given dish, a fruit or anything which occurred to her at the moment. It was the husband's responsibility to satisfy his wife's unusual cravings. This custom, incidentally, is also common to folk cultures of other nations.

There were no doctors to attend the sick or to deliver a baby, but there were a variety of folk healers from *parteras,* or midwives, to *médicas, curanderas, arbolarios,* and *sobadores.* The *curanderos,* male or female, had a good deal of empiric knowledge regarding ailments and their cures, usually in the form of herbs and rubefacients. Except for complications after birth or dangerous infections, these village healers managed to take care of their own people. The *arbolarios* and the *sobadores* were greatly relied upon in years past, and they still are consulted by many who are skeptical of modern medicine. The *arbolario,* whose name should be *herbolario,* is particularly effective in counteracting a witch's hex by the use of herbs and other magical rites. The *curandero* is more of a general practitioner with a bit of folk psychiatry thrown in. The most effective of these healers is the *sobador.* He is a folk chiropractor who knows how to put a dislocated joint back in place and who can also give a very soothing rubdown, which, for ten times the price, becomes a "massage," in our effete society. For those who complain of a backache after a hard day's work, he administers an *apretón de arriero* by having the patient stand with his back to him, hands laced behind his neck and elbows forward together. The *sobador* encircles his patient's arms from behind, hoists him off the floor and gives him a bear hug. The patient's back cracks like popcorn and when he gets back to his feet exhales a deep breath and declares that he is good as new. This treatment is called a "wagon-driver's hug" because when men on the Santa Fe Trail developed a severe backache from riding rough wagons over the plains, they were given this hug to relieve muscle tension.

Colorado folk communities were held closer together by the extended family relationship called *compadrazgo,* that is by becoming "co-parents" at a child's baptismal ceremony. The layette, called a *canastilla,* was never to exceed $14, and as the child was returned from the church to his or her parents, there was always an appropriate exchange of folk verse.

Aquí les traigo esta prenda
Que de la iglesia salió
Con los santos sacramentos
Y el agua que recibió.

I bring you this precious jewel
Just returning from the church
After receiving the sacraments
And holy baptismal water.

The courtship and marriage customs were adhered to until recently, particularly among the rural folk. After a *pretendiente,* "pretender" became a *novio* or suitor, he would have his parents or other close relatives speak for the girl's hand in his behalf by presenting a *carta de pedimiento* to the girl's parents. If the answer was *sí,* both sets of parents would arrange a *prendorio,* an announcement-party-type meeting where the girl's relatives sat on one side of the room and the boy's on the other. The girl went to each of the young man's relatives after being introduced to the gathering by her father and shook hands saying, *"Servidora de usted,"* "At your service" or *"Aquí tiene usted su criada,"* Here is your servant." The other person, if he or she knew the routine would answer, *Y yo soy su servidor,* "And I am your serviteur." On the other hand, the whole thing would end abruptly if at the *pedimiento* the young man was given *calabazas,* that is, he was literally "squashed." The young man took his turn around the room introducing himself to his girl's relatives in the same manner. Bashful young people went through this ceremony apprehensively and blushing. Like most Hispanic gatherings, the ceremony ended with refreshments and sometimes with a dance. By means of this presentation, all those participating became *primos* or *primas.* This accounts for another form of extended family relationship which sometimes leads uninformed outsiders to believe that the whole village consists of blood relationships.

The period between the announcement party and the marriage ceremony is called a *plazo* or time limit set by mutual agreement. During this time, which is quite short, the groom is supposed to give the bride a *per diem* called *el diario,* and he usually splurges a bit in order to show what a good provider he can be. At the wedding, the *padrino,* or best man, pays for the entertainment, the groom pays for the *donas,* which in this case means the bride's wedding dress. It is still customary in many families both in Colorado and in Spain for the groom to present her with the *Arras.* In the Middle Ages, the groom gave his bride 13 gold coins in recognition of her merits, but in Colorado and New Mexico it is customary to give *catorce reales,* or $1.75, literally fourteen *reales.* It is a breach of etiquette to refer to *arras* as "one dollar seventy-five."

As the procession leaves the church, children approach the *padrino,* shouting *"pastilla!"* and in southern New Mexico, *"bolo!"* The procession is essentially the same as the one described in the old ballad when Doña Jimena married El Cid in the eleventh century. After a dinner and a ball that evening, the couple retires to the bride's parents' home where they stay for three days or a week, at the end of which it is customary for them to take home the matrimonial mattress.

In a short account, only a few traditions and lore can be mentioned briefly. A culture that lives by custom has a rich heritage of practices and a value system which has become an inseparable part of their social structure. Many of these customs and folkways are not questioned, nor do they think of defending them because *"es la costumbre de nuestra gente,"* that is, "it's the way of our people."

It is interesting to note that despite centuries of living in a region occupied by different Indian tribes, there is very little, if any, Indian influence in the traditional behavior of Hispanic residents in Colorado. There are a few material accretions which were adapted in colonial days, but as soon as trade contacts were established with the Mexican centers through *El Camino Real* or literally "The Royal Highway," the settlers supplied themselves with products which were more familiar to them. On the other hand, contact with Anglo-American culture since the days of the Santa Fe trade enabled them to assimilate the material contributions of this culture very rapidly. Today, Hispanic people of Colorado still preserve some of the philosophy of life and values of their traditional culture, but materially they are hardly different from the rest of the population.

Notes

[1] Arthur L. Campa, "Spanish Religious Folktheatre of the Spanish Southwest (First Cycle)," *University of New Mexico Bulletin, Mod. Lang. Series,* 5 (no. 1, Feb. 15, 1934).

[2] Arthur L. Campa, "Spanish Religious Folktheatre in the Southwest (Second Cycle)," *University of New Mexico Bulletin, Mod. Lang. Series,* 6 (no. 2, June 15, 1934).

[3] Edwin B. Place, "A Group of Mystery Plays Found in a Spanish Speaking Region of Southern Colorado," *University of Colorado Studies,* 18 (no. 1, Aug. 1930): 1–8.

[4] Richard B. Stark, *Music of the Spanish Folk Plays in New Mexico,* (Santa Fe: Museum of New Mexico Press, 1969).

[5] Arthur L. Campa, "Los Comanches, A New Mexican Folk Drama," *University of New Mexico Bulletin, Mod. Lang. Series,* 7 (no. 1, April 1, 1942).

[6] Gilberto Espinosa, "Los Comanches," *The New Mexico Quarterly,* May 1931: 130–142.

[7] Espinosa, "Los Comanches," p. 133.

[8] Arthur L. Campa, "Spanish Folksongs in Metropolitan Denver," *Southern Folklore Quarterly,* 24 (Sept. 1960, no. 3): 178.

[9] Olibama López, "The Spanish Heritage in the San Luis Valley," (M.A. thesis, University of Denver, June 1942), p. 72.

[10] Marcel Gautheir, "De quelques jeux," *Revue Hispanique,* 33: 385.

[11] Richard B. Stark, *Juegos Infantiles Cantados en Nuevo México* (Museum of New Mexico Press, 1973).

[12] Arthur L. Campa, "Spanish Folksongs," p. 185.

8 The Santero Tradition

John Wilson

In 1851, three years after the Treaty of Guadalupe Hidalgo, the village of San Luis was established in southern Colorado by Hispano settlers from New Mexico. Settlements at San Pedro, San Acacio, Guadalupe, and Conejos followed soon after. The mountains, physical barriers surrounding the valley except to the south, kept this area a cultural part of New Mexico well into this century.

The settlers brought with them techniques of irrigation, herding, adobe construction, and a unique religious folk art that had developed during nearly two and one-half centuries of isolation from the mainstream of Hispanic culture. This art, transplanted at its prime, had developed as a result of a spiritual need for visual religious symbols in the Spanish colony of New Mexico. The colonists, often without the services of a priest, kept an active religion with the aid of sacred images, commonly known as santos, which were placed in homes, private chapels, moradas,[1] and churches.

New Mexico, unlike the other settlements in the new world, was twice removed from the mother country. The political center for the expeditions was Mexico City rather than Spain, and the nearest supply center was Chihuahua, which was 600 miles south of Santa Fe. The difficult round trip required five months of traveling time. The demand for the necessities of life and lack of a water route or an easy land route into New Mexico permitted the importation of few fragile Baroque carvings.

During the Pueblo Indian Revolt of 1680, most of the religious images brought from Mexico were destroyed. The small wood carving of the Virgin known as La Conquistadora is an exception; it was carried by the Spaniards on their retreat to the area near El Paso and returned to Santa Fe with the reconquest in 1692. Another figure dating from a slightly later time is that of San

Miguel in the Church of San Miguel in Santa Fe which is mentioned in an account in 1709.

The returning Franciscan missionaries, wanting visual materials for the religious training of the Indians and decorations for their missions, painted on tanned buffalo, deer, and elk hides, using single image, nonnarrative figures in a linear Renaissance manner reminiscent of the frescoes at the church in Acolman, Mexico. It has been established that hundreds of these paintings were made, but only about fifty remain, many as fragments. Though competent and historically interesting, these works lack the vitality, intensity, and originality that was to be fully developed in the later work of the New Mexican santero, a maker of santos.

Two eighteenth-century carvers of note were the Mexican priest, Fray Andrés García, and the Spanish captain, Bernardo de Miera y Pacheco. Fray García is known for his rosy-cheeked figures and his knowledge of jointed figures and hollow-framed carving techniques. Miera y Pacheco's theatrically posed, robust figures, carved from solid pine logs, indicate his knowledge of Baroque and Renaissance art works in Spain.

An example in Santa Fe of provincial Mexican carving is the altarpiece originally made for the military chapel of Nuestra Señora de la Luz, also known as the Castrense, commissioned by the Governor and Captain General of the province, Francisco Antonio Marín del Valle, in 1761. The altarpiece, carved from local stone by imported Mexican carvers using low-relief painted panels and engaged columns, influenced all subsequent altarpieces in New Mexico, whether they were designed to hold paintings and sculptures already in the possession of the church, or were made for images to be commissioned.

A demand for santos, the works of Fray García and Miera y Pacheco, and religious prints from Mexican presses stimulated an indigenous folk art that, in the nineteenth century, far surpassed these provincial interpretations of European art.

There are similarities in the bultos, three-dimensional sculptures, from the various Spanish colonies, as one would expect, whether they were made in Mexico or other Latin American countries, the Philippines, or New Mexico. Usually, they were based on Baroque archetypes, no matter how distant in time and space. As examples, Saint Joseph was depicted as an old man before the Counter Reformation. In Baroque art, he was rejuvenated and contrasted with the gentleness of the Christ Child, as was Saint Anthony of Padua. There are a great many sculptures of the richly draped Immaculate Conception, as she was declared patroness of all Spanish possessions. The figures are usually polychromed wood and richly decorated. Hands were carved separately and pegged on, and often heads were treated in the same manner. Other materials were added to heighten realism, such as hair, glass eyes, teeth, clothing, and jewelry. There was a strong tendency to express suffering and the tragedy of the crucifixion.

In New Mexico, there were no fine quality woods readily available for carving and practically no proper carving tools. The dried root of the cottonwood tree, alamogordo, was used because of its softness and uniform grain. Unlike the sculptures in the other colonies, each section of each member of the body was carved separately and pegged and glued together with animal glue. Even the joints of the fingers were made separately on larger sculptures. This made possible sanding and shaping with sandstone and permitted greater animation in the figures. The surface of the santo was covered with a gesso made from baked gypsum and animal glue and painted with locally manufactured vegetable- and mineral-based water colors. Only indigo blue, also used by the weavers, was imported. The surface was coated with a rosin varnish, which gave a mellow golden tone to the figures. New Mexico, unlike the other colonies, had no gold for gilding the holy images. Very little metal was used in decorating the santos until the coming of the Anglo-American with his tin cans, although simple silver crowns were used occasionally.

Full-skirted figures of the Virgin were often carved to the waist and set on a slat-framed conical form that was covered with cloth dipped in gesso, not unlike the large processional figures from Europe. This form is also used in figures of the Nazarene Christ and other bultos a vestir, which were made to be clothed. In later Colorado figures, solid wooden trunklike skirts were left relatively uncarved in the clothed bultos.

Usually drapery was formed by dipping cloth in gesso and moulding it onto the figure; however, a mid-nineteenth-century sculpture of the Immaculate Conception in the Church of St. Francis at Ranchos de Taos, obviously based on a two-dimensional model, has the drapery applied in a planar fashion on the front and back of the figure. The drapery has been cut from thin, flat boards to reproduce the frontal silhouette seen in the original picture. From the front, the drapery is not too unconvincing, but from any other angle it appears the Virgin is holding a rather strange heraldic device.

The Penitentes required articulated figures of Christ to reenact His suffering in a type of lay mass. Their earliest figures had flexible leather joints, while later versions had cloth joints. This jointing is found frequently in other bultos a vestir. Still later Colorado examples had wooden hinged elbows and pegged moveable shoulders. A group of Colorado bultos in the Taylor Museum in Colorado Springs have unusually finely carved heads, hands, and feet, although the commercial house paints used for coloring lack the subtlety of earlier New Mexican pigments.

The nearly geometric elements representing the organic units of the body are carved with a clarity and restraint, even in the facial features, that echo the underlying structure of the assembled figure. The hieratic pose of the santo holding its particular symbolic attribute is given a further sense of power and dignity by the elongation of the total form. The symbolic nature of these attributes allows for a definite size differentiation that stresses the importance of the saint. The soldiers in the crucifixion of San Acacio, the horse in bultos of Santiago, and the angel and oxen used in depicting San Ysidro are diminutive compared to the central figure, giving a vertical stress and general simplicity to the composition.

Pine was used in the panel paintings, known as retablos, and in the constructed altarpieces. The form of the panel was often a simple rectangle, or it might have been capped with a shell form or lunette. The rather short and stocky figures painted on the gesso-covered retablos were outlined in dark color, and the resulting areas were filled in with transparent watercolor. This method of painting, used on both retablos and bultos, demanded a sureness of line that allowed for no overpainting or correction. There was little or no attempt at depicting three-dimensional space in the fully developed works or art. The images were painted with a calligraphic line, usually in a three-quarter view that permitted a linear treatment of the facial volumes.

Santos were not considered to be aesthetic commemorative figures of saints. They were sacred images more in the sense of icons in the Eastern Church. Scrapings from images were charred and used as a medication in the food of the sick; the figure of the Christ Child was placed in bed with a sick child to aid his recovery, and figures of saints, such as San Ysidro, were taken to the fields when aid was needed for the crops. The good character of the santero was considered when commissioning a work in order that it would be more effective. With the exception of the figures of the Sorrowing Virgin and Christ, santos depict the sacred power of the saints, and aside from the usual attributes to identify the individual images, do not dwell on earthly suffering.

Part of the vitality of the santo may have been a result of the practical awareness of the santero. Figures of Santiago, San Acacio, and San Ysidro often wear the clothing contemporary with the time of their creation in the nineteenth century. Although the santos more frequently wear the moccasins typical before 1850, a later santero depicted his santos in the newly arrived hobnailed boots. As acts of continuing devotion, the santos have been dressed and adorned with every available material: velvet, homespun, commercial calico, and nylon. Today, paper flowers have been replaced by plastic flowers.

Santos, so appreciated today for their beauty, strength of form and simplicity, have not been so well received in the past. From its inception in the eighteenth century, the unique nature of this religious art was severely criticized by outsiders. Records remain from 1776 in which the ecclesiastical visitor from the diocese of Durango, Mexico, Fray Atanacio Domínguez, haughtily denounced the quality of these unusual art works. In the early nineteenth century, various visiting prelates from Mexico declared that animal skins were unfit for depicting saints. These condemnations, along with definite ridicule, were heightened after the annexation of the Southwest by the United States at the close of the Mexican-American War. Bishop Lamy, his priests, and other new settlers were aesthetically offended by the crudeness of the locally produced images and had them removed from many churches, replacing them with plaster images more acceptable to Europeans and Anglo-Americans. Many of the offending santos were taken from the churches and placed in moradas by the Penitentes.

The availability of new materials, such as sawmill lumber, commercial house paints, glass, and wallpaper used by the later santeros contributed to the decline of quality in santo production. The desire for conformity, the new, and the commercial led people to buy mass-produced lithographs and plaster images, and the art of the santero, born of spiritual necessity, was discontinued at the beginning of the twentieth century.

Notes

[1] A chapterhouse of the Penitentes, a brotherhood functioning in the Third Order of St. Francis. The traditional santos for the moradas were the Nazarene Christ, the Crucifix, the Sorrowing Virgin, St. John, Christ in the Sepulcher, and the skeletal figure in the death cart called Doña Sebastiana.

9 Peasant Religion: Retablos and Penitentes
Thomas J. Steele, S.J.

Peasants are one of the constants of civilized history, dating back as a recognized class of society for millenia before Christ, appearing in practically all of the civilized areas of the world both in the eastern and western hemispheres. A peasant society can be described as a small agricultural village which is neither wholly isolated from a more developed society nor wholly complete in itself. The peasant society instead forms a portion—indeed the foundation—of the larger compound society, and consequently it must be defined within that larger context. Peasants may therefore be contrasted with primitives, whose society tends to be far more isolated and more complete in itself.

The peasant society, properly, is one that has some significant relationship to a town or city, usually a market town. Peasants produce not only for themselves, but also in hopes of exchange and gain so that they can achieve for themselves a certain success within a village and make possible for their children a greater success within the total and much more extensive system of political-military-taxgathering-ecclesiastical power of which the farming village is only a subordinate part. By means of his agricultural surpluses, the peasant indeed supports the non-agricultural specialist workers and rulers, and in the typical total society of this sort in past ages, the peasant was arguably the origin of all economic values. Plainly, industrialization and technology create the main values of the new total system according to processes that are entirely non-agricultural. When this change takes place, as we will see later, the notion of the Physiocrats that the land is the source of value usually retains a sort of half-life as an agrarian ethical ideal with a significantly nostalgic cast. The town and city that the peasant always keeps as a part of his awareness are bearers of what has been well named the "great tradition" of the larger compound society, a tradition of wisdom and religious knowledge, a tradition of wealth and power, a tradition of legal justice and the possibility of its opposite; consequently, the peasant who has frequent dealings with town or city is often in need of the patronage of some powerful person who is more acquainted with the economic and judicial workings of the great tradition and who will be able to protect him from being victimized.

The peasant spends his life in close relationship to the land. He draws his name from the *país,* the neighborhood in which he spends the overwhelming majority of his life, centered on the village of which he is above all a part, and he spends it in close relationship to the farm which, in the typical peasant tradition, has been controlled by his family for several generations, passing down from father to son; the result is both a deep traditional attachment to the particular parcel of land and a social structure normally patrilineal, patrilocal, and patriarchal. The religion which comes to be associated throughout the world and throughout history with the peasant is (whatever that of the great tradition might be) utilitarian and moralistic—that is to say, practical and directed to very particular social roles and the duties that one who occupies a social role must perform faithfully if the social order is to retain its stability. It supplements a religious system which does not tend to question the ultimates, since the peasant can assume that they are cared for by the great tradition which he knows *of* but does not himself know. Because the kind of farming that is carried on in a typical peasant system demands a fair degree of co-operation, this religion will tend to curb aggressiveness, diminish any thrust toward individualism, socialize the members of the peasant society by rendering them dependent upon the group, and issue sanctions to them which foster the routine fulfillment of routine tasks. As Robert Redfield has summed up in *Peasant Society and Culture,* a peasant's values center on "an intense attachment to native soil; a reverent disposition toward habitat and ancestral ways; a restraint on individual self-seeking in favor of family and community; a certain suspiciousness, mixed with appreciation, of town life; a sober and earthy ethic."[1]

The variation of this sort of society in which the eighteenth- and nineteenth-century Spanish Coloradan or New Mexican lived labored under a greater than ordinary isolation from the "great tradition" referred to above. The farming villages in New Mexico were also far more isolated than is usual in peasant cultures from anything that might be recognized as market towns, as well as from each other. There is a story told of a little mountain village in the northern part of the colony which was neither attacked nor overcome during the Pueblo Rebellion of 1680, and it was not even aware that anything at all had happened until the Spanish settlers returned a dozen years later; the village was used to being left alone. The story is almost certainly not true, but it suggests the vastness of isolation in the furthest backwaters of the Spanish past. In so isolated a world as this, the aid of a powerful and knowledgable protector against the larger society was rarely necessary; Frances Swadesh says that "the emergence of patrons as a powerful class appears to date from the mercantile development stimulated by the Santa Fe Trail." Further, debt peonage, which often is a sign of the patron relationship and which was the standard social relationship for the bulk of the population of Old Mexico, was very uncommon in New Mexico and Colorado, occurring only rarely in the Rio Abajo region; peonage becomes a notion applicable to New Mexico only when Anglo agri-business forced the people off their small farms and into the role of migrant braceros.[2]

Furthermore, in what market towns there were, trade was carried on more by barter than by cash. In the villages themselves, transactions were carried on by gift exchange and work sharing rather than even barter. There were very few things that the people of the farming village needed from the market towns and the even greater world that the towns mediated. The people had to have some tools, particularly those of metal, such as saws and axes, and metal itself that might be worked up within the village—iron, brass, and lead to be used as solder and for bullets. Weapons also had to come from the larger society—guns and swords. Some dyes were imported into the colony to be used to tint the woolen cloth made by both the Spanish and the Indians; these dyes frequently turned up among the materials of the santeros. Any fine clothing for special occasions or feast days had to be purchased or traded for. From the local area, the villagers had to obtain a few more things, especially salt, pottery from the local Pueblo Indians, and santos made by the semi-specialist santeros. In the village itself, there were a few specialties—medical attention and medicines from the *curandera* or *curandero,* the local expert in folk cures of the area; blacksmithing, working up the metal that had been secured in town; and midwifery. Apart from these things, however, each family—each extended family—would provide the vast majority, practically everything, of what they would need to live. The animals they had, sheep, goats, cattle, burros, and horses, would provide work, meat, grease for candles, and hides and wool for clothing. Timber was cut to be used for fuel and for making furniture and portions of the house. Finally, the earth itself provided the adobe and rock for the house, multiple crops for food and other uses, and the remainder of the dyestuff not imported. The skills to exploit these raw materials were provided by the members of the family itself—the minor necessary specialties uncalled-for in a one-crop or wage-work economic system which can purchase in a cash market all that it needs. Spanish peasant life was, by contrast, one of self-subsistent villages made up of self-sufficient families in almost every area of practical daily living; as Karl Marx wrote of nineteenth century French peasantry, "Each individual peasant family is almost self-sufficient; it itself directly produces the major part of its consumption and thus acquires its means of life more through exchange with nature than in intercourse with society."[3]

For the old village society, the weakness of every peasant society was aggravated by another factor. During the years of isolation, the area experienced a significant decline in effective energy use due to a recession in the technology of tools (farming implements especially) and of weapons. A great deal more manpower and man-hours were required to perform the same tasks of cultivation and defense than had been needed at the beginning of the colonial period. In the early days, the colony had been relatively well supplied with weapons with which to subdue the Pueblo Indians and coerce work from them—which the Spanish later had to do themselves; further, the farm tools—plows, pitchforks, scythes, sickles, hoes, and so forth—demanded more labor when they were homemade than they had when they were imported from Mexico and Europe. The Colorado and New Mexico Spanish were not invention-minded in the way that contemporary English and Americans were—such as James Watt, Eli Whitney, Robert Fulton, Cyrus McCormick, and Samuel Morse—mainly because there was not the economic substructure to reward the exploitation of such inventions as these men had made. The Spanish were resourceful, though: they had to be in order to even continue to survive in the face of a practically total abandonment by the "great" Spanish tradition. The population of New Mexico, counting Spanish and Pueblo Indians, appears to have declined in the first two centuries of the colony's history. Disease unassociated with malnutrition doubtlessly played some part of this decline, but the energy crisis fostered by a tool-and-weapon collapse must be held chiefly responsible for this major population decrease.[4]

For the Spanish villager of a century and more ago, the "great tradition" existed psychologically as an awareness on the farthest horizon of consciousness, as the fundamental guaranteeing and validating factor among many others within a continuity which began with the royal court of the king in far-off Madrid and the papal court of the pontiff in Rome (and even Heaven itself), passed through the viceroy in Mexico City and the bishop in Chihuahua or Durango, to the governor and vicar-general in Santa Fe and the alcalde and priest of the nearest town, and ended with the people of the village in manual contact with their land.

The peasant attachment to the land has been mentioned already as something that needs to be defined very carefully. The romantic era, beginning in the late eighteenth century and reaching a fever pitch in the nineteenth, set a very high value on the land. First, the above-mentioned economic view of the Physiocrats, a French school of economics that existed prior to the Revolution, when rendered obsolete as an economic theory, maintained its existence in the form of the ethic of agrarianism, which pointed to farming—and above all, the one-family farm— as a source of tremendous social and personal moral value. Secondly, land in the form of scenery corresponded to the eighteenth- and nineteenth-century notion of sensibility, the faculty that Wordsworth presupposed, that Emerson and Thoreau tried to develop into an American lifestyle, and that is an attribute of the vast majority of the heroines of nineteenth-century novels and even of such highly masculine heroes as Natty Bumppo, Huck Finn, and the monster in Mary Shelley's *Frankenstein*. Romanticism in this way led to a resacralization of nature after its demythologization at the hands of the rationalistic enlightenment and the technological advances which led to the industrial revolution. Apropos of the nineteenth-century peasant, a romantic viewer and writer could consequently make statements like this of Sister Joseph Marie: "The *Padres* and the *Conquistadores* left a cultural deposit in the Southwest which is a blend of religious devotion and adventure, a kind of Romantic Movement in the making."[5] Such a statement gives a seriously distorted notion of peasantry and of the area during the last century. As Father Walter Ong points out in *Rhetoric, Romance, and Technology,* "Romanticism appears as a result of man's noetic control over nature, a counterpart of technology, which matures in the same regions in the West as romanticism and at about the same time, and which likewise derives from control over nature made possible by writing and even more by print as means of knowledge storage and retrieval."[6] A precondition for Romanticism, in other words, is what sums itself up in the mathematicizing of the universe by Newton (*Principia,* 1687) and the invention of the steam engine by James Watt (1769). The rationalistic Enlightenment and the Industrial Revolution serve as psychic preconditions for Romanticism. For the first time in his multimillion-year career, man is able comfortably to confront nature, which hitherto has been overwhelmingly threatening, knowing that he can always fall back upon the comparatively safe world promised him by Newton, Watt, Diderot, Franklin, and the other lion tamers. Granted that the nineteenth-century Spanish peasant had a closeness to the land and that he was endowed with a large number of quaint customs surviving from or reverting to or at least reminiscent of the Middle Ages (that period dear to Romanticism), it must be remembered that nobody is quaint to himself, nobody is picturesque to himself, nobody is romantic to himself—except perhaps a member of the court of Versailles dressed up as a shepherd or shepherdess and playing with carefully laundered lambs. The Spanish of the nineteenth century are people *about whom* romantic sentiments were experienced by the sightseers and recorded by the authors of travel books for the sentimental reader. The closeness to the land of the Spanish is not that of the Byronic exile but that of the isolated peasant who is untouched by Romanticism because he is unaffected by the Enlightenment and industrialization which are its necessary presuppositions. He cares about *his* land in *his* village, not about nature *in globo.* Nature in general is to the peasant a mysterious and discomforting unknown.

Father Ong goes on to say that "Strong disapproval for the cliche is a regular concomitant of the romantic state of mind, subconsciously convinced that what is already known does not require repetition because what is known is stored in books, whereas art is necessarily a venture into the unknown." Totally devoid of any Renaissance or Romantic hunger for novelties, the New Mexican or Coloradan peasant, like all peasants, had instead a desire for what Eric Wolf, writing in *Peasants,* refers to as "that sense of continuity which renders life predictable and more meaningful." It is precisely this sense of continuity which is served by the ancient Greek rhetorical commonplaces—the aphoristic and proverbial gatherings of inherited wisdom of preliterate and pretypographical societies; as Father Ong points out:

> Oral cultures necessarily place a premium on standardization or fixity, for in the absence of writing the major noetic effort of a society must be not to seek new knowledge but to retain what is known, not to let its scant, hard-won store disintegrate or slip into oblivion. In this economy of thought, commonplaces serve an important function. They are major devices for standardizing knowledge, for keeping it in fixed forms retainable in the memory, so that it can be retrieved orally at will. Indeed, commonplaces are seen to be the most basic or central standardizing devices in the entire noetic economy once we recognize that commonplaces include epithets, which are omnipresent in an oral culture. We here understand epithets in the usual sense of expected or standard qualifiers, (the *mournful* cypress, the *clinging* vine, the *sturdy* oak, *wise* Nestor, *wily* Odysseus) or standard surrogates or kennings ("tamer of horses" for an ancient Greek warrior, "the Mantuan" for Virgil, "whale-road" for the sea). Epithets are mini-commonplaces.[8]

I would like to suggest in this context that the santos are a set of visual commonplaces, in which the verbal epithets of the commonplace are replaced by the visual attributes of the santo. It is my contention that the santos as a group make up for New Mexico and Colorado a nearly complete motivational system having to do with the control of the world exercised on behalf of mankind by God and the various saints. The santos make up a system which is both pictorial and, because of the legends, prayers, and associations passed down by word of mouth about the vast majority of the saints represented by the santeros, also oral.

The majority of these saints are patrons of various particular needs. Recently, I did a small amount of questionnaire work in Colorado and New Mexico, testing the possibility of recovering knowledge on this subject. I asked the question with regard to a list of saints, for what favors was each of them prayed to—for what good was this saint asked, for protection from what evil was that saint petitioned. In this way, I hoped to find out as completely as possible the hopes and fears which the Spanish of the last century associated with each of the saints. Unfortunately, a great deal of the knowledge, if indeed it ever did exist for each saint, seems to have been lost forever. I was, however, able to recover enough information, both through my questionnaires and by consulting written sources, to become convinced that when compared with a generalized motivational system drawn up for an agrarian, peasant society, the saint-related system of hopes and fears offers a nearly complete account of the motivational psychology of the Colorado and New Mexico Spanish.[9]

The saints' names that made up the body of the questionnaire were those represented by the santeros—the saint-makers—of the old Spanish Southwest. These folk artists derived from the Mexican version of the baroque school of painting and sculpture, but in the hands of the peasant New Mexicans and Coloradans, there developed an independent school of religious folk painting and sculpture. This art, fashioned almost exclusively from home-crafted local materials, is of three sorts, *retablos, bultos,* and *reredoses.* A *retablo* is a painting made on a pine panel, sawed at top and bottom, the rest hand-adzed, the front smoothed, covered with gesso (a mixture of gypsum and animal glue), and painted with watercolors, most of them homemade from carbons, earth oxides, and organic substances, some (as has been noted) made from dyes imported into the territory. A *bulto* is a statue assembled from carved cottonwood root, covered with gesso, and painted like a retablo; bultos were frequently clothed. Sometimes the nether portions were constructed of small pine laths clad with gesso-soaked cloth and painted when dry. A *reredos* is a large structure of pine columns, niches, and panels to be placed behind an altar; they are finished like retablos.

The proximate objects of imitation in the New Mexico santero tradition were artistic: the previous work of the santero himself and the representations of the subject at hand by other santeros with which the given santero was familiar. The ultimate imitated object of each santero painting or statue is the saint or other holy person.

In most cases, this was some saint, a human person who had attained Heaven after a holy life. Since Spanish southwestern peasant art was religious rather than aesthetic in purpose, so that the goal was to create an instrument of holiness and power, an instument for help in need, rather than an artifact for detached contemplation, the connection between the saint in the picture and the saint of reality was a matter of great importance. Granted that the artifact may be intrinsically holy, not merely because of what may be done with it (prayer) but because it was made by a holy santero working within this multiple holy tradition, a new dimension of the santo's sanctity appears upon consideration of the exact mode of existence of the object of imitation and the santo's relation to it. The degree of sacred power of a ritual article or action is gauged by two norms: its nearness as imitation to the original and the degree of power and holiness of that prototype.

There are two modes in which New Mexico cult objects are validated. The first is the simpler; it has to do with the relationship of pictures and statues of the saints, the angels, the Virgin, and God to those holy persons themselves. The principle stated above, that the power of a cult object or action depends upon its nearness to the original and the power of the original, applies quite readily. The question of nearness was cared for by the tradition of santero art, for the santero can assume that he is making his santo right if he is making it "the way it's always been done." The question of power insures that the santo will imitate not the saint as he or she was formerly active during an earthy lifetime but the saint presently living at the peak of power and holiness in heaven.

For it is not the saint in this our world, having merely the power of a holy human being, but the saint established in heaven, in the timeless "now" of eternity, who is able to give the maximum power to the bulto or retablo which imitates him, and therefore maximum help to a people in distress. Before death, Spanish piety believed, holy persons have only a very limited power, but after death God assigns certain of them responsibilities in definite earthly matters and the authority to fulfill them throughout the world for the rest of time. Hence the saints of santero art are shown not in moments from their earthly lives but in the timelessness of eternity, not in the earthy geography of their weak mortality but in the celestial environs of the unearthly paradise. The celestial saint has in a sense "recovered" and summed up timelessly all the moments of his earthly history and (more important) all the power and responsibilities for earthly affairs which God has given him to exercise in all places for all subsequent history. For the Spanish, then, the saints are mainly sources not of good example but of aid. The various items they hold—skulls, rocks, crosses, books, pennants, and so forth—are not implements with which they are shown performing some edifying activity or other of their earthly lives; these items are instead attributes which serve to establish the saint's eternal self-identity, and very often they are signs as well of the responsibilities the saint is currently fulfilling on behalf of people on earth.

European religious art of the Renaissance era suggests that if Saint So-and-So, pictured in a moment from his earthly history, was once a mere mortal like us, we can attain his eminence by imitating him; this can easily tend in the direction of Pelagianism, that constantly recurring Christian heresy which holds that man saves his own soul by living a good life in imitation of Christ and other holy persons. Santero art seems on the other hand to say, Saint Such-and-Such is now in heaven and is assigned by God to aid me; this holy retablo is of itself and by its own sanctity both my powerful claim on him and his potent presence at the spot of need. Since a ritual or ritualistic object is holy and powerful to the degree that it represents (and hence becomes) the ritual-giving action or sacred being from the pattern-setting time or place, the santero founds his likeness upon what is more real and most holy—the saint in heaven.

It may be noted at this point that not only ordinary saints but most of the other holy personages are treated in this fashion: the Blessed Virgin, for the reason that she is, like the rest of the saints, more powerful now than she was on earth; and the angels and God the Father and Spirit, all of whom have never had other than a heavenly existence.

The second mode of validation is that associated with the santero statues of Christ, the crucifixes, and (particularly) the carved bultos of Jesús Nazareno (Jesus the Nazarene or Nazarite, what European art knows as the Ecce Homo). For all their traits of stylization, these figures, and especially the latter, have a tremendous life-likeness rarely encountered in other New Mexico religious art, which tends instead to be highly iconic. The Jesús Nazareno figures derive their life-likeness from the lavishness of very carefully wrought detail; from their size—they are nearly as large as a man, far bigger than other santos; and from their articulation, for they are hinged with leather at the shoulder like huge puppets so they can be carried through the various stages of scourging, crucifixion, deposition, and burial. The validation of these Christ-figures stems not from heavenly being (as it does in the case of saints) but from a particular set of earthly actions, the Passion. It is not Christ in his eternal pre-existence or in his present glorification who guarantees these santos, but the earthly Christ in his performance of the only complex of actions that is recognized by Christians as a truly pattern-setting and power-inducing earthly and historical deed: his passion and death. In the Jesús Nazareno bultos, the hinging of the shoulders suggest that it is not so much the person Christ who is imitated by the bulto as it is the action-sequence of the Passion, Crucifixion, Deposition, and Burial. This complex action (in a fuller theology, with Resurrection added) is the validating basis of Christian salvation and Catholic sacramentalism, and consequently it stands in the Catholic Christian religion as the equivalent of the action-complex of the culture hero of a primitive tribe.

The pattern-setting action of any culture hero always occurs in a special kind of pattern-setting time which, like eternal now of the saints in heaven, can have access to any other time and indeed become identical with it, can absorb this lesser historical time into itself. Just as any and every earth navel is *the* earth navel, any and every world center is *the* world center, so any and every time which wishes to have access to the sacred time can do so, can *become it again* in its own way.

Within his special kind of time, the culture hero performs an action which established a rite and its mythic accompaniment. The myth validates the rite rather than explaining it. It often contains an authorization, in the form of a command, a request, or a grant of permission for the subsequent performances of the ritual (or the primal action in ritual form, if that is what is is): "And this day shall be unto you for a memorial: and ye shall keep it a feast to the Lord throughout your generations: ye shall keep it a feast by an ordinance for ever" (Exodus 12:14); "Do this in remembrance of me" (I Corinthians 11:24); "the hero is completely engrossed in ritual, and after teaching it to his brother—he repeats it by having his brother sing over his sister so as to rehearse under the hero's directions"; the sacred animals tell the hero, "these things we have given you are what you shall use henceforth."[10]

This theological framework permits the most productive appraisal of the Penitentes and of the santero art most closely associated with them. The Penitentes—the popular name for La Cofradía (Confraternity) de Nuestro Padre Jesús Nazareno—originated as far as can be known in about 1790-1810.[11] The Penitentes seem to have arisen to fill a vacuum in religious direction caused by the lack of enough priests during the eighteenth century, which was later aggravated by the ousting of the Franciscans by Spain and the Spanish priests by Mexico, and the departure of Mexico-trained secular priests after the American annexation. The Penitentes used the Jesús Nazareno bultos to perform the stages of the passion of Christ during their devotions in the earlier weeks of Lent, but the focal moment of the Penitente year was the re-enactment of Christ's crucifixion on Good Friday, when one of the Brothers was tied to a full-sized cross he had carried to the Calvario, was raised up on it, and was left for some time, frequently until he fainted. This is, of course, the ritual which has given rise to most of the sensationalizing journalism about the Penitentes.

Francis of Assisi's concern with the passion of Christ led to his fostering the devotion to the Way of the Cross—a series of 14 episodes of the last hours of Jesus, both scriptural and mythical, from the condemnation by Pilate to the placing of the dead body in the tomb. These "stations" concerned the people more during Lent than at any other time of the year, and as that penitential season drew to a close, the entire town often co-operated in performing the devotion. In certain areas of southern Colorado and northern New Mexico, "some plazas staged a cycle of plays during Holy Week that depicted the wholy story of the capture, trial, and crucifixion of Christ."[12] The best-documented of the old plays is that in Tomé, from which survive a complete scenario, précis of the five standard sermons, texts of *alabados,* and even some movie footage. The play was performed annually from the eighteenth century to 1955.

The ceremonies begin with a Tinieblas and procession on Wednesday evening. After the Holy Thursday morning Mass, an afternoon ceremony enacts the capture and imprisonment of Christ. All the parts are taken by the townspeople except those of Christ, Mary, and John the Evangelist, which are taken instead by large statues carried around on pallets. At nine in the morning on Friday, after the Mass of the Presanctified, the *bulto* of Christ, hands tied, is led out of the church to a spot beneath the balcony that spans the front door where Pilate is seated with his attendants and Barabbas. After dialogue with the Jews, Pilate sentences Jesus to death (the First Station of the Way of the Cross), and the performance proceeds around the village plaza, ending after the Ninth Station (the Third Fall) with a sermon. The Friday afternoon ceremony enacts the remaining stations, the stripping and crucifixion, the death and deposition, and cortege and entombment; an evening sermon commemorates Nuestra Señora de la Soledád, Mary the widow bereft of her Son.

Saturday offers only slight additions to the standard Catholic services, but on Sunday, the ritual concludes with the enactment of the resurrection. The bulto, with the head of the suffering Christ of Friday replaced with a transfigured one, returns toward the church from which the statue of the Virgin comes to meet him; Saint John, carried by two men, "runs" between them to bear the glad tiding to Mary over and over again.

All the foregoing suggests that the Penitente crucifixes and Jesús Nazareno bultos and the Penitente ceremonies themselves are best evaluated together, as parallel manifestations of the same religious dynamic. Most of the New Mexico saints are, as has been said, represented in repose, so that even San Acacio and Santa Librada are not depicted in the moment of their "painful" crucifixions so much as shown possessing their crosses as attributes; but the Penitente crucifixes and especially the Nazarenos are definitely action oriented, showing a highly dramatic Christ and often made with hinged limbs so as to be put through the various torturous stages of flagellation, crowning with thorns, mocking, crucifixion, deposition, and burial. The events of Christ's passion and death evidently occupy a status as pattern not equaled by the earthly deeds of any other holy person. Particularly, when the Penitente brothers or the assistants at a passion play move the Jesús Nazareno bulto through the various moments of Christ's earthly passion, death, and entombment, the activity is almost certainly to be understood as a folk equivalent of the Catholic Mass: the action, no less than the articulated statue itself, is validated by the primal Christian even in such a way as to become its ritual symbol, a symbol in which that primal event is truly present. This kind of activity originally took place in New Mexico without authorization by the official Church, and there is no provision in any official Catholic theology of the sacraments for it; but anthropologically, the Penitentes were undoubtedly performing a ritual of exactly the same sort as are the sacraments: making present in their own day the identical action upon which the Christian religion is based.

Therefore, especially when the same events are not re-enacted by the nearly lifesize "puppets" made by the santeros or mimicked by actors, but undergone by actual men, the ritual should be seen not as a Pelagian effort to gain one's own salvation by doing for oneself what Christ did, but as a memorializing of him in such a way as to make present again the original crucifixion itself, not *another* event. Just as in Catholic theology the given particular contemporary Mass is not adequately distinguishable from the Sacrifice of Calvary, so the Penitente crucifixion ritualizes and hence *becomes* the original Calvary. Granted that the person tied to the cross may be Hermano Espiridion Miera of our little village, insofar as he matters, he is Jesus Christ. There are not two holinesses, one of Calvary, the other of the Penitente ritual; that of the latter is identically if only by participation that of the former, the original ritual-giving and pattern-setting action of the only earthly time which can set patterns. And in like manner, there are not two powers and holinesses, the one of the saint in heaven, the other of the retablo or bulto on earth, but only one— and indeed, a kind of singleness of being.

In conclusion, I would like to suggest that any serious study of the New Mexico Spanish of the nineteenth century discovers a people with a special relationship to the deity and the saints who are portrayed in santero art, and I insist that this relationship needs to be taken seriously into account when the people are spoken or written about. The saints, as they are aligned with the needs, the hopes, and fears associated with them, constitute a particular motivational economy which, while it is not complete in all respects, is a necessary supplement for any and all other accounts of the Colorado and New Mexico Spanish of the last century: the "People of the Saints," as George Mills accurately names them, cannot be known apart from their saints. The santos—the wooden saints, retablos, and bultos—were components of a power system which reached from earth to heaven and controlled hell, and in so doing, protected the culture (including the power system itself) from that worst of all failures, the loss of the people's confidence in their way of life. The Spanish of the last century did not trust in or attempt to put into practice a physical control over their world through technology, however rudimentary, but their culture shows what every living culture shows: that however passive and fatalistic it may seem, especially to an aggressive and nature-dominating culture, every culture enables its people to posit a refusal to yield to basic defeat, a refusal not to endure. Though help may be needed, from the past, from the future, from another world altogether, the vital culture insists that help is available through known strategies. The Spanish people in the Southwest of the nineteenth century sought help in prayer, and they endured.

Notes

[1] Robert Redfield, *Peasant Society and Culture* (Chicago: University of Chicago Press, 1960), p. 78. Frances Swadesh, "The Social and Philosophical Context of Creativity in New Mexico," *Rocky Mountain Social Science Journal* 9 (1972): 15. Swadesh comments that "In New Mexico, the most admired personality configuration centers on reserve, coupled with sensitive perceptions of the feelings of others, frequently communicated by nonverbal means." On the relationship of peasant to town, an interesting Anglo sidelight is offered by Robert Penn Warren's elegiac "The Patented Gate and the Mean Hamburger," which presents the agrarian tradition in a positive light, the town in a negative; describing mountaineer sharecroppers in the market town: "They will stand on the street corners and reject the world which passes under their level gaze as a rabble passes under the guns of a rocky citadel around whose base a slatternly town has assembled." *The Circus in the Attic and Other Stories* (New York: Harcourt, Brace, 1947), p. 121.

²Swadesh, "The Social and Philosophical Context of Creativity," p. 12; see also Irving A. Leonard, *Baroque Times in Old Mexico* (Ann Arbor: University of Michigan Press, 1959), p. 222.

³Karl Marx, "The Eighteenth Brumaire of Louis Napolean," in Karl Marx and Frederic Engels, *Selected Works* (New York: International Publishers, 1968), p. 172.

⁴D. W. Meinig, *Southwest* (New York: Oxford University Press, 1971), p. 13; Eric R. Wolf, *Sons of the Shaking Earth* (Chicago: University of Chicago Press, 1959), p. 195, states that "between 1519 and 1650, six-sevenths of the Indian population of Middle America was wiped out"; pp. 198-211 give a cogent argument in terms of energy use. For other particulars, Wolf, p. 160, notes that "only one plow, of the many types of Spanish plows, was transmitted to the New World," and Irving A. Leonard, *The Books of the Brave* (Cambridge: Harvard University Press, 1949), p. 242, states that the Spanish Crown "had forbidden the manufacture of arms in the colonies and had severely limited the importation of them from the homeland."

⁵Sister Joseph Marie, *The Role of the Church and the Folk in the Development of the Early Drama in New Mexico* (Philadelphia: University of Pennsylvania Press, 1948), p. 3.

⁶Walter J. Ong, S.J., *Rhetoric, Romance and Technology* (Ithaca: Cornell University Press, 1971), p. 20. Copyright 1971 by Cornell University. Used by permission of Cornell University Press.

⁷Ong, *Rhetoric,* p. 21; Eric R. Wolf, *Peasants* (Englewood Cliffs: Prentice-Hall, 1966), p. 98; Swadesh, "The Social and Philosophical Context of Creativity," p. 16, says: "New Mexican perceptions of the relationship between Man and Nature do not apparently lead to the celebration of Nature for its own sake, which is characteristic, for example, of the poetry of Wordsworth."

⁸Ong, *Rhetoric,* pp. 261-62.

⁹See my *Santos and Saints* (Albuquerque: Calvin Horn Publisher, 1974), pp. 85-95, 207-09.

¹⁰Gladys A. Reichard, *Navaho Medicine Man* (New York: J. J. Augustin, 1939), p. 76; Alfonso Ortiz, *The Tewa World* (Chicago: University of Chicago Press, 1969), p. 14.

¹¹The good accounts of the Penitentes are Fray Angélico Chávez, "The Penitentes of New Mexico," *New Mexico Historical Review* 29 (1954): 97-123; George Mills and Richard Grove, *Lucifer and the Crucifer: The Enigma of the Penitentes* (Colorado Springs: The Taylor Museum, 1966); Bill Tate, *The Penitentes of the Sangre de Cristo* (Truchas: The Tate Gallery, 1966); Marta Weigle, *The Penitentes of the Southwest* (Santa Fe: Ancient City Press, 1970—with a good

the Southwest *(Santa Fe: Ancient City Press, 1970*—with a good bibliography*); and Lorenzo de Córdova, Echoes of the Flute* (Santa Fe: Ancient City Press, 1972); Chávez, *My Penitente Land* (Albuquerque: University of New Mexico Press, 1974); Weigle, *Brothers of Light, Brothers of Blood: The Penitentes of the Southwest* and *A Penitente Bibliography* (Albuquerque: University of New Mexico Press, 1976).

[12]Robert Adams, *The Architecture and Art of Early Hispanic Colorado* (Boulder: Colorado Associated University Press, 1974), p. 22. —An eyewitness account of a New Mexico drama may be found in John A. Chester, S.J., "Holy Week at San Miguel," *Woodstock Letters* 10 (1881), 274-80; a valuable account of a San Luis Valley passion play appears in Olibama López Tushar, *The People of "El Valle"* (Denver: Olibama López Tushar, 1976), pp. 71-73.

10 Alabados of the San Luis Valley

Yvonne Guillon Barrett

The *Alabado* is a religious hymn predominant among the Spanish-speaking people of the southwestern United States. According to tradition, the meaning of the word is derived from *Alabado sea* ... (Praised be...) which is the first incantation used in Spanish hymns dedicated to the Blessed Sacrament. Later, particularly in the Southwest, the word *alabado* came to be any form of hymnal chant at religious festivities, wakes, or funeral processions, its contents coming to vary considerably and the alabados now variously dedicated to Christ, to the Virgin, or to a given saint. Further, the motifs no longer are solely of praise, as in the original ones, but are also of thanksgiving, forgiveness, and protection, as well as other expansive demonstrations of spiritual and temporal yearning.

Even though the *alabado* is a form of popular religious poetry, surprisingly it has not been extensively researched in the United States, aside from efforts to incorporate them into analyses of popular or traditional poetry or to relate them with isolated examples of religious practice. In fact, the most successful efforts to examine *alabados* appear to have been the collection of J. B. Ralliere[1] and the study of Juan Rael.[2] Although Father Ralliere's publication is restricted to compiling a representative variety of hymns, it lacks references to origin or source; yet to date, it has had eight reprintings. The last one, in 1933, was reedited to permit a slightly different classification.[3] The study by Rael, on the other hand, includes 89 *alabados* selected according to popular appeal from more than 200 collected throughout New Mexico and southern Colorado; these are classified into eight categories with an autochthonous musical transcription appended. The Colorado portions came from Antonito, Conejos, Isla, Alamosa, Manassa, San Luis, and Cerritos—all are towns and villages of the San Luis Valley.

According to Rael, the music was recorded during the summer of 1940, the melodies deriving from the collaboration of six local singers, all members of the Flagellants Society. The transcriptions were executed and categorized by Eleanor Hague, a musicologist, who also contributed the musical explications. To provide English-speaking readers with a better idea of the content of these *alabados,* four in the collection have been translated.[4]

Although there is insufficient evidence of genesis for the *alabados* in Colorado, it is not adventuresome to postulate that they spread into the North American culture via two separate routes: (1) by means of the Spanish missionaries of the seventeenth century and (2) by way of the Penitentes, or Flagellant Brotherhood. In fact, it is to the latter that is owed the presentation of the major collection to date.

As to the first of the two cultural routes, it is well known that in the atmosphere of zeal to convert natives to Christianity, the Catholic missionaries established certain specific precedents for the use of prayers and the chanting in the daily mission life. Thus, there were the *Cántico del Alba,* or the dawn prayers; the *Alabado,* or song of divine praise sung at various times throughout the day; the *Bendito,* or grace before and after meals; and the *Angelus* at sundown. After the evening meal, the missionaries and their congregations would gather for the *doctrina* where *alabados* would again be sung by the entire community.[5] Although there is little record of the activities of the first missions in Colorado itself, it can be assumed that these too followed this mission-style religious pattern of life. In Colorado, the first stable mission to be established probably was composed of friars who accompanied Don Diego de Vargas, Governor of New Mexico, to Culebra Creek in the present San Luis Valley. If this is true, then it can rightly be assumed that the *alabados* were chanted in Colorado *circa* 1694.[6]

Apparently, by the end of the eighteenth century, formalized mission education in the Southwest was coming to its close. Therefore, catechizing as a tradition automatically came to be relegated to the frontier cabin homes where religious education was conducted mainly by the mothers and family in general. It is possible that at this crucial transitional cultural stage the various classifications of hymns used by missionaries would all be regrouped and become known as *alabados* regardless of their previous more formalized categorizations and come to be sung by oral tradition as part of a daily ceremony.

As to the second of the two religious-cultural routes, the other source of *alabados* in Colorado (and the ones that have remained in written form to this day) arrived with the community of *Penitentes.* This brotherhood seems to have been an outgrowth of the Third Order of Saint Francis and is known by various names, the most succinct one being *Los Hermanos Penitentes de la Tercera Orden de San Francisco* (The Penitent Brothers of the Third Order of Saint Francis). These *penitentes* settled in the Southwest very early, as can be testified to in the *memorial* of Fray Alonso de Benavides to Pope Urban VIII in 1634. Therein, the Commissioner of the Holy Inquisition writes about the flagellation taking place among Christian folk during Holy Week.[7] Since the fraternity is composed of lay brothers, those who came to Colorado settled mainly in the San Luis Valley and had to devote themselves to such means of livelihood as grazing and other forms of agriculture. Today, the order is nearing extinction, but those who remain in San Luis continue to adhere to the Spanish culture in their language, traditions, and folklore. This is particularly true in religious matters where Catholic practices predominate. It is not surprising to find that in the chanting of *alabados* they continue to preserve the words and music of their centuries-old Spanish forerunners.

The hierarchy of the Penitentes comprises several offices, one of which is the *rezador,* or reader-of-the-prayers, and whose duty it is to read the prayers and to sing, or to lead the singing, of the *alabados.* These readings take place on specific occasions— initiations of novices, celebration of wakes, funerals, observances of Lent, and particularly the Holy Week. The *alabados* sung at these services vary according to the circumstances and are not exclusively songs in praise as their name implies. Although, as a rule, only the *rezador* and the brothers of the congregation may participate, there are other special religious events such as Good Friday where the entire community, including women and children, is admitted to chant.

While some *alabados* are very old and come directly from Spain, others are imitations, or improvisations, by local poets.

The music generally is composed in the flatted minor-key forms and is chanted in liturgical fashion; it is usually adapted from church music and therefore is not original.[8] The *alabados* of the *penitentes* are usually handwritten and handed down from *rezador* to *rezador* or to members of their immediate family. The majority of those are quite long and only with difficulty can be committed to memory. Because of their frequent use, personal collections do not last in legible state for long and must be recopied periodically. This gradually results in a variance of style, wording, and spelling because of the poetic license of the copyists or to their deficient command of the written language. Frequently, identical hymns can be found in several separate collections; because of continuous usage and rapid deterioration, however, no old manuscripts remain from which to trace the evolutionary changes to their originals in Spain.

The predominant verse and strophic forms of the *alabados* is the eight-syllable verse used in traditional Spanish folk poetry. This form appears with a variety of stanza and rhyme schemes, such as the quatrains, quintillas (five-line stanzas), sextains with alternate rhyme, and the typical *decima* (a ten-line strophe with the abbaaccddc rhyme). Other lesser forms include lines of five, six, seven, and ten syllables following the patterns of early religious poetry in Spain. Among the predominating forms is the classical *romance*, particularly in those hymns dedicated to the Passion and the Crucifixion of Christ. The *alabados*, describing the suffering of Christ, the Virgin and the Apostles, etc., are usually sung during the ceremonies of Holy Week, and are variations of the *romances* on the same theme found in the *cancioneros* of sixteenth- and seventeenth-century Spain. The dramatic aspects of the Passion are notable and follow the traditional realism of Spanish literature. Among such variances of a peninsular *romance*, we note the *alabado* "Por el rastro de la sangre" which has sustained several metamorphoses and is traceable to sources in Spain. We have found an earlier version in a *romance* of the *Cancionero de Ubeda*, published in 1588.[9]

> *Por el rastro de la sangre*
> *que Jesucristo dejaba,*
> *va caminando su madre*
> *quebra el coracon miralla.*
> *Las palabras que decía*

> *son de mujer lastimada:*
> *¡Ay, Hijo, redentor dulce!*
> *¿dónde está tu linda cara?*

(Along the trail of blood that Jesus shed, the mother walks and the heart breaks to see her. The words she has uttered are of a woman broken: "Oh my Son, sweet Savior! Where is Thy face so fair?")

Juan Rael has found another version by J. M. Cossío and Maza Solano in their *Romancero popular de la montaña*.[10] Here there is a slight variation in both stanzas, particularly in the second, where, instead of a plaintive rhetorical question, there ensues a dialogue with an unknown woman, thus lending it a more dramatic form:

> *Por el rastro de la sangre*
> *que Jesucristo ha derramado,*
> *camina la Virgen pura*
> *en busca de su hijo amado,*
> *En el medio del camino,*
> *una mujer ha encontrado:*
> *—Dime, cristiana mujer*
> *si a mi Jesús has hallado.*

(Along the trail of blood that Jesus shed, walks the Virgin pure in search of her beloved son. Halfway up the road, to a woman she has met says she: —Tell me, Christian woman, if my Jesus you have seen.)

Aurelio Espinosa has published several variants of this same haunting ballad found in the Southwest and elsewhere in the Spanish-speaking world.[11] On the other hand, Rael was able to locate companion versions in the San Luis Valley, which, though altered, read from the same basic format. One of these from Manassa is interesting for its linguistic and descriptive changes:

> *Por el rastro de la sangre*
> *que Jesucristo* **redama**,
> *camina la Virgen pura*
> *en una fresca mañana.*

> Encuentra a San Juan Bautista
> y de esta manera le habla:
> ¿No has visto por aquí
> al Hijo de mis entrañas?[12]

(Along the trail of blood, that Jesus shed, walks the Virgin pure upon a morning fresh. She meets St. John the Baptist and this to him she says: "Have you seen my precious son pass this way?") The substitution of *redama* for *derramado* is a clear case of metathesis common to popular speech patterns. In like manner, the description of the "fresh morning" so illustrative of the indelible, rural countryside aura, evokes a feeling of purity and spirituality that these *alabados* commonly exude.

Both the original Spanish and the San Luis versions describe and itemize Christ's agony along His way to Calvary. However, the Colorado version of Manassa has additional verses appended which transformed the original Spanish ballad of Ubeda into a religious hymn. The same is true of the ballad discovered by Cossío and Maza Solano in Santander. Inasmuch as the additional transition of this ballad from monologue to dialogue is a feature also found in the New World versions, it is possible to postulate that these came from the region of Santander, Spain, all stemming from their sixteenth-century ancestor. The *alabados* derived therefrom are really versified sermons, interrupted with meditations and explanations, with the purpose of inducing piety, fear, and atonement of the sinners who contemplate the agony of Christ and the mysteries of redemption. Moreover, the San Luis version has an invocation to the Holy Virgin, very much in keeping with the medieval tradition still permeating the Spanish Catholic world.

> (*Santander*)
>
> *El que esta oración dijese*
> *todos los viernes del año*
> *saca un ánima de pena*
> *y la suya de pecado;*
> *la de su padre y su madre,*
> *la de todos sus hermanos.*

*Quien la sabe y no la dice,
quien la oye y no la aprende,
el Día del Juicio verá
lo que en ella se contiene;
con una vara de acebo
palos hasta que se quiebre.*[13]

(He who chants this prayer, each Friday throughout the year, redeems a soul from Purgatory and his own from sin. He who knows it and teaches it not, he who hears it and learns it not, shall know on the Day of Judgement the meaning of this prayer; he shall be beaten with a branch of holly tree till it breaks.)

(*San Luis*)

*Quien esta oración cantare,
todos los viernes del año,
saca una ánima de penas
y la suya de pecado.*

*El que sabe y no la enseña
el que la oiga y no la aprende,
el Día del Juicio sabrá
lo que esta oración contiene*

*Madre mía de Guadalupe,
Madre de Consolación,
Señora de los Dolores,
yo te ofrezco esta oración.*[14]

(He who chants this prayer each Friday throughout the year, a soul from Purgatory redeems and his own from sin. He who knows it and teaches it not, he who hears it and learns it not, shall know on the Day of Judgement the meaning of this prayer. Oh, Mother of Guadalupe, Oh, Mother of Consolation, Oh, Lady of our Sorrows, to Thee I offer this prayer.)

Among the other verse forms used for describing Christ's Passion is the quatrain found in the beautiful alabado *Ayudad almas queridas* (Come and join, dear souls), preserved in the towns of Antonito and Cerritos. The first strophe is an exhortation to the reader to join Mary in her sorrows for her Son.

*Ayudad, almas queridas
a sentir a nuestro Padre,
que es Jesús de Nazareno,
Hijo de la Virgen Madre.*

*El Jueves Santo en la tarde
cuando a mi Jesús prendieron,
María, su dulce Madre,
el corazón le partieron.*

(Dear souls, join in mourning for our Father, for he is Jesus of Nazareth, Son of the Virgin Mother. On the afternoon of Holy Thursday, when my Jesus was taken away, Mary, his sweet mother, felt her heart break.)

The remainder of the *alabado* is a narration of Christ's Passion interspersed with monologues and dialogues uttered both by Jesus and His mother. Mary does most of the speaking, sometimes bewailing Pilate's judgement, others exhorting the mothers of the world to share her sorrow, or again talking to her Son. In all of the dialogues, there is naive and simple expression of love on the part of both mother and Son.

Amid other stanzaic forms that review the Passion is the more elegant quintilla of *Niño pues vais a pagar* (Child, you will pay) sung in most of the Valley (Alamosa, Isla, Antonito, Conejos, Manassa, and San Luis). The narration is in the first person, with Jesus telling of his sorrows from the moment of his trial to his death, and in so doing emulating the literary tradition of Franciscan poetry.

According to Rael, the original *Alabado* consisted of 27 stanzas and the Manassa version is missing only one stanza, number 20. On the other hand, those of Alamosa, Isla, and Antonito do not contain stanza 27; the example of Conejos ends at stanza 21 and thus is a peculiar pattern, closing *in medias res* with the falling of Christ on his way to Calvary.

*Al quererme levantar
como la fuerza era poca
caí para mas tormento
y, faltándome el aliento,
di en el suelo con la boca.*

(When I tried to get up, and my strength was drained, I again fell to new torture, and being out of breath, my face struck the ground.)

The version of greatest variety is the one we found in San Luis where stanzas 2 and 7 are missing, yet one more is added between 25 and 26, and several have changes of position as well as wording. While all of these renditions contain the pathos of the Passion and portray to the reader the same tragically vivid image of Christ, they lack the lyrical qualities of the one previously described, or as contained in *La Pasión,* a hymn written in octavillas (eight-line stanzas). This *alabado* found by Rael in Cerritos and Isla, has a two-line refrain wherein the protection of God is invoked and repeated at the end of each strophe.

> *Escucha con atención*
> *lo que padeció Jesús,*
> *desde el huerto hasta la cruz*
> *en su sagrada pasión.*
> *Lágrimas de devoción*
> *nos de a todos el Señor*
> **Por tu pasión, Dios Mío,**
> **abrázame a vuestro amor.** (refrain)

(Listen carefully to the suffering of Jesus from the Garden to the Cross. May the Lord give us tears of devotion for his sacred Passion. For your Passion, dear God, hold me close to your love.)

Another strophic variation still more elegant, the gloss, predominant in the *cancioneros* of the sixteenth and seventeenth centuries is used in *Bendita sea tu Pureza* (Blessed be your purity), an *alabado* not dedicated to the Passion but to the Virgin, and generally sung at wakes to invoke Mary's intercession on behalf of the deceased.

This *alabado* is also found with marked variations in several parts of the Spanish-speaking world; our version, however, has the distinctive quality that each verse of the first stanza is glossed at the end of each consecutive decima, and since the decima is composed of ten verses, the glossed *alabado* contains eleven stanzas.

Bendita sea tu pureza
y eternamente lo sea
pues todo un Dios se recrea
en tu graciosa belleza.
A ti, celestial princesa,
Virgen sagrada, María,
yo te ofrezco en este día
alma, vida y corazón.
Mírame con compasión
no me dejes, madre mía.

(Blessed eternally be your purity, for God basks in your Gracious Beauty. In this day I offer you, Celestial Princess, Sacred Virgin, Mary, my soul, my life, and my heart. Look at me with compassion, do not leave, Mother.) The devotion to Mary portrayed in these lines is prevalent in most Spanish religious poetry, where Mary is Queen of Heaven, Mother of Pity, Protector of Purity, and always a refuge for sinners.

Studies of religious *cancioneros* of the sixteenth- and seventeenth-century Spain reveal the same poetic forms and the same authentic and simple fervor as we have seen above and as found in the various collections of *alabados*.[13] However, one principal difference vis-à-vis the San Luis versions is that, while the Spanish hymns usually credit their authors, the *alabados* of the Valley were, and remain today, anonymous. This appears to confer upon the latter greater authenticity as popular religious poetry, and very much in keeping with the tradition of those early poets who aspired to serve and contribute to the extent of their talents and without formal recognition. Considering that the same spiritual candor and simplicity of the early *cancioneros* of Spain have been transmitted to their Southwestern heirs, however, the *alabados* remain a splendid contribution of religious devotion from the people of Old Spain to the people of modern Colorado. Today, the San Luis Valley is still a haunting cultural repository, a museum of Old Spanish culture and folklore.

Notes

[1] J. B. Ralliere, *Colección de Cánticos Espirituales,* (Tomé, New Mexico, 1897).
[2] Juan Rael, *The New Mexican Alabados,* (Stanford, Calif., Stanford University Press, 1951).
[3] J. B. Ralliere, *Cánticos Espirituales. Dispuestos en nuevo orden sin añididuras por un Padre D.K.C.D.J.* (El Paso, Texas: Editorial Revista Católica, 1933).
[4] Hymns 3, 36, 39, and 65 have been translated by Mrs. Elsie T. Stebbins.
[5] *The Catholic Encyclopedia,* Vol. 10 (New York: McGraw Hill, 1967), p. 101.
[6] J. Manuel Espinosa, "Journal of the Vargas Expedition into Colorado, 1694," *Colorado Magazine,* 16 (May 1939): 81-90.
However, most historians agree that some entries were made into Colorado by Franciscans before the Vargas expedition, but either they returned to New Mexico or were killed by the Indians and probably did not establish firm missions. See William Jones, *The History of Catholic Education in the State of Colorado* (Washington, D.C.: The Catholic University of America Press, 1955), p. 2-8.
[7] *The Memorial of Fray Alonso de Benavides, 1630,* with an English translation by Mrs. Edward E. Ayer (Albuquerque: Horn and Wallace, 1965). On pages 101-102, Benavides tells the Pope of the remarks of an old sorcerer who thought the Christians were crazy because of their flagellations: "el debia de haber visto alguna procesion de desciplina de Semana Santa en algun pueblo de Cristianos...!" See also the English translation on p. 21, "he must have seen some procession of penance (discipline) during Holy Week in some pueblo of Christians...."
[8] Rael, *New Mexican Alabados,* p. 138.
[9] Juan Lope de Ubeda, *Cancionero y Vergel de Plantas divinas* (Alcalá de Henares, 1588), p. 4.
[10] José María de Cossío y Tomás Maza Solano, *Romancero popular de la montaña,* vol. 2 (Santander: No publisher, no date), pp. 263-64.
[11] Aurelio Espinosa, "Romancero Nuevomejicano," *Revue Hispanique,* 40 (no. 97, June 1917): 218, 219.
[12] Rael, *New Mexican Alabados,* p. 192.
[13] Rael, *New Mexican Alabados,* p. 193.
[14] Cossío y Maza Solano, *Romancero Popular,* p. 264.
[15] See the collection of religious poems and hymns compiled from the *cancioneros* of the sixteenth and seventeenth century by Justo de Sancha in *Romancero y Cancionero Sagrados,* (Madrid: Biblioteca de Autores Españoles, 1872).

11 Tradiciones Hispanas En Valle del Río Grande

Arthur L. Campa

Tiene el Río Grande su nacencia en la hoya del sur de Colorado generalmente conocida por el nombre de *Valle de San Luis,* formada por las vertientes de las cordilleras de *San Juan* al occidente y la de *Sangre de Cristo* al lado oriental. De ambas vertientes nacen los arroyos y los pequeños ríos tales como el Culebra y el Trinchera que pasan por las cercanías de *Del Norte, Trinchera,* y muchas otros pueblos. Estas aguas son parte de los afluentes que en el sur de Colorado forman el histórico *Río Grande.* Sigue su curso este río atravesando el estado de Nuevo México de norte a sur hasta llegar a la ciudad de El Paso, Texas, sitio donde cambia su cauce con dirección al sudeste desembocando finalmente en el Golfo de México después de recorrer por montañas, cañones, y llanuras por más de 3,000 kilómetros.

Existieron durante el siglo pasado, y aún existen hoy, muchas tradiciones y costumbres que los pobladores del siglo diecisiete trajeron consigo cuando fundaron sus villas, aldeas y rancherías a las márgenes del Río Grande. Algunas costumbres nuevas han surgido de las adaptaciones que los antiguos pobladores hicieron al establecerse en una región nueva escasamente poblada por pequeños pueblos de indios agricultores y tribus cuasi-nómadas como los Navajó, los Apaches, y más tarde, los Comanches. Los indígenas contribuyeron muy poco a la cultura tradicional española de esta región salvo productos naturales que los colonos incorporaron a su propio modo de vivir. Entre esto pueden incluirse también la caza del bisonte y ciertas adaptaciones de vivienda que han continuado hasta hoy en el norte de Nuevo México.

Hay que notar de paso que la cultura hispánica del Río Grande, y sobre todo en el valle río arriba, era por lo general una cultura tradicional que se estableció en 1598 cuando don Juan de Oñate fundó la colonia del Nuevo México trayendo consigo ochenta y tres carros, alrededor de seicientos pobladores y soldados, y mas de siete mil bestias y ganado diverso desde la ciudad de México. Puede apreciarse la distancia que separaba a esta colonia en el norte de la provincia de Nuevo México tomando en cuenta los dos años que tardo la expedición para llegar desde la ciudad de México. Hubo un intervalo de doce años, de 1680 hasta 1692, cuando los indígenas se sublevaron hasta ser reconquistados por don Diego de Vargas. Desde fines del siglo diecisiete permanecieron sin interrupción hasta llegar a formar parte de los Estados Unidos en 1848. A pesar de la ocupación norteamericana, los antiguos colonos continuaron su vida tradicional con poca o ninguna intervención de la nueva cultura, salvo en las grandes ciudades donde se concentraron los de habla inglesa. Claro está, que hoy día ha cambiado mucha esta cultura tradicional, pero en las pequeñas aldeas aisladas en la sierra y en los valles apartados todavía existen muchas modalidades que datan del tiempo de su colonización original.

Como esta región no produjo las riquezas minerales del imperio Azteca ni del de los Incas, los pobladores se dedicaron al cultivo del suelo y a la cría de ganado vacuno y lanar sumándose a esta industria algunas pequeñas de artesanía popular como el tallado en madera, ebanistería muy sencilla y tejidos. Durante el siglo pasado, y hasta hace cincuenta años, todavía se usaban ciertos procederes en el campo y en las aldeas que atestiguaban su origen hispano-colonial. Los aspectos tradicionales de la cultura del Río Grande se dividen a grandes rasgos en costumbres relacionadas con la agricultura, con la preparación de víveres, con la vida social y religiosa y también con ciertas prácticas de curación y medicina popular. A todo esto pueden añadirse otros aspectos del folklore como las supersticiones y el habla popular.

En una región semi-árida como el sudoeste, el agua es una de las mayores preocupaciones de los agricultores. Para mejor utilizar el agua del Río Grande y sus afluentes, los agricultores que tenían tierras de regadío establecieron un sistema de acequias para la distribución del agua a las tierras de cultivo. Desde el sur de Colorado hasta El Paso, nombran aún al canal principal "La acequia madre" de la cual se desprenden las acequias menores que forman la red de toda la región. La administración de las aguas del río, antes de la intervención del gobierno federal, estaba en manos de los agricultores los cuales se reunían en la primavera y en el verano para tomar las disposiciones necesarias en la repartición del agua. En la región del valle de El Paso, aguas abajo en el pueblo de Ysleta, se reunía la "Junta del Agua" a la cual acudían los terratenientes de toda la comarca. Durante la primera guerra mundial, la junta estaba presidida por don Luis Foa, según se hispanizaba su nombre francés Foix. Don Luis era el Juez de Paz del pueblo de Ysleta, y como también era agricultor, conocía los problemas relacionados con la distribución del agua. En esta junta se nombraba el Alcalde de la Acequia de esa jurisdicción, un vecino de la región que montado en su caballo vigilaba la repartición de agua y la condición de la acequia bajo su responsabilidad.

El agua se repartía en rotación por el Alcalde, según el tipo de sembrados servidos por la acequia. Para facilitar esta vigilancia, uno de los bordos de la acequia llevaba una vereda y todos los linderos de propiedad se mantenían abiertos para no evitarle el paso a su caballo. En caso de sucitarse alguna disputa sobre el uso o el abuso de las aguas de la acequia, el Alcalde era el árbitro que decidía la contienda, y como en el caso del Concejo de Aguas de Valencia, su desición era final. Como todos los agricultores hacían uso de la acequia desde que se desprendía de la Acequia Madre, tenían la responsabilidad de "sacar la acequia" durante la primavera antes de echar el agua para regar. El Alcalde se encargaba de ver que esta labor de limpieza se llevara a cabo en su debida forma.

Terminada la "sacada de la acequia" había otra labor importante que era renovar la represa en el río y remover el ensolve para hacer llegar el agua a la Acequia Madre. A esto llamaban "La fatiga" y era un proyecto colectivo en el que todos los que se servían de este canal principal proporcionaban tiros de caballos, hombres, y herramienta según disponía el Alcalde de la acequia. Luego se elegía el "mayordomo de la fatiga" que era puesto aparte del Alcalde, y por una semana acampaban a la entrada del río hasta hacer llegar el agua a la Acequia Madre. Al empezar el riego, el Alcalde ponía la primera compuerta para "dar el agua," al que primero le tocaba—comunmente a los rancheros que tenían hortalizas. Antes de terminar el riego, el que la usaba daba aviso al Alcalde cuando estaba listo para "pasarla" y luego decía si quería usar "el romaniente" o remanente que venía por la acequia. Así, sucesivamente el uso y repartición del agua continuó haciéndose desde tiempos coloniales hasta que el nuevo sistema federal se inició, aun dentro de este nuevo sistema quedó incorporado no solo el sistema tradicional sino hasta las leyes que rigen hoy el uso del agua en el sudoeste.

Otra costumbre entre los rancheros del Río Grande, sobretodo en sitios donde había ranchos de mayor extensión, era la de "echar peonadas." Como todos los residentes eran agricultores, no era fácil emplear peones para la cosecha. Cuando el trigo estaba maduro, y listo para segar, el dueño iba con su vecino y le pedía peonadas, o un cierto número de hombres para meter el trigo a la era. Estas peonadas no se pagaban con dinero sino con peonadas correspondientes según el número de hombres y el número de días que se debían. La cosecha del trigo se hacía de manera enteramente tradicional. Había unos que no hacían más que cortar; los segadores con hoz de mano iban cortando el trigo en manojos que los gavilladores recogían y ataban en haces antes de llevarlo a la era. Los trilladores eran otros especialistas que con su manada de cabras o potros daban vuelta al torno de la era trillando hasta estar listo el grano para los aventadores. Los hombres aventaban la paja con la horquilla y las mujeres hacían el último procedimiento con bandejas hasta limpiar el grano y ensacarlo.

El trabajo era duro; se trabajaba de sol a sol, pero durante el día los trabajadores o peones, como les llamaban a éstos antes de la Revolución mexicana, podían "sestiar" sin que se les tachara de ser perezosos. La costumbre del cigarro era *sine qua non* para todos, y de ella se aprovechaban también los no fumadores. En medio de una milpa, con el sol de plano, anunciaba uno de los trabajadores que "iba a hacer un cigarro." Todos suspendían el trabajo mientras "torcían un cigarro" de su cuenta o esperaban a que el compañero fumara. Metódicamente, el fumador sacaba su saquito de "punche" y luego escogía una hoja de maíz del rollo que traía, la encarrujaba y con mucho acierto iba sacudiendo el tabaco para no desperdiciarlo. Con los dientes cerraba la jareta del saquito, lo guardaba y empezaba a torcer el cigarro, es decir a enrrollarlo una, dos o tres veces hasta estar cierto de que no estaba ni muy apretado ni muy suelto. Con la punta de la lengua enhumedecía la orilla de la hoja, lo cabeceaba con la uña del pulgar y ya estaba listo para encender con fósforo o con islabón y yesca. Solo uno encendía; los demás pedían "lumbre," salvo los menores o bisoños quienes no podían pedir lumbre a sus mayores a no ser que la ofrecieran. Con la mayor satisfacción echaba la primera bocanada de humo recargándose sobre el cavador o la pala para gozar como se hace hoy en la institución nacional del "coffee break." Esta costumbre del cigarro se respetaba por mayordomos y por no fumadores.

Aunque el sudoeste es una región semi-árida, había "temporales," "reviliones," y "tempestades" que impedían la siega o la cosecha de ciertos productos. Era importante por lo tanto saber cuándo sembrar y cuándo segar de acuerdo con el tiempo. Los antiguos rancheros del Río Grande sabían que para tener buenas cosechas había que sembrar ciertos granos cuando la luna estaba en menguante y otras cuando estaba en creciente. A más de eso, había que saber de antemano qué tiempo se podía esperar durante el año venidero, y para ello había especialistas que sabían "echar las cabañuelas," una costumbre antigua traída de España. Consistía este sistema de observar el tiempo durante el mes de enero dividiéndolo de la manera siguiente.

El tiempo de los doce primeros días del mes correspondían a los doce meses del año. Del trece en adelante, los días representaban los meses del año en reverso. Del 25 al 30 cada medio día representaba el tiempo de cada mes sucesivamente y las primeras doce horas del 31 de enero también representaban el tiempo de los doce meses del año. Se calculaba el tiempo del año a fin del mes de enero tomando el promedio de las observaciones hechas durante el mes. Pero como estos pronósticos del tiempo solo decían el tiempo de cada mes, había otras maneras de saber lo que el tiempo sería de un día para otro. Si por la tarde veían retozar a los potros y los becerros era porque llovería el día siguiente. Si cantaba un gallo al empezar la noche era señal de que el tiempo cambiaría al día siguiente. "Anillos" al torno de la luna quería decir que habría tempestad, y si la leche fresca se agriaba era porque iba a llover. Así que por medio de las cabañuelas y los otros signos que los agricultores conocían podían gobernar sus actividades para lograr los mejores resultados sin tener que consultar al meteorólogo de hoy día.

Hoy día el ama de casa puede sacar del refrigerador una comida ya preparada que dentro de treinta minutos en el horno está lista para servirse. Con café instantáneo y leche en polvo adereza el almuerzo o la cena, y luego pone un pastel en el horno que al terminar la comida servirá de postre con helado de crema sacado del mismo refrigerador de donde ha salido la comida entera. Al leer la historia de sus antepasados, esta mujer moderna que ahora habita el valle del Río Grande se pregunta cómo podían vivir estos pobladores de hace dos o más siglos sin las comodidades modernas.

El hecho es que los antiguos habitantes del Río Grande también buscaban la manera de ahorrarse tiempo, amenizar sus quehaceres domésticos, y asegurar el abastecimiento de provisiones para los largos días de invierno. Como no había refrigeración ni supermercados, se conservaban los comestibles de dos maneras, o "curados" o secos, según la especie. Durante el verano, cuando abundaban los tomates maduros se abrían éstos por el medio y se secaban al sol para almacenarlos junto con todos los víveres en la bodega. De las calabacitas, que en Sud América llaman zapallos, hacían "rueditas" tajando esta legumbre cucurbitácea y secándola al sol. Los ejotes, o "vainitas" en el Perú y "judías" en España, había que someterlos a un procedimiento un poco más complejo. Primero se sancochaban en un baño de agua hirviendo y luego se ponían en sartas por medio de una aguja de coser y una hebra de hilo fuerte. Estos "collares de ejotes" se secaban en perchas, y ya secos se ponían en sacos para consumirse durante el invierno.

El elote, maíz verde, o choclo sudamericano, también se conservaba de distintas maneras, algunas de las cuales se habían adaptado de la cultura indígena. Cuando todavía estaba verde pero "sazón" se hervía la mazorca de maíz y después de deshidratarse al sol se desgranaba y luego se almacenaba como los demás granos. A esto le llamaban "chacales" en la región de El Paso y "chicos" más al norte. De este grano se hacían guisos y platos semejantes al garbanzo y hacía las veces del maíz congelado de hoy. El chile se preparaba según el gusto personal. Los que querían chile verde para comer en el invierno tostaban los chiles sobre un comal, los pelaban y luego los ataban del "tronconcito" o tallo poniendo seis en cada manojo. Al hervirse recobraba su sabor original y con un poco de queso o con carne seca se condimentaban los antiguos un plato que no tiene mal sabor aún hoy.

Una manera de preparar el maíz que no ha pasado todavía a la historia, y que se originó con los indígenas de toda la región del Río Grande hasta México, es el pinole. En la región de El Paso cosechaban un maíz muy dulce que llamaban "viejito" porque se arrugaba mucho al secarse. Este lo tostaban y luego lo molían añadiendo un poco de "piloncillo" o "panocha" como llaman a la azucar morena. De la harina de pinole preparaban una bebida para la mesa que llamaban "atole de pinole," preparada con leche si la había, o con agua. Para darle más sabor le ponían un poco de canela y clavo de comer. Algunos tomaban el pinole como el cereal moderno, es decir una cuenca de harina de pinole con azúcar y leche que satisfacía más que el notorio "breakfast of champions" de hoy día.

De todas las frutas, fueran durazno o no, hacían orejones tal como se hace hoy día, y con éstos se garantizaban las empanadas y los pasteles en el invierno cuando no había fruta fresca. La conservación de la carne siempre era, y es hoy, un problema que los antiguos resolvían de dos maneras tradicionales. Cuando los "ciboleros" iban a la caza de estos nobles animales de los llanos, llevaban perchas consigo donde colgaban las "cecinas" de carne a secar. A este carne le llamaban "charqui" que los norteamericanos más tarde convirtieron en "jerky." Lo mismo hacían cuando "beneficiaban" una vaca. De aquí venia la carne seca del siglo pasado que tantos apetecían asada sobre un brasero y servida con atole blanco, es decir el atole hecho con masa de maíz.

La carne de puerco era más complicada por la manteca que tenía, y al "beneficiar" un puerco era más que tarea, era una ocasión de festejo que en muchos pueblos pequeños llamaban "la matanza del cochino" a la cual invitaban a todos los parientes y a los amigos vecinos. Todos ayudaban cuando empezaba la matanza. Se apartaba una fanega de maíz para cebar a cada puerco destinado a la matanza y se le daba todo el maíz que pudiera comer hasta tener que comer sentado el último almud por estar tan gordo. Todo mundo venía temprano, se encendía la lumbre debajo de una enorme vasija de cobre que llamaban "cazo." Los chicos no tenían más que hacer que "atizar la lumbre" hasta que hirviera el agua. Se corría la voz que el agua estaba hirviendo y el cerdo, que ya había comido su última cena de maíz como un condenado a muerte también había tomado todo el agua posible para que "tuviera mucha sangre." Esto era importante para hacer morcilla, dulce o salada según el gusto. Una vez limpio de toda cerda, y limpio por dentro y por fuera, el matancero tajaba las lonjas que las mujeres cortaban en pequeños trozitos. Estos pasaban al cazo donde se freían hasta soltar la última gota de manteca. Del bagazo de las lonjas se hacían los chicharrones que iban sacando con un cedazo en un palo. Este era el momento que todos esperaban. De aquí salieron los primeros "burritos" o tacos que se inventaron, pues la tortillera echaba alteros de calientes tortillas de maíz, mientras otras preparaban la salsa de chile "caribe" que servía para condimentar el chicharrón caliente en tortilla de maíz con su sal y salsa de chile con tomate. Venía el convite y todos se acercaban para gozar la matanza del cochino con un burrito en una mano y una taza de café negro en la otra.

Los costillares y mucha de la carne se hacía cecinas y se adobaban en una preparación de vinagre, chile colorado, y especies. Puesta al sol y seca, esta carne se envolvía en tela y también pasaba a la bodega para usarse durante el año. No tenían carnes congeladas estos habitantes del Río Grande pero no dejaban de comer algunos platos que aun hoy día son apetecibles.

Los víveres, secos, curtidos o "curados," como ya se ha dicho, se guardaban en bodegas, pero otros comestibles había que guardar en "almárcigos" o "almácigos." Sobre una excavación rectangular de dos pies de hondo se construía un armazón de techo de dos aguas el cual se cubría con jara, ramajos o cachainilla según eran accesibles estos materiales. A este techo se le echaba tierra hasta parecer una loma al lado de la casa. En un extremo se dejaba una puerta que durante el tiempo de frío también estaba bien cubierta de tierra. En esta bodega se guardaban los camotes, tomates verdes, cebollas, y otros productos que conservar en su estado natural. Los más prevenidos almacenaban manzanas, calabazas, nabos, betabeles, melones, y sandías que se podían conservar por largo tiempo. Era la costumbre sembrar tarde algunas matas de una especie de melón llamado "de invierno" y sandías de corteza dura llamadas también de invierno o "chilacayotas." Estos productos se conservaban en los almácigos hasta navidades y aún más tarde. Los que envasaban frutas y conservas también almacenaban estos productos en el almácigo. La temperatura variaba muy poco en estas bodegas donde se ponían las provisiones a salvo del tiempo, de los niño traviesos y de los animales del rancho.

Muchos son los productos que en la mayor parte de la zona del Río Grande, y sobretodo en las principales ciudades, ya han pasado a la historia pero todavía hay algunos que saben preparar el requezón del suero de leche, asaderos de leche de apoyo, quesos de cabra, arrope de uva, y otros muchos productos que son el resultado de una tradición hispánica de muchos siglos.

Como en tantos países de fondo hispánico, la región del Río Grande también tenía diversas maneras de conservar la salud. No había médicos pero si "médicas" parteras, curanderas, sobadores, "arbolarios," o herbolarios que conocían todas las maneras de curar y sabían que cocimientos, hierbas, tes, cebos, y ungüentos recomendar para un enfermo. Las parteras y las curanderas son bien conocidas en todas partes hoy pero no tanto el sobador o el "arbolario." Aquel era conocedor del esqueleto humano, y cuando alguien se "falseaba" una conyuntura, él sabía como sobar y donde estirar para poner un hombro, un tobillo, o una rodilla en su lugar. Luego, como el osteópata del pueblo, seguía dando tratamientos que no distan mucho de los que hoy dan sus hermanos más estudiados y con más títulos. Había un tratamiento bastante eficaz que se suministraban los arrieros, es decir, los que iban en los largos viajes por tierra por el mentado "Santa Fe Trail." Estos arrieros que iban sentados todo el día en incómodos carretones sufrían dolores de espalda al fin de la caminata y para restablecerse se daban "apretones de arriero." El que iba a recibir el apretón, ponía las manos entrelazadas sobre el cuello o la nuca y luego juntaba los codos hacia el frente. El que daba el apretón le pasaba los brazos sobre los del paciente, y recargando el cuerpo sobre él le daba un soberbio apretón que le hacía tronar la espina dorsal como una metralla. Con esto quedaba el arriero descansado como si le hubieran "quitado los nudos de la espalda."

Los "arbolarios" se ocupaban, no tanto de dar cocimientos sino de curar de espanto o desembrujar a los embrujados o curar el "ojo" en aquellos quienes habían sido víctimas del temible ojo. Los eruditos del pueblo conocían centenares de hierbas y cocimientos. Sin embargo, había algunas hierbas muy notorias que todo el mundo conocía porque "jamás fallaban." Para los dientes se mascaba la "lengua del toro"; para una infección de la piel, allí estaba la "yerba de la golondrina"; para el mal del estómago solo bastaba tomar el "te de popotillo"; y para las reumas se sobaban con cebo de coyote, o manteca de zorrillo o aceite de vívora, según el gusto de la persona.

Las costumbres sociales, que ya he tratado en otro estudio, son más conservadoras, y muchas de ellas aun siguen observándose en muchos pueblos del sudoeste.

12 *Aguilar and Its Western Valley of Trujillo Creek*

Anne Lucero

As one travels south on Colorado Interstate 25, between the historical towns of Walsenburg and Trinidad, a sign that designates Exit 14 points the way to a little town which bears the Spanish name of Aguilar. In describing its location in relation to the area, someone once made the statement, "Aguilar is where the mountains begin and the great plains end." This is quite true, for if one drives west on Aguilar's main street and continues on it, one will proceed to the mountains, the fantastic area of the Spanish Peaks and the beautiful western valley of Trujillo Creek. If one drives in the opposite direction, one can see far into the distance; the horizon seems unreachable. We know it is part of the wonderful lowlands and plains that contain and sustain life, as do the mountains, in their own particular way and form.

In our beautiful Centennial State of Colorado, we find many little towns and farming communities which are of significant importance in their historical background. This is so because these little towns and communities at one time gave strength and essence to the territory that in 1876 became the State of Colorado. The Hispanic people settled in areas of distinctive beauty and convenience. Colonies of entire families settled and made their "placitas" the heart of their community. Many were the reasons for such settlements. People had traveled together on caravans of wagon trains sharing the hardships and dangers of the vast territory and unconquered land. Many settlements were made up of entire households. Once they reached their destination or a place of beauty or convenience, a "plazita" arose, bustling with activity and life. Some became trading posts for barter with Indian people and French and Hispanic pioneers. Others were railroad stations after the railroads began. Being a place of barter caused the birth and the infancy of the little town of Aguilar.

Aguilar is situated below the foothills and mountains of the beautiful "Cumbres Españolas" or Spanish Peaks. The beautiful valley of Trujillo Creek lies to the west, at its right, like a right arm or a main branch.

Aguilar was pioneered by settlements of Hispanic people from the great land of New Mexico. José Ramón Aguilar, Casimiro Romero, Francisco Gonzales, Miguel Coca, Leonizo García, Francisco Sandoval, and Francisco Mestas were some of the very first who settled in the region. At that time, the little town was a trading post. Many of the Hispanos had considerable property, such as big flocks of sheep, herds of cattle and goats, and many beautiful horses. They found in the plains east of Aguilar wonderful grazing land. Straight toward the east, they saw the waters of the Apishipa River, glistening with alkaline, and so they named the area *Salado*, "salty" (waters). Crestone, or Hogback, is part of this big grazing ground which is separated by mounds or crests of sand and rock and a few chaparrales, low-growing shrubs and trees. Throughout the mid-1860s through the 1890s, people from New Mexico as well as other places continued to settle near Aguilar. Many were homesteading the land and forming permanent settlements. At this same time, many people from Europe had immigrated to this country, and they too were coming to the West. A continual flow of people was reaching Aguilar and spreading in every direction. To the west were the mountains and the secluded beautiful virgin soils and forests of Trujillo Creek which the Hispanos referred to as "la sierra" or the mountain.

The first known name of the Aguilar community was *Puerta del Cañón*. Perhaps the first settlers found the placita as a gateway to the mountainous region which they hoped to explore. Sometime later it was known as Estranger; later it was called Achulz, and finally Aguilar.

Aguilar was incorporated as a town in 1894 with J. H. Hibbits as its first mayor. The town was named after José Ramón Aguilar, an early pioneer who came from New Mexico and became a prominent man in Las Animas which had become a county in 1866. José Ramón Aguilar won the admiration and respect of many people in the surrounding areas. He was a great leader and statesman. He served as County Commissioner of Las Animas County as well as State Representative for two terms during 1881 to 1887.

A few years after the death of his first wife, the beautiful Nicolasa Coca, daughter of Miguel Coca, he married the gracious and beautiful Bersabé López. From this marriage, several daughters and a son were born. The big adobe dwellings which were home to this Aguilar family is still standing, but the land that José Ramón Aguilar owned is no longer owned by his family. The family is scattered throughout the United States. A handsome and distinguished looking nephew, José María Aguilar, still resides in this little town of Aguilar.

Aguilar continued to grow and prosper as the Hispanic people spread in every direction. The plains east of the town became the grazing grounds for big flocks of sheep and herds of cattle and large numbers of horses. A gallant man of much prestige in those days was Miguel Coca, who owned sheep and cattle. Some of his descendants still live in Aguilar. José de La Luz Vargas, Procopio Valdez, Jerónimo Romero, and Miguel Coca controlled the plains and were big livestock operators of the late 1860s thru the 1890s. Casimiro Romero and José Ramón Aguilar owned much of the land which makes up the town of Aguilar and occasionally the older people of Aguilar still refer to parts of the town as "the Romero Addition" and "the Aguilar Addition." This is especially noted during election years when two voting precincts exist and are often referred to as the Romero Addition at the west part of Aguilar, and the Aguilar Addition on the east side.

Aguilar continued to grow and flourish with the Hispanic culture as people made their way into the beautiful mountain areas, and began to farm and establish themselves. People of other nations and cultures began to arrive and mingled freely with the Spanish. Many of these people began to buy property and establish themselves in business. Among the earliest business people were A. I. Lindsey and his brother; they established a lumber yard. The Lindseys were the first to realize the richness of the forests in the valleys to the west of Aguilar.

Before long, beer saloons, stores, and hotels made up the main street of Aguilar, and people were proud of their little town. Most of these were plain religious folk, and a place to worship as a congregation was built, a beautiful adobe chapel in the simple, charming Spanish style. It was dedicated to Saint Anthony of Padua. Beautiful paintings of the face of Jesus adorned the painted walls. The entrance faced the east. Leonizo Garcia donated the land for the cemetery. The very early Hispanic pioneers were buried around the chapel. The grave of Miguel Coca was at the very doorsteps of the adobe structure. Later the bodies were taken out to the regular cemetery. A new chapel was built in later years, and now it is the parish of the town and serves as a mission for the country to the west.

The secular education during early days was very important to the Spanish people of Aguilar. One of the first teachers, before a school district was organized, was Pablo Coca, son of Miguel Coca. Education was bilingual, and translation from Spanish to English was one of the main subjects taught. This made the actual reading program quite involved, and it progressed very slowly. The program was deep, and it enriched the understanding of its learners. Handwriting was considered of prime importance; this is evident by the beautiful writing in the records of some of the old pioneers of Aguilar. Arithmetic was also of great importance, as it involved the transactions of business in every individual life. The first grade-school building in Aguilar was located on the east part of Main Street. It is now the present Texaco Station. The first high school was built where the still-existing old swimming pool is located.

At the turn of the century when the surrounding hills near Aguilar were found to be rich in coal, Aguilar became the home of people from many countries: Italians, Slovanians, Greeks, Austrians, Blacks, and a few Japanese, as well as people from Mexico. The mines attracted many people for their vast supply of bituminous coal. The mines in the surrounding area of Aguilar were Broadhead, Peerless, Shaft, Royal, Empire, Jewel, and Southwestern. Not too far away, within a distance of eight to ten miles, were Delagua, Hastings, and Tollerburg to the south; and Rapson, Rugby, and Colorado mines to the north. Many people from these mining camps made Aguilar their Saturday night stop. Aguilar was bustling and booming with business and a new culture. During the years from 1915 thru the 1930s, the coal industry around Aguilar prospered.

The lot of the miner was not an easy or a pleasant one, but a living was carved from it. Money was hard earned and often easily spent. From long hours of digging and shoveling the black dusty coal in the darkness of the mines, the miners came out with the coal dust stuck to their whole bodies. Tired and bent, they returned home at the end of a long day to warm their bath water on top of the coal stove, and then they bathed in a tin tub.

The merchants of Aguilar prospered. Saloons, liquor stores, hotels, and grocery stores lined the busy main street of Aguilar. The tree-lined streets of older days became like a carnival on Saturday nights and pay days. Beer saloons provided tables under the trees for their customers as gallons of beer at fifty cents per gallon were consumed. Model T cars that belonged to the miners were parked on the busy main street, while saddle horses, horse-drawn buggies, and wagons remained tied to hitching posts and hitch hooks. Many horses stomped deep holes in the ground as they remained tied to hitching posts until midnight or early morning hours of the next day.

Local law was always strictly enforced with sheriffs, night watchmen, and truant officers. But in spite of laws and curfews, Aguilar like any other town, large or small, had its lawlessness. There were drunken bouts, robberies, gambling, and even killings during the early days. The reasons for such wickedness were deep and sometimes personal for the people who engaged in them. The jail house of Aguilar many times remained full of men who stayed drunk until early morning of the next day.

The coal industry around Aguilar brought the railroad into the heart of this small town. At all hours of the day and night, the entire community heard the whistle and clanging of the bell of the Colorado and Southern as it made its run to the west part of town where the freight depot was situated. The railroad tracks went as far as the Broadhead Mine at Green Canyon west of Aguilar. At Lyn to the east, a few miles out of Aguilar, was the passenger depot for the Aguilar community. For many years during the booming days of Aguilar, Samuel García was night watchman for the C & S and Burlington yards in Aguilar.

During the prohibition period of 1920 through 1933, while Aguilar was still in its flourishing days, many people began to manufacture "white mule" and dealt in the illegal practice of its distribution. Aguilar found itself with an uncontrollable menace.

Thousands of gallons of "white mule" were dumped in basements or onto the streets when the liquor agents discovered them.

As this difficult period was leveling off, the country was in the grips of the Great Depression. Many of the mines closed, and the companies vacated the camps they had set up to house their employees. Aguilar was left nearly desolate, and the hustle and bustle of former years became a thing of the past.

During the days when Aguilar reached the heights of great prosperity, Main Street with its many stores, hotels, beer saloons, and theaters offered the best to its community. Most of the buildings were two-story brick buildings. In each building, a shop or store occupied the ground floor and the second floor offered rooming accommodations. The Main Hotel, the Alpine Hotel, and the Arcade were some of these places which housed two different businesses.

The Shaddy Clothing Store was a fashionable store of that day, while Prato's Meat Market sold choice meat that was purchased from the farmers of Trujillo Creek. Rico Valentine owned a large store and warehouse. Pascacio Gallegos operated a dry cleaning establishment where blue serge suits and woolen shirts were cleaned. The State Bank of Aguilar offered banking services to its community until it was forced to close during the depression. Years later, Safeway and J. C. Penney established stores in Aguilar, and for several years, these prospered, as did the town for a time; new businesses sprang up. Shoe shops, dress shops, and beer parlors continued to do business. Automobiles, however, were now taking people away from Aguilar; Walsenburg and Trinidad were but a few miles away.

As an echo of the voice of the past, Aguilar today remains a small community of a few hundred people. There are high hopes as promises of the rebirth of the coal industry circulate the entire southern part of Colorado. Aguilar anxiously awaits the industry, for it knows there are plentiful deposits in the surrounding area. Strip mining is already taking place near the old Jewel mine north of the town. All hope that in the not too distant future, Aguilar will see new glory and boom again. The streets of Aguilar might once again be aglow with neon signs and lights as automobiles of every make park on its streets, replacing the horses, buggies, and Model T cars of the old days.

To all the hustle and bustle, and the swing of the pendulum, the beautiful "Cumbres Espanolas" or Spanish Peaks have stood as two witnesses. To what all this land and its inhabitants below have experienced and seen, the beautiful peaks have in silence witnessed. In a beautiful, sometimes deceiving, magical way of fairy-book material, they have seemed close and within reach. To the west of the little town of Aguilar and the valley of Trujillo Creek, they set as objects of attraction, beauty, wonder, and romance. Side by side we see them as symbols of parallelism. They are but a piece of the Maker's creation. They are a restful sight for weary eyes, and an inspiration for the artist and the poet.

The Indians, whom the Spaniards found here, worshipped the peaks and considered them sacred. They believed that the rain gods dwelled there, and when the fog and mist completely covered the peaks, the Indians knew that the gods were angry. The Indians in their close association with nature considered the two peaks as the two breasts of a woman, and thought of them as the breast of the world. The Indians called them the "Huajatollas." Throughout the pages of time, imaginations of people have attributed much to these magnificent peaks. Lucas Lucero, a former sheepman from the southern part of Colorado, found the profile of an Indian chief and his squaw on the contour of the two peaks as he gazed far into the distance while watching over his flock. The imagination of Fernando Vigil, one of the grandsons of an early pioneer Juan de Jesús Vigil, attributed an eloquent personification to these two peaks by saying, "The cumbres are the breast of our local area, and like a mother, they nourish the valley with the fruitful and productive land which we have in Trujillo Creek." Trujillo Creek is at the very bosom of these Huajatollas. The creek gets its start from the dripping of the snows and springs near the peaks. This water that helps to nourish the valley is one of man's main necessities.

Near the beautiful Spanish Peaks is the western valley of Trujillo Creek, which played an important part in the growth and development of Aguilar. In many ways, Aguilar and Trujillo Creek have been depending on one another. Since the very beginning when Aguilar was called "Puerta del Cañón," this

Hispanic-orientated community served as the gateway to the canyons which were hard to reach by difficult trails and roads. "Puerta del Cañón" was the place to obtain food supplies, horseshoes, and wagon wheels as the pioneers traveled to the mountains. Bolts of chambray and gingham for dresses, shirts, and aprons, and high-top shoes for men and women were sold to the country women. In turn, the merchants carefully counted the silver coins, paper money, and gold pieces which the friendly pioneer ranchers from Trujillo Creek paid them.

The beautiful valley of Trujillo Creek is made up of three smaller narrow valleys of interesting hills and ridges, and forms the letter Y at the main part of Trujillo Creek. Nice clear brooks empty into the main river of the valley for about five miles which then empties into the Apishipa River. Trujillo Creek is beautiful mountain country with an elevation of 7,400 feet; the elevation increases toward the Spanish Peaks, which reach the height of 13,623 feet on the west peak. This valley of Trujillo Creek has a natural beauty and charm. There are ridges of striking pine trees and interesting rock formations. There are sloping hillsides of oak brush and native grasses. There are forests of pine trees, Douglas fir, balsam, and juniper, as well as beautiful white-bark aspens. The fertile land is composed of black rich soil. This soil was all a dense forest which the Hispanic settlers cleared with their crude walking plows and oxen teams in order to plant their first crops.

The changing seasons bring beautiful scenes into focus in the Trujillo Creek valley. Spring and summer have the beauty of luscious green sloping hillsides and budding trees. The beauty of many wild flowers is a breath-taking sight as one sees morning primroses, blue penstemons, scarlet gilias, Indian paint brush, and purple fleabanes along roadbanks and hillsides. The golden glory of rich colors makes the autumn season one of the most beautiful parts of the year in the valley of Trujillo Creek. The clean white beauty of winter snows and frost sharpens the profile of the interesting mountain ridges and valleys. To reach the Trujillo Creek valley during the season of ice and snow can be an unpleasant and frightening experience, for the winding dirt roads become snow-packed and dangerous. Only people who know of such conditions during winter weather can travel these roads with confidence. These roads are maintained by the working crew of Las Animas County.

This beautiful valley was settled by the Hispanic people from New Mexico. During the early 1860s, José Ramón Trujillo first set foot on this beautiful valley as he traveled with a group of land surveyors. He was a courageous and intelligent man. The unconquered and unknown mountainous land which he saw far out to the west probably attracted his curiosity, while the natural beauty of the area captured his heart. He returned to Mora, New Mexico, and reported his findings to his superiors. After a year or so, José Ramón Trujillo returned to Trujillo Creek with his wife Ysabelita and a few others on an ox-drawn covered-wagon caravan. Within a short time, other pioneers continued to come west, and another Trujillo family, that of Juan Trujillo, arrived. About seven and a half miles west of "Puerta del Cañón," or Aguilar, they settled and farmed a "plazita" which was called "La Plazita de los Trujillos," for the Trujillos were numerous. There were signs of Indian dwellings all about them, but most of the land around was densely covered with oak brush, willows, and pine trees. The area to the west was one dense bluish-green forest. The creek which they discovered near the sloping hillside was shallow and wide as the beavers had built their ponds nearby. The tall cottonwoods and willows were gnawed at the base and would be down within a short while. The people rejoiced at the abundance of crystal-clear water, and they referred to the creek as the "rito." In time, they were all calling the entire valley "El Rito de los Trujillos" for the Trujillo families had increased and had populated the small "placita." These Trujillo families built the first adobe homes at the "plazita" and lived their entire life in Trujillo Creek. Some of these houses remain in this valley, some are inhabited and remodeled, and some are only ruins. Their construction gives evidence of the adobe craft and a simple but charming Spanish architecture. Here in this small "plazita," school and church were held in the same building. This same building was also used for the post office. As more settlers continued to arrive, they penetrated the valley to the west and began to clear the land and to homestead the area. The clearing of land, cutting down forests and oak brush, was a laborious task.

These are the names of the early Spanish pioneers of Trujillo Creek: José Ramón Trujillo, Juan Trujillo, Juan de Jesús Vigil,

Blas Felipe Quintana, Quirino Maes, José María Vigil, Juan Bautista Vigil, Juan Luis Borrego, Domingo Aragón, Fermín Bueno, Manuel Sánchez, Tomás Bustos, Tomás Cárdenas, Aduato Armijo, Estevan Cárdenas, Abran Cárdenas, Leandro Borrego, Pablo Martínez, José Romero, Francisco Abeyta, Samuel Johnson, and Jacobo Johnson. These were the men who with their crude implements of iron and wood, with oxen and horses, cleared the land of brush and forest and named the beautiful valley "Rito de los Trujillos." These were the early pioneers who built the community, who mingled with the friendly Indians, who were here before us and shaped and made the beautiful valley of Trujillo Creek a peaceful and wonderful place for still other generations and other people. Their efforts and contributions to this beautiful valley were of significant importance.

Years later, people from other countries joined these settlers in beautifying and cultivating of the land, and they too contributed much to the growth of the beautiful valley of Trujillo Creek, but the region remained primarily Spanish. These early pioneers had great determination and courage as they set about to build adobe homes and log cabins from the forest they cut down. Many claims for homesteads continued to be approved, and people felt a greater sense of security. Within a short time, the beautiful western valley of Trujillo Creek was populated with people of the Hispanic culture.

Juan de Jesús Vigil, his wife Romana, and their large family arrived from the beautiful valley of Mora, New Mexico, in the mid-1860s and settled in the area where their son-in-law, José Ramón Trujillo and his wife were living. Trujillo Creek was a new home for them, as Juan de Jesús began to build a large adobe house for his family. Within a short time, his sons, Isidoro, Hilario, Telésforo, Celedón, and Manuel acquired homesteads. They too built comfortable adobe homes and planted beautiful orchards and gardens. The adobe house which was the home of Juan de Jesús Vigil still stands, and it is owned by his great-grandson.

Blas Felipe Quintana, his wife Doloritas, and their large family left Santa Cruz, New Mexico, and came to join Juan de Jesús and Romana, for Doloritas and Romana were sisters. Blas Felipe also had a large family. They settled at the end of the north Trujillo Creek fork. Blas Felipe Quintana became a mail carrier a few years after his arrival in Trujillo Creek. On his beautiful sorrel horse named "Ray," he delivered mail from Hicks, west of Trinidad, to Abeyton and Trujillo Creek. Blas Felipe was critically injured during a mail delivery when wild ducks frightened his horse; the injuries in time caused his death. The beautiful apple orchard which Blas Felipe planted in Trujillo Creek is still producing fruit.

Quirino Maes and his family came from his ranches near Mora and Guadalupita, New Mexico. He drove his flocks of sheep and cattle and settled near the rolling plains of San Luis. The bitter cold winter weather of the valley compelled him to seek a warmer climate, and so he moved eastward. He crossed the mountain ranges and settled near Aguilar for some time. Before long, news of a beautiful valley to the west reached him, and he again moved, this time to the valley of Trujillo Creek. He lived there for the rest of his life. His sons Salvador and Santiago stayed on the land, and Salvador acquired much more land.

Salvador became a very prosperous rancher and a well-known man. His main occupation during the autumn season was custom threshing for the entire community, as well as other communities near Aguilar and Trinidad. He operated a steam-engine threshing machine which required a crew of seven or eight men and a water boy, which was always one of his favorite grandsons. Every year the entire community prepared their big stacks of grain for Salvador Maes as he went from one place to another, threshing the beautiful golden grains which the rich land produced.

The beautiful and productive western valley of Trujillo Creek with its rich black soils and plentiful water produced great fields of hay, corn, wheat, oats, and barley, as well as potatoes and other vegetable crops. Piles of corn of several varieties were placed near garden fences and were husked by hand during moonlit nights of those early days.

These early pioneers raised their own food on the land and sold their surplus to the Aguilar merchants or traded for sugar and coffee and other supplies. Their corn supplied much of their food, as well as food for their livestock. The blue corn supplied flour for their nourishing "atole" and "shaquewe." The white corn made "pasole" and "nistamal," and the yellow corn was feed to cattle, chickens, and hogs which supplied the finest of hams, meats, and sausage.

The Trujillo Creek valley was a land which was under irrigation during spring and summer months. Juan Mestas, who worked for the Board of Water Commission, carefully alloted the farmers their share of water. Faithfully he traveled in his one-horse buggy, checking the main head gates and visiting the farmers. The cool, clear waters of the Trujillo Creek River nourished and helped the rich mountain soil produce in abundance, and the beautiful valley was a fruitful place.

From the "llano estacado" and great plains of Texas came the gallant "vaquero" Juan Luis Borrego, and his aging father Félix Borrego. They brought their family and their personal property of beautiful Texas cattle, horses, and 50 head of mules. When they reached the grazing lands of eastern Aguilar, they found many of the Hispanic people grazing their livestock there also. Agreements were made, and Juan Luis also began to graze his stock on this land. For a few years, they shipped cattle and mules back to Texas. Sometime later, they heard of the beautiful western valley of Trujillo Creek and went to homestead a portion of this valley. His sons, Epifiano and Salomón, farmed the land and always remained in the cattle business.

José María Vigil was another important man in the settlement of Trujillo Creek. He was married to Guadalupita Maes, the beautiful daughter of Quirino Maes. He and his family came from El Rito, New Mexico, and settled near the "plazita" in Trujillo Creek. The beautiful open valley which is seen as one enters Trujillo Creek was cleared of forest and brush by José María Vigil and his family and friends whom he welcomed to the beautiful land. It has been said that Vigil was a person of great integrity and truly believed and literally accepted the motto of "Live and Let Live." On the land which he homesteaded, he welcomed many others who arrived a short time later. He gave them land to live on and build their homes. The land which he orally gave perhaps never was confirmed in a legal transaction, but people lived there in peace and with an abundance of food. The land which José María homesteaded is still owned by his descendants, and the home which he built is still the home of his grandchildren and great grandchildren. The descendants of the many people whom he welcomed often return to the valley and point to the places where they had lived. The many kindnesses that José María Vigil showed are often remembered. His memory lives in the hearts of many of his people and friends.

At one time, Aguilar received many of the wholesome products which were raised in the fertile soils of the beautiful Trujillo Creek valley. The food was pure and fresh. The people were honest and reliable as they prepared their products for sale. Cream, milk, butter, cheese, and eggs found an easy market with the merchants of Aguilar. Even though refrigeration from electricity was not available in this mountain valley, the perishables were kept fresh in the old-type ice boxes until they were taken to market. Many yard goods which sold for 25¢ per yard, and hats and shoes for less than $2.00 each were often exchanged for butter and eggs. Many of the merchants bought the wheat, corn, and oats from the farmers and resold these at good profits. Meat was also sold in this manner before government regulations were enforced.

Saw mills, which produced many types of lumber for home building and other uses, were operated near the beautiful forests of Trujillo Creek. Many of the farmers of the area worked at cutting logs for the mills, and others hauled lumber to Aguilar and the surrounding areas. The Lindsey Lumber Company bought much of this lumber. From one tree, a beautiful red spruce, 1,100 board feet of lumber were produced. There were beautiful huge trees such as this which had been in the forest for hundreds of years until the pioneers cut them down with two-man saws and axes. Teams of strong work horses or mules were used to haul the logs to the nearby mills. One timber business which operated in the Trujillo Creek valley was known as Colorado Timber Company.

When the coal mines began to operate near Aguilar, the farmers and ranchers continued to prosper. Many ranchers and farmers went to the hills to cut mine timbers of various sizes. They cut pieces for props, sprags, capieces, and cross-bars. For many days, these men worked in the hills and forests, getting their timber ready. The mine timbers were carefully placed on wagons, securely tied with chains and ropes, and then taken to the mines. Wagon-loads of mine timbers made early morning journeys to the various mines. It was a common thing in Trujillo Creek to see farmers going at predawn hours of the morning with big loads of timber on their horse- or mule-drawn wagons. Teams of beautiful horses or big strong mules with fancy harnesses were used to pull these huge loads of timber. During these days, horses and mules were given extra attention and care, as they were the only means of transportation. They were fed choice hay and grain and were kept in the stables at night. They were brushed and petted and given names of their own. "Duke" and "Diamond" and "Mora" and "Ramo" were the names of two teams which have been remembered in the Trujillo Creek valley. These teams hauled many loads of timber to the mines.

For many years, the beautiful forests of the Trujillo Creek valley have been thinned out, but the new growth is a constant process of nature. In the latter years, only a few mine timbers have been cut, but new demands have begun. Securing trees for landscaping of city homes has become a big business. Trees and tree boughs for the winter celebration of Christmas are taken from these forests. As long as the earth remains, the forests will replenish themselves, and one generation of people will succeed another, perhaps with demands for new products from the forests.

Some of the coal companies near Aguilar set up company stores of their own in some of the mining camps. These stores were well supplied with nearly everything the miners and their families needed. Their prices were often higher than prices in the Aguilar stores, but they offered the convenience of credit and they were usually within walking distance from the miners' homes. On miners' pay day, the company deducted the grocery bill from the miners' wages, and sometimes there was little money left.

The timber men from the Trujillo Creek valley who supplied the mine timbers also bought many of their necessities at these company stores. Sometimes the farmers traded their timber for a supply of groceries at the company store. They stopped in Aguilar only to get their mail or for a drink at the saloon.

The charming blue chapel in Trujillo Creek, which stands among the tall pine trees, was built by the early Hispanic people of the western valley of Trujillo Creek. It was built near the end of the last century. The land for this chapel was donated by José María Vigil and his brother, Juan Bautista Vigil. These two brothers had adjoining land. When the financial and building discussions were made about the chapel, José María Vigil also donated a choice ox to the party who would make the adobes. Other people who gathered for the discussion of the proposed building pledged their services, money, and other things that were necessary. Celedón Vigil, a skillful builder and carpenter of that period, made 3,000 adobes which went into the building of the beautiful chapel. Celedón was the son of Juan de Jesús Vigil, one of the early pioneers. Many of the people in the valley helped in the construction, and most of the materials used were from the immediate area of Trujillo Creek.

Within two years, the chapel was completed. The people rejoiced to see their place of worship overlooking the area of the "plazita" to the east and the beautiful valley and Huajatollas to the west. A petition from the faithful women of the valley was granted as the chapel was dedicated to The Lady of Mount Carmel. The beautiful clear-toned bell which graced the steeple tower was donated by Michele Passarelli who had married Carmelita, the beautiful eldest daughter of Blas Felipe Quintana, one of the earliest pioneers of Trujillo Creek. In the late 1940s, when one of the lower adobe walls showed signs of weakening, a stucco job was done by Lorenzo Baca and his son, both of Aguilar. The outside of the chapel was painted blue. This color had been the favorite color of the "Carmelitas" who had supervised the church affairs in early days. The interior of this chapel has never had major repairs or modeling. It has the simple beauty and charm of early Hispanic churches throughout the area.

During the early days before this chapel became a mission of St. Anthony Church in Aguilar, the priests who offered Mass in Trujillo Creek rode in a one-horse buggy. They tied their horses and buggy in the church yard. The priests used the sacristy at the back of the chapel for their rooming quarters, which consisted of a wood and coal heater, a sleeping cot, two chairs, and a kerosene table lamp. They visited the people in the community and ate their meals at various homes. Their visits were happily anticipated and spiritually rewarding.

The early Hispanic people were of strong religious convictions. They had customs and beliefs that went back hundreds of years in origin. Some of these were the "Carmelitas," "Hijas de María," and the Penitentes. They celebrated many days in honor of saints. They had religious all-night wakes, processions, and luminarias. The "Carmelitas" and "Hijas de María" were religious orders for women and unwed young girls, whereas the order of Penitentes allowed only men. Some of the "moradas," "depositos" and "calvarios" are still standing in the Trujillo Creek and Aguilar areas. The processions and honoring of saints has continued until very recent years. The people from the beautiful valley of Trujillo Creek have celebrated July 16th in honor of the valley's patron saint—The Lady of Mount Carmel—until just recently, and Aguilar has celebrated the 13th of June in honor of St. Anthony of Padua. Beautiful handmade banners and "nechos" were carried during this procession as people sang beautiful hymns and recited prayers.

The all-night wakes or vigils in honor of patron saints were held in various homes. One of the saints which was honored in earlier times in Trujillo Creek was St. Isidro, patron saint of the farmers. A hand-crafted wooden statue and its miniature ox team and wooden plow were taken through fields and roadsides of the Trujillo Creek valley. It was truly and sincerely believed that St. Isidro interceded for a successful year of good crops.

The "luminarias" or bonfires which were lit during early evenings reflected an old belief. There were usually nine evenings in which a luminaria was lit and burned, and sometimes there was a series of twelve "luminarias." This was called a novena of prayer and sacrifice. The bonfires attracted much attention, and many people practiced this during the month of December, when it is believed that Christ was born. Many people who remember days in the "plazita" vividly remember the lighting of "luminarias." The Padre Estevan Bueno and Padre Alfonso Trujillo often took part in some of these religious ceremonies and customs of early days.

The sad tolling of the chapel bell made the residents aware that someone had passed away within the Trujillo Creek valley. Immediately, a messenger would get the full details about the death and relate it on horseback to the entire community. Friends and neighbors then gathered to offer assistance and to comfort the bereaved family.

A simple wooden casket was constructed by some of the men who came to offer assistance. The women bathed and prepared the body for burial and placed it in the coffin. After an all-night wake and the singing of Alabados and praying, the body was taken to the Trujillo Creek cemetery north of the plazita.

Many of the early pioneers are buried in this cemetery. Some of the graves are marked by native stones and have a few letters and numbers carved by hand. There are graves which date back to the 1880s. The cemetery is taken care of by residents of the community. In 1973, the late Francisco Passarelli designed the entrance gates which lead into the cemetery.

The secular education of the Trujillo Creek community was always considered important, and many people who received most of their elementary education in this country school have made contributions to society because of their noble and productive personal resources in their chosen fields.

The first schoolhouse was a one-room building where only the three Rs were taught. School was in session only three months of the year for the first few years. This school was a building at the placita. It still stands and is the home of a school teacher of this valley who now teaches in Aguilar. Trujillo Creek school was reorganized with Aguilar in 1961.

The two-room adobe schoolhouse which was built in the 1890s served the community for many years and provided a place for the education of the families of the early Hispanic settlers. It once had an average daily attendance of 75 pupils who walked to and from this school a distance of six to eight miles per day.

School teacher's wages were from $40 to $75 per month for nine months of school. One school teacher of the early days was Demecio Sánchez. His memory lingers in the minds of many of the senior citizens who are in their seventies and eighties today. This distinguished-looking man, who taught for many years, married a beautiful daughter of Salvador Maes and built his home and a little country store near the Plazita de Trujillos. One of his sons is a citizen of the Aguilar community today. Other teachers still in the minds of living senior citizens are Sara Martínez, Juan Valdez, and Eloy and Grace Romero.

During the days of the Works Progress Administration, the old adobe schoolhouse was replaced with a new stone building which still exists, but it is closed to the Trujillo Creek community. The entire educational system was changed with reorganization, and the children from this valley began to be transported by bus to Aguilar in 1961. The Trujillo Creek School House is now privately owned and is being remodeled and restored as a personal home.

Although the early pioneers of Aguilar and Trujillo Creek suffered hardships and their means of earning a living were at times quite difficult, these people possessed joyful hearts and spirits. Their religious beliefs were active and strong; often through these religious activities, they found ways and opportunities for much fun and gaiety. To terminate some of their religious celebrations, they held dances at the schoolhouses or at regular dance halls. People gathered to square dance and do other types of dances such as the varsoviana, cradle dance, scarf dance, waltzes, and polkas. The well-remembered and well-loved music of violin and guitar was played by the bands of those days.

The wedding celebrations of early days with their marches, dances, and "entregas" were times of much enjoyment and great pleasure. Different types of ball games and playing horseshoes were often the invigorating outdoor sports for men and boys. Story-telling was another form of entertainment within family circles, as well as the old puppet shows, or "títeres." At one time, the merchants, residents of Aguilar, farmers, and ranchers of Trujillo Creek met at "Los Alamitos" for yearly picnics. "Los Alamitos" is a group of cottonwood trees between Aguilar and Trujillo Creek. This lovely nook of trees and shade provided a rest area for travelers during the horse and buggy days of 1860 to 1900.

During election years, state and county officials solicited votes through public addresses at schoolhouses or other public places. After the campaign speeches, dances were held. Violin and guitar music was provided by residents of the community. The campaign speakers mingled in a happy and friendly manner with the people. The late Mauro Córdova, who served as County Commissioner for this valley, District No. 2, made campaign speeches to the people. He promoted the building of many roads and bridges, and he named one of our beautiful mountain passes "Córdova Pass" in memory of his father, José J. Córdova, who served as County Commissioner during the late 1920s.

The many county officials who solicited votes by this means brought joy, confidence, and good cheer to the Aguilar and Trujillo Creek communities. They won their positions through the giving of themselves, their time, and their talents. During the early days, election years meant excitement, fun, and good will.

In the early days of Aguilar and Trujillo Creek, the Hispanic people were carefree and happy. Often as they went about their daily life, they sang or whistled their favorite songs. Some of their favorites were "Cielito Lindo," "Adelita," "La Paloma," "Las Mañanitas," and "La Golondrina."

These people found time for many activities, but at the end of the day, families knelt together and bowed their heads in prayer in symbol of submission to their great Provider. As the prayers ended, the younger stood up and went to their grandparents and parents to ask for the "bendición" or blessing. In turn, they were given the blessing by saying "Dios te bendiga," ("God bless you"). A "bendición" was also asked for when people went on a journey. The blessing was kindly given and the trip began. Juana María, an Indian mid-wife who lived among the early pioneers of Trujillo Creek, often gave her blessings to the children she had helped bring into the world. She often told these children that the Great Spirit would be with them and guide them.

Times change and people change with them, but the basic needs of individuals remain unchanged. The great human needs of understanding, kindness, acceptance, and love remain the same. The people of the small community of Aguilar and the beautiful western peaceful valley of Trujillo Creek still communicate these needs to one another, as merchants and farmers continue their business and friendly relationships with each other.

The present generation of Aguilar and its western valley of Trujillo Creek have come to know the modern way of life. Transportation, communication, and electricity have changed the former way of living. It is only a twenty-minute drive from Aguilar to Trujillo Creek, compared to a half-day trip during the horse and buggy era. The dial of the telephone puts the residents of Trujillo Creek in communication with Aguilar in minutes. Electricity has lighted homes and business places, and the Trujillo Creek Community has all the conveniences of the city. Many of the old buildings of Aguilar have been replaced with modern ones. A new and attractive Community Center is in place where the Main Hotel once stood. A new doctor's office, a new Post Office and a new telephone building have replaced several of the old buildings on one side of the street. There are no more theaters and no opera house. Several of the two-story brick buildings have been demolished and vacant lots are now in evidence.

Aguilar is still a united little town. It still has the City Mayor form of government. It is proud to have a kind, young, and competent doctor. It has an accredited grade school and high school which educate more than 300 students. The Catholic religion is the dominant religion, but other religions are also represented.

Two grocery stores, a bakery, and drug store are on one side of the street. The J. C. Penney building houses a general clothing store with its shelves and counters of the old days. A few saloons and a barber shop still remain. Near the place where the C & S freight depot stood, there is a large complex of low-income homes.

Only two or three Hispanic senior citizens in their nineties remain. Their memories are fading with the passing of years. On pages of historical records, the deeds of many of the early Hispanic pioneers will be made known. Several years before Colorado became a state, Hispanic people were already naming towns, rivers, and ranges. Records and memories of the past have become a historical heritage as a period of one hundred years has lapsed.

13 Spanish-Surnamed Americans in the First Hundred Years of Government

Charles S. Vigil

It is logical to assume that Spanish penetration into southern Colorado was frequent and extensive. The apparent lack of commitment to the region prior to the nineteenth century implied by the absence of permanent settlements can be explained by the logistical problems involved in the distance of this far outpost from the cosmopolitan centers in Mexico. Even today, the journey from Colorado or New Mexico to Mexico City is awesome, especially when viewed from the imagined perspective of the transportation potential of the sixteenth and seventeenth centuries. In any case, the southern one-third of Colorado, roughly along the drainage basins of the Arkansas, Rio Grande, and Gunnison Rivers, had close contacts with the Spanish-speaking inhabitants of the well-organized, well-populated settlements of northern New Mexico, making this area of the state a not too remote outpost, well within the territorial influence of Santa Fe. It should not be surprising, therefore, that while the Anglo population east of the Mississippi was still sublimely ignorant of the area, or, later, considered the territory of Colorado to be a desert wilderness unfit for human habitation, the southern part of the state was populated by Spanish-surnamed people, speaking the Spanish language, locating themselves with reference to geographic features and places bearing Spanish names, and considering themselves to be, without reference to ethnic origins or national allegiances, native-born occupants of the soil on which they lived and from which they drew their sustenance.

It is natural then that the records of early political activity in what was to become the State of Colorado reveal an interesting, but extremely sketchy, story of participation on the part of Spanish-surnamed individuals. As the territory was defined and moved toward the organization of the system of counties and electoral districts around the population centers, Spanish-surnamed people were active in the various councils and legislative bodies which led to the establishment of the Colorado Territory and finally to statehood. The tier of counties along the southern border of the state was populated mainly by the Spanish-surnamed, and they filled most of the county offices and a few of the state offices originating in and from these counties. Among the names of legislators in the territorial government of 1861 are J. M. Francisco from La Veta and Casimiro Barela from Trinidad. Francisco, who has remained relatively obscure because his history has never been told, was evidently from Virginia and had been a colonel in the military. At one time, he was a candidate for the United States Senate, and his prominence in La Veta is marked by a museum memorializing him there.

The name of Casimiro Barela figures very prominently in the politics of the early years of Colorado. Although at one point in his political career he gave his birth place as Mexico, in his biography, he claims Spain as his birthplace. Barela served in the territorial or state legislature, apparently without interruption, from 1861 to 1916, when he was defeated in his candidacy for re-election as State Senator from Las Animas County. He was instrumental in the decision to publish all laws and business of the state in English, German, and Spanish. In the 1890s, Barela was elected president pro-tem of the State Senate and became Interim Governor of the State for a brief period during the absence of the Governor and the Lieutenant Governor. It is interesting to note that in 1904 Barela changed his party affiliation from Democrat to Republican, and although his action stirred up considerable debate and he was accused of selling out by prominent Democratic leaders, his political base was solid enough that he was re-elected as a Republican. A measure of his prominence and the importance of his contribution is that he was selected as one of the 13 leading citizens of the state to be honored by being in the 13 windows of the state Capital Building by the original commission appointed by Governor Charles S. Thomas.

Aside from the personal participation of Senator Casimiro Barela, it is essential to point out that his many years as an active political figure were accompanied by a continuing attrition in the numbers of Spanish-surnamed state legislators. In the Legislative Assembly of January 3, 1876, there were 12 Spanish-surnamed legislators in addition to Casimiro Barela: Manuel Lucero, Clemente Trujillo, Felipe Baca, Lorenzo A. Abeyta, Mariano

Larragoite, John Manzanares, Pedro Raphael Trujillo, José A. Velásquez, Donaciano Gurule, Nicanora [sic] D. Jarramillo, Mauricio Apodaca, and Preenciseo Sánchez, all representing constituencies in the southern counties. By 1915, this number had been reduced to three, including Barela. By 1921, the only Spanish-surnamed representative was Andrés Lucero of Las Animas County.

This trend was temporarily stemmed in the mid-1920s. In the 1920-1925 period, the Klu Klux Klan was the dominant force in Colorado politics, causing a shift in the balance of political power in favor of the Republican party, and persuading most of the candidates for public office to follow the middle of the road rather than risk defeat in fighting the K.K.K. There were a few brave souls in the political ranks; among them was Frank J. Medina, who had served long and faithfully as the mainstay of the Democratic machine in the City and County of Denver and had been the Federal Liquor Commissioner for the district including Colorado in the period when prohibition was first installed. He was from Boston, of a Spanish father and an Irish mother. Later, Medina served as Chief Clerk in the House of Representatives. He fought the Klan with everything he had.

In 1925, José Eliseo Martínez, popularly called Joe, emerged as the new champion of the Spanish surnamed. Undoubtedly he was the ablest and most vocal of all the Spanish surnamed who had served the people. His grandfather had been in the first legislative session, and his grandmother was still living in Weston; he bridged the gap from the early participants in the endless struggle for justice. He was an immensely popular Democrat. Although he was in the minority, he was so highly regarded that when he was one of the sponsors of the first state junior colleges in Colorado—as he said, "so that the Americans of Spanish surnames can be educated"—he was able to secure the support of many Republicans. The colleges were established, one in Trinidad, and as he foresaw, countless young Spanish-surnamed Americans have marched through the halls of the Trinidad State Junior College.

Later he initiated the bill establishing the first boxing commission in Colorado, a sport of which he had been a part since his days at the University of Colorado where he proudly wore the silver boxing trunks of the school he loved. Pedro

Quintana (Eddie Mack), a junior lightweight champion from Regis College in his day, who was born in the San Luis Valley, was strongly in favor of this bill. When it was signed, he appeared with Governor Billy Adams and Joe Martínez to receive a pen from the Governor.

In 1927, there was an increase in the legislative ranks: Reginaldo García from Conejos, Pedro Gonzales from Huérfano, and Joe Martínez of Trinidad were in the legislature. In 1929, Representative Joe Martínez became Senator Joe Martínez, and Andrés Lucero, also from Trinidad, was serving in the House. In 1931, Senator Joe Martínez was still fighting for the people and Andrés Lucero was in the House, along with Joe A. Barron from Walsenburg. Barron later became County Judge in Huerfano County, serving at the same time that J. Frank Torres was County Judge in Trinidad. Senator Joe Martínez became very ill in 1932 and did not run for re-election.

In 1933, Herman J. Atencio and Joseph A. Barron were the only Spanish names serving the people in the House, but J. M. Madrid, who had served in the House earlier, was elected to the Senate and served there with distinction. A man of very impressive bearing, he was some six and one-half feet tall, thin, with aquiline features and a kindly face. He was born in New Mexico, where he and José Urbano Vigil had been friends before they both came to Colorado with their families. A. M. Guerrero of Walsenburg came to the House in 1935. The contribution of all these legislators was significant in this period of grave depression when all peoples were seeking work, food, and help.

In 1937, Juan N. Noriega was elected to the Senate from Trinidad, Las Animas County. Noriega had been born in Spain and came to the United States to settle and work in the coal mines when he was 14. Later he organized laborers and took credit for much progress for organized labor in the state. Earlier he had been jailed when the International Workers of the World were at their strongest. Noriega was a self-taught American, and he resented being called Spanish-American, Mexican-American, or any kind of "hyphenated" American.

During the years that followed, the war years and thereafter, representation of the Spanish surnamed in the state legislature ebbed once again. In the 1941 and 1943 sessions, there were no Hispanos in the Senate; Jesús C. Valdez from Trinidad and David Vigil from Walsenburg served in the House, joined by Joe La Crue from Trinidad in 1943.

However, in 1963, Ed Johnson assisted by Charles S. Vigil, proposed the constitutional amendment creating districts which was passed; subsequently senators and representatives were elected by districts in Denver and elsewhere, rather than at large. Thus districts with large percentages of Spanish surnamed were able to elect representatives and senators with Spanish names: what had theretofore been a rarity now became an easier matter. The history of Spanish-surnamed representation in the legislature changed, and the following years are a record of increasingly effective political activity.

Prior to election by districts, it was difficult for a Spanish name to be voted into office. Since the passage of this constitutional amendment, many Spanish named have been candidates, and most have been elected. Candidates at large for any major state offices were virtually non-existent, except for Casimiro Barela who was selected once as a Democrat to run for State Treasurer, but he was defeated. José Urbano Vigil once attempted to run for State Auditor but was not designated. In 1954 and 1958, Charles S. Vigil, who had served under Presidents Truman and Eisenhower as United States Attorney with a record perhaps unequaled by any previous United States Attorney for excellence in handling the office and for successful prosecution of cases, both civil and criminal, was the Democratic candidate for Attorney General. His efforts to be elected failed by narrow margins. In 1956, he was a candidate for Congress from the Third District but again the votes were lacking.

A significant factor in the history of participation by the Spanish surnamed in the political process of the state has been lack of cohesiveness. Perhaps the real reason for this lack among the Spanish surnamed is the spirit of independence, the thought expressed in "every man a king." This is a much more profound feeling than the one generated by ethnic names which often invoke antagonism against Mexicano, against Mexican-American, against Spanish American, against Cuban, Puerto Rican—

against Hispanos in general. Yet it is true that all Spanish surnamed are proud of their names, which are after all truly Spanish and nothing else.

Land grants bind together all the Spanish-speaking people of the New World, since these were the means to populate the land. The explorations—the names given to Colorado itself, to counties, towns, mountains, valleys, and plains—all these show the heavy influence of Spanish and the Spanish people. The Dominguez-Escalante expedition, which went through part of Colorado and which is now receiving a great deal of study, rivals in spirit, courage, and excitement any expedition carried out in the New World. Of continuing historical significance also is the Adams-Onís Treaty, a model for later treaties, carried forward magnificently by Onís to protect the rights of both the Spanish and the Mexican. The rodeo and branding came from the Spanish settlers. The religious influence and the making of modern images such as *santos* (or painting them on wood as in the *retablos*) were imported from Spain and Mexico, since Spanish *santos* were made of wood long before the first Spanish farmer came here.

All of the diverse elements which the Spanish record shows: the efforts of individual heroes; the folklore, of which the *Alabados* are a part; the story of the land grants; the *santos* and the *Penitentes*; the farm culture; workers such as the *santeros*; the Spanish in coal, gold, and silver mining; ranching and the raising of cattle, from the longhorns to the white faces; sheep and sheep herding; the Spanish of Río Arriba; journalists and journalism of the early days, all these are traditions to be upheld proudly by the contemporary Spanish of Colorado, culminating in a legacy so strong for Colorado that it must match all that is good in contributions by any other ethnic group.

Professors like Dr. Arthur L. Campa at the University of Denver have sought to present the laudable spirit and endeavor of the Spanish in Colorado and, indeed, in America. Dr. José de Onís at the University of Colorado has made similar contributions in his numerous articles and books on the Spanish in America. It would be grossly negligent not to mention Edward P. Costigan, the son of an Irish father and a Cuban mother. Educated at East High School in Denver, Costigan went on to become a lawyer, noted for his representation of labor unions, even though nominally a Republican. He served on the Tariff Commission as a Republican member in the era of President Wilson. He became a Bull Moose, later a Democrat, and in 1930 was elected United States Senator from Colorado. He became a very liberal supporter of Franklin D. Roosevelt and served until 1936, when unluckily he was stricken with illness; he then did not contest for the seat which was taken by Edwin C. Johnson who, while Governor wrote to the Rocky Mountain News a letter saying that Spanish-named Americans were not Mexicans.

Divisions created by being called various names are often promoted by self-seeking politicians. When the day comes that the Spanish surnamed consolidate their forces on the basis of the cohesiveness of pride in their Hispanic name, customs, heritage, habit, and culture of a many-faceted facade, that day will mark the attainment of a milestone in political maturity for Spanish-surnamed Americans in Colorado. The day will come when the Spanish name will be a mark of distinction and honor, when the owner of such a name will not seek to change it or to claim an alien background to achieve some better acceptance in the community of politics.

The political scene in Colorado embraces all these elements, and the current Spanish-named officials, including among many others, Valdez, Cisneros, and Gonzales, will add a significant chapter for future generations to ponder, study, and honor.

14 The Spanish Language of the San Luis Valley

Anthony Girard Lozano

The San Luis Valley in Colorado, its people, and their language, as they underwent four centuries of history, are a living reminder of the Hispanic origin of Colorado. Entering the San Luis Valley from New Mexico, you trace the steps of the early settlers as they traveled into south-central Colorado. To the east, you can see the jagged outline of the Sangre de Cristo range of mountains against the blue sky, a sky that seems always to be sunny. You can follow the Río Grande River northwest to its source. Between the eastern mountains and this river, while still traveling north, lie the towns of Jaroso, Mesita, and San Luis. The latter is the oldest permanent settlement in Colorado; it was founded in the nineteenth century by Hispanos from northern New Mexico, where their ancestors had settled in the sixteenth and seventeenth centuries. These were the settlers who gave the names to the high peaks—Culebra Peak (13,890 feet), Trinchera Peak (13,546 feet), and Blanca Peak (14,363 feet), which you can see on the eastern horizon. You can sense their imagination and ingenuity as they named these sites—"Serpent Peak," "Deep Cut Peak," and "White Peak." Did they call the range "Blood of Christ" because of the red reflection on these mountains at certain times of the day? Why did they name this river the "Big River"? Was it the size or the need for water in this dry land that gave it its importance? Alamosa is farther north on the west side of the river. As you come closer to the San Juan Mountains ("St. John Mountains"), you come to the town of Monte Vista ("Mountain View") from which you can see the western range. Just before entering these mountains, you see the town of Del Norte ("From the North"), taken from the full name "Rio Grande del Norte." The headwaters of the river are in these mountains. This valley, 115 miles long, extending from the New Mexican border to Poncha Pass, where the Sangre de Cristo range and the Sawatch range meet, is a wedge-shaped enclave of Hispanic language and traditions in southern Colorado. To leave this valley in the north, you must travel through Poncha Pass. A town somewhat to the northeast from here was appropriately named Salida, ("the Exit").

It was not easy for the Hispanos to settle this valley. The Ute Indians fought bravely for this land, a land that required irrigation to meet the needs of the new settlers, a cold land that required the careful selection of new crops. Andrews (pp. 17–18) gives us an idea of the adaptation these early settlers had to undergo:

> When the Spanish settled the upper drainages of Culebra Creek, they found a more severe environment than the one from which they came. The milder temperatures of their northern New Mexico settlement areas did not prevail here. While summertime temperatures reached into the high eighties and low nineties, the months of December, January, and February almost always included a few below-zero temperatures. For these three months during the thirty-year period from 1891 to 1921, temperatures were recorded as low as -30° F.

The great mountain range on the eastern side provided some protection against the hordes of "North Americans" during the homestead period. The geographic conditions we have described served to accent the isolation of the Hispano settlers. They outnumbered the North American settlers who entered the valley in the late nineteenth century. The concentration and isolation of this group of Hispanos contributed to the maintenance of their language, a dialect which has its origins in sixteenth-century Spanish. From this valley, twentieth-century Hispanos have in turn moved to other towns and cities in Colorado where they continue to speak Spanish. To tell the story completely, we will have to ferret out the history of these people over a period of four hundred years, a period during which their language was drawn into the currents of history but remained essentially a rural dialect of Spanish.

Colorado Spanish provides striking characteristics that set it aside from other Southwestern dialects at the same time that we can detect similar historical forces that have played a part in developing all of the dialects of Southwestern Spanish. Newer historical forces continue to shape the nature and maintenance of

Colorado Spanish. Colorado Spanish and the other Southwestern dialects belong to the major dialect which includes Mexico and the Southwestern United States. Without going into great detail, Mexican and Southwestern dialects have in common phonological, grammatical, and lexical characteristics. In order to describe the Spanish dialects of the Southwest, a scholar has to avoid interviewing both informants whose dominant language is English on the one hand, and those who speak a standard dialect of Spanish on the other. This is not easy to do, because there exist many degrees of bilingualism and because, unlike Hispanos in the San Luis Valley, speakers in other parts of the Southwest have lived in close contact with speakers of urban Mexican Spanish. For example, during and after the Mexican Revolution, many middle- and upper-class Mexicans took refuge in San Antonio, Texas. The language spoken by Mexican-Americans is fascinating because of its complexity, its historical development, its variety, and its contact with English. What were the historical events that determined the development of Colorado Spanish?

Trying to visualize the conquest of New Mexico, you can imagine those days as you leave Zacatecas, Mexico, the city where de Oñate gathered his men in 1598. As you travel northward through the huge desert in the state of Chihuahua, you can see the group of 400 men with 50 wives and children (Espinosa, p. 8) who accompanied him. Even today, this desert is formidable. The traveler feels the solitude produced by the neverending landscape, an emotion that those colonists must have felt. What dialect or dialects of Spanish did they speak as they traveled to their new homes? Espinosa (p. 9) says that these settlers came from Castilla, Andalucía, Asturias, León, and from the western Spanish-Portuguese area in Spain. According to Canfield (pp. 65–66) the largest numbers of colonists from Spain came from Andalucía and Extremadura. Basing his information on Boyd-Bowman's study, he mentions León, Castilla la Nueva, and Castilla la Vieja, which also contributed to the stream of colonists in the sixteenth century.

> Con el recuento de pobladores españoles según su procedencia peninsular, hecho últimamente por el profesor Peter Boyd-Bowman, se nota que el grupo preponderante de los colonos españoles era de Andalucía, y que otro contingente numeroso procedía de Extremadura. En los primeros años de

194   The Hispanic Contribution to the State of Colorado

> la colonia en las Antillas casi la mitad de los pobladores eran de la misma ciudad de Sevilla. A través del siglo XVI sigue muy fuerte la corriente andaluza, extremeña y leonesa, que con las dos Castillas constituían la masa de los emigrantes a Indias. Con razón se habla de la influencia andaluza en la colonia americana.

It is difficult to pinpoint more accurately the exact place of origin of the early settlers of New Mexico and Colorado. As suggested in conversations with Professor José de Onís, the home towns recorded for the colonists when they left Sevilla may not be accurate, because they may have given the names of local towns rather than their place of origin. In the prolog to the same book by Canfield (pp. 15–16), Tomás Navarro makes the following criticism of Canfield's study:

> Su concepción de la pronunciación hispanoamericana bajo dos momentos sucesivos determinados por el predominio de la modalidad andaluza sobre la castellana y el de la criolla sobre la peninsular necesitaría demonstración más completa. No parece que el primer momento, de predominio andaluz, se apoye en más testimonio concreto que el del seseo. Aunque el vocalismo antillano respondiera tambien a ese mismo origen, el de los demás países figuraría en todo caso más propiamente acogido al tipo castellano.

Since dialect mixing is known to have occurred in Spanish America, we cannot rely on dialect information alone and would have to search for more historical or anthropological data to determine the exact area or areas of origin.

Many of the archaisms found in Colorado date back to these early days. The archaisms found in Colorado Spanish attest to its importation into New Mexico in the sixteenth and seventeenth centuries as well as to its isolation from urban Mexican Spanish for at least a century. Southern Colorado has not undergone the large influx of twentieth-century immigrants from Mexico that has been experienced in Texas and California, thus setting it apart from other Southwestern regions. The Nahuatl term *cajete,* originally meaning a round vessel, came to mean bathtub, but it is known as a *baño* in Texas and a *tina* in Mexico. The term *cajete* seems perfectly appropriate for the round bathtubs used in the

American West in the nineteenth century. The term for suspenders, *pretales* (metathesis of *pertales*), is no longer used in Mexico or Spain where they are known as *tirantes*. A rug is known as a *jerga* in Colorado, while it is known as an *alfombra* or *tapete* in Texas and elsewhere. This term, *jerga,* is also an archaism. In Argentina and Chile, *jerga* refers to a saddle blanket, a meaning not too far distant from a small rug. Other archaisms include *trujo* for *trajo* (brought), *asina* for *así* (thus), *mesmo* for *mismo* (same), *vide* for *vi* (I saw), *onde* for *donde* (where), and *naiden* for *nadie* (nobody). The author of *El Quijote,* Cervantes, who lived from 1547 to 1616, used many of these archaisms as can be seen in the words in italics in the excerpts below.

Mas el Barbero (que ya auía dado en el **mesmo** *pensamiento que el Cura) preguntó a don Quijote.*
(**Quijote,** *II, III, 2*)

La levantavan dos grandes manadas de ovejas y carneros que por aquel **mesmo** *camino de dos diferentes partes venían.*
(**Quijote,** *I, II, 75*)

Hermano músico mire lo que canta y no moteje a **nayde** *de mal vestido.*
(**Ilustre freq,** *IV, 172*)

Pero hasta agora no ha llegado a mi noticia ningún verso infamatorio contra la señora Angélica, que **truxo** *rebuelto el mundo.*
(**Quijote,** *II, III, 7*)

Trúxome *la mano por el lomo, abrióme la boca.*
(**Coloq. perros,** *IV, 243 v*)

Al despertar del sueño assí importuno, ni vi monte, ni monta, Dios, ni Diosa, ni de tanto poeta **vide** *alguno.*
(**Viaje Parnaso,** *VI, 66*)

Ross describes a large number of words with pronunciations unlike modern standard varieties of Spanish. Many of these are archaic pronunciations directly traceable to the sixteenth century. The following 14 words in current use in Colorado are taken from Ross (pp. 22-27) and are only a small sample selected from his extensive inventory. These 14 words are listed in Boyd-Bowman's glossary of sixteenth-century lexicon which was compiled from 50,000 pages of colonial documents. The date shown under "Boyd-Bowman" below represents the date documented by the latter in his glossary.

Modern	Colorado	Boyd-Bowman
1. frasáda	fresáda	1651
2. añadír	añidir	1654
3. konfesyón	konfisyón	1687
4. leksyón	lisyón, lesyón	1678
5. ímpetus	ímpitos	1642
6. decír	desír	1641
7. pedír	pidír	1628
8. bestír	bistír	1670
9. prinsipál	prensipál	1628, 1634, 1651
10. prinsípyo	prensípyo	1645
11. ospitál	espitál	1651, 1678, 1680
12. oskuridád	eskuridád	1694
13. oskúro	eskúro	1625-1694
14. rrótulo	rrétulo	1672

As you travel northward through Mexico you come to Juárez and El Paso (The Pass), where three generations later the colonists took refuge (Bancroft, pp. 174-223) after the Indian Pueblo revolt drove them out of Santa Fe, the "Holy Faith." The modern-day traveler continues northward through the arid country seeing the bright green oases around the small towns. The mountains with their Spanish names run from north to south on the western horizon. Albuquerque, named after the duke of Alburquerque (sic), lies ahead. Traveling northward past Albuquerque, the land is still arid. Santa Fe, founded in 1610, is at the entrance to the northern part of New Mexico where there is more water, the lifeblood of the western United States.

The San Luis Valley begins in northern New Mexico and extends into southern Colorado. The Río Grande River has its origin in the San Juan Mountains west of this valley and flows south through New Mexico, Texas, and finally reaches the Gulf of Mexico. The mountains surrounding this long valley are impressive. The flavor of the valley is unlike other parts of Colorado. The adobe houses and the strings of peppers hanging from the eaves give a distinct Hispanic air to the region. The San Luis Valley is also famed for the severity of its cold winters. It is in this valley where the modern descendants of the earliest Hispano settlers of Colorado continue to speak Spanish and maintain the customs and a style of life traceable to the Hispanic heritage. This setting, with the long valley surrounded by high mountains, is perhaps the most dramatic in Colorado.

Borrowed words in a language are the linguistic traces and relics which are left of old contacts with other peoples and civilizations. Such lexical borrowings remind us that the Spanish of Colorado was brought by its speakers via Mexico at a time when the latter was considered the jewel among Spain's colonies. Into the Spanish of the time entered the Nahuatl names for exotic foods unknown in Europe before the Conquest. Since Nahuatl was the language of the Aztec Empire, it had a strong influence on Spanish vocabulary. During the harvest known as the *pizca* to the Aztecs, the *elotes* were gathered, or *se pepenaron*. These *elotes*, the ears of corn, were perhaps ground by an Indian woman using the *metate*, the stone used for this purpose. She would then cook an *atole*, a soup made of maize, or would heat the corn tortillas on an earthenware *comal*, known to us as a flat griddle. If this woman needed water, she may have gotten it with a pot tied to a *mecate* (a rope). On a rainy day, the *zacate* (grass) in the fields would have gotten wet, and she may have had to walk through the *zoquete*, the mud near her home. All of these terms, including *pizca, pepenar, elote, metate, atole, comal, mecate, zacate, zoquete,* and others are Nahuatl borrowings used daily in Colorado Spanish.

As mentioned earlier, de Oñate led the conquest of New Mexico in 1598-1599 (Bancroft, pp. 110-145). Travel between central Mexico and New Mexico was dangerous and time consuming, thus leading to the isolation of New Mexico. Separated from cultural and historical events in central Mexico, this northern colony was also isolated from developments in the language that took place in the capital. New Mexico was cut off from the notion of a national standard language, which led to the establishment of the Academia Real de la Lengua in 1714, the purpose of which was to dictate "correct usage" in Spanish.

Agrarian society developed in New Mexico in the seventeenth and eighteenth centuries. The local Indian languages in New Mexico do not seem to have lent many words of New Mexico Indian source. Ross (p. 155) makes a similar observation and lists only *champes* (a fruit from a rose used to make marmalade), *chaquelue* (a type of thick pottage made from maize), *ocha* (a wild celery), and *tegua* (a moccasin):

> *Las lenguas indígenas de la región aportaron pocos vocablos al español de Colorado (con la excepción de los nombres de hierbas medicinales). El enorme caudal de nahuatlismos que el español mexicano había absorbido ya en el sur había hecho innecesaria la adopción de muchas palabras locales.*

Contact with North Americans began in the early nineteenth century, when the United States still occupied only the area toward the east of the Mississippi. At the time of these early contacts with citizens of the United States during the first half of the nineteenth century, many Spanish words were borrowed into English, as the Hispanos introduced ranching, mining, and irrigation into the Southwest. Thus, the extensive vocabulary used for ranching in English comes in large part from Spanish, as described by Bentley in *A Dictionary of Spanish Terms in English*.

The second half of the nineteenth century brought a new political reality into the picture. Events in Texas (Perrigo, pp. 113–134) would eventually have their effects on the history of New Mexico and Colorado. In 1836, the Republic of Texas became independent of Mexico. This independence was won by immigrants from the United States as well as by local Mexican citizens.

The ties between Texas and New Mexico were never close even under Spanish and Mexican rule. Vast distances separated the two colonies. In 1841, an army of Texas attempted to invade New Mexico and lay claim to all of the latter territory east of the Río Grande (Bancroft, pp. 319–329). They were captured by the Mexican authorities, and Texas was never able to establish its claim to land in New Mexico. Political divisions of this type coincide with the development of separate dialects. In 1846, Texas became a part of the United States—the first significant step taken in Washington that would eventually lead to the Mexican-American War and the consequent annexation of all of the Southwest by the United States.

The different periods of colonization also contributed to the dialect differences described below. The colonies in New Mexico were founded more than a century earlier than those in Texas, and the Spanish spoken in New Mexico and southern Colorado retains to this day more archaisms than does the Texas dialect. The Hispano migration from New Mexico to Colorado took place in 1851, the date of the first permanent settlement in the latter. The variety of Spanish spoken in Texas also developed more rapidly and in a sense became more modernized because of the constant immigration from Mexico that has continued through the twentieth century.

Among the linguistic features which distinguish one dialect from another are different subsets of vocabulary. Thus the choice of lexicon is different in the dialects spoken in Texas and Colorado. For example, *sartén* (frying pan) is used in Texas versus *puela* in southern Colorado. The latter is found in sixteenth-century citations. The Nahuatl term, *guajolote* (turkey) is used in Texas, while *ganso* refers to the same animal in Colorado. Giving a new meaning to *ganso,* which meant "goose" in Spain, the early settlers of New Mexico and Colorado were able to name an animal unknown in Europe. In Texas, the generic term for "fish" is *pescado,* while it is *trucha* in Colorado. The latter term means "trout" in Spain and Mexico. Due to the importance of this type of fish in the mountain streams of Colorado, *trucha* came to be used to refer to all fish. *Camalta* (from *cama alta*) refers to a bed in Colorado but is known simply as a *cama* in Texas. The use of *camalta* (high bed) in Colorado was probably necessary to distinguish it from a *petate* (sleeping mat). *La plebe* refers to children in Colorado while *los niños* or *huercos* is used in Texas. These vocabulary differences between Texas and Colorado attest to the separate status of Colorado Spanish. Colorado Spanish could also be compared and contrasted to other regional dialects spoken in the Southwest.

New Mexico and Colorado were under Mexican rule for only 23 years (Bancroft, pp. 310–343). Mexico became independent of Spain in 1822 and New Mexico and Colorado did not fall into

North American hands until 1846. The separate regions of Mexico often felt more allegiance to the local government than to Mexico City. The Mexican identity and the strong patriotism in modern Mexico were not forged until after the Mexican Revolution which began in 1910. Consequently, regions on the frontier such as New Mexico and Colorado could not be expected to have developed strong loyalties to the then newly independent government in Mexico City in 1822. This, in turn, may have led to stronger loyalties to Spain than to Mexico. Such regionalism has historically also been true of Spain. Nevertheless, the Nahuatl words found in New Mexico and Colorado Spanish provide strong evidence that Mexico, under both Spanish and Mexican rule, played a major role in the history of these states. The contacts between New Mexico and central Mexico lasted from 1598 to 1846, the former depending for its political, military, and ecclesiastical existence on the latter. The archaisms found in the Spanish spoken in these two states does not warrant emphasizing the peninsular origin of this dialect and downgrading the importance of the Mexican contribution. The Hispanos in New Mexico and Colorado were driven to denying their Mexican origins by the prejudice held against Mexicans in the Southwest. The truth is simply that both Spain and Mexico contributed to the establishment of Spanish-speaking settlements in these two states.

A phenomenon known as dominant language theory refers to the effect of the language of the conquerors on that of the conquered. The American conquest of New Mexico and Colorado in 1846 was accompanied by the introduction of a new form of government, by a new Catholic hierarchy, by the railroad, and the influx of large numbers of North Americans who were "more than equal" under the law (Bancroft, pp. 408-473). Although Spanish was maintained as an official language in New Mexico and Colorado, the dominant language became English since the government and political control had fallen into the hands of the North Americans. Once a language becomes politically or culturally subordinant to another one, it begins to incorporate many words from the dominant language; thus an extensive number of English words began to enter New Mexico and Colorado Spanish in the second half of the nineteenth century.

English has had a strong impact on the vocabulary of all the dialects of Southwestern Spanish since the mid-nineteenth century. For example, the adoption of the American monetary system required two new borrowings alongside the Spanish terms. The American coins included the cent, nickle, dime, quarter, half-dollar and dollar. With the addition of *nicle* and *daime,* the new coins were included in the Spanish list and became the American *centavo, nicle, daime, peseta, tostón* and *peso.* The American dollar eventually came to be known as the *dólar* in Mexico, but *peso* was kept in the Southwest for both the Mexican *peso* and the American dollar.

The retention of words of measure such as *pulgada* (inch), *yarda* (yard), *milla* (mile), and *libra* (pound) are simply an indication that the metric system has still not been adopted in the United States. The use of these words sounds old and quaint to Spanish speakers from other countries who measure in terms of *centímetros, metros, kilómetros,* and *kilogramos.* By a strange twist, these Spanish archaisms are maintained due to the influence of American technology which in this instance happens to be outdated. It is not a question so much of English language but of cultural or technological interference.

Ethnocentric attitudes directed against New Mexicans contributed to the delay in granting statehood to their territory, although this region had been governed under a system predating the colonization of the East Coast by the British. Several reasons led to this delay as described by Perrigo (p. 309):

> One was the realization that public education was not making great headway, as indicated by the revelation in 1880 that only one-fourth of the one hundred and sixty schools had been provided with buildings and that the average attendance was only a little above three thousand out of a total population of over one hundred thousand people. The use of the Spanish language in homes, schools, business houses and courtrooms also gave many visitors the impression that this territory had not yet become properly "Americanized."

As a consequence, New Mexico was not to attain statehood until 1912, although Colorado was admitted in 1876. Southern Colorado, of course, had been part of New Mexico. The process of English borrowing mentioned above and the negative attitudes held against Hispanos and their language in the late nineteenth century provide us with examples of dominant language theory. These conditions continued into the next century.

Turning now to the twentieth century, we find that the technological advances in the United States along with its status as a superpower have maintained a high level of English borrowings in Southwestern Spanish as well as in standard varieties of Spanish worldwide. Many English words dealing with the automobile and other motor vehicles are used daily in Colorado Spanish, including *bómper* (bumper), *bos* (bus), *reque* (wreck), *requiar* (to wreck), *troca* (truck), *troquiar* (to truck), and *yaque* (car jack). Other twentieth-century inventions are also adopted, along with their English names. The geographic and political separation from Mexico led to the maintenance of the local variety of Spanish, while the language in central Mexico became more standardized and, following the norms established in Spain, lost words which came to be termed archaic. In spite of this separation and isolation, Colorado Spanish continues to be an authentic variety of this language. Even the influence of English has not been sufficient to destroy the Spanish of the San Luis Valley. What is remarkable is that the Spanish of the San Luis Valley has been maintained intact in spite of so many adverse conditions. Colorado Spanish and all of the dialects of Southwestern Spanish share a strong phonological and syntactic base that is unquestionably Spanish. In other words, the pronunciation and the sentence patterns are virtually the same as those in Mexican Spanish. On the other hand, the effects of English as the language of the dominant society have been profound, causing large numbers of English words to be borrowed into Spanish, replacing Spanish as the language for higher social activities, and forming an integral part of the *code switching* in the speech of English/Spanish bilinguals.

Notwithstanding this code switching, which is an interplay between English and Spanish, Colorado Spanish is neither a mixed nor new language. Its grammatical base, its overwhelmingly Hispanic vocabulary, and its completely Spanish pronunciation attest to this. A mixed language is a merger of two languages in such a way that neither one of the original languages predominates, and it can only be described as a new creation. One test that can be applied is the one for mutual intelligibility. If Southwestern Spanish were extremely divergent from the urban dialects spoken in Mexico and elsewhere, we would expect there to be difficulty in mutual comprehension because of the degree of difference. However, this is not the case. A fluent speaker of Colorado Spanish who avoids using Anglicisms can easily understand and be understood in the Hispanic world, although his Spanish is typically rural or *popular,* to use the Spanish term. This ease in communication is one indication that this Southwestern dialect is simply a type of rural Spanish and not a mixed or new language. This rural dialect has been maintained primarily by oral tradition.

Although Colorado Spanish has been highly isolated from Mexico, two factors in the twentieth century have added some modern effects. Pachuco vocabulary from the street gangs of modern El Paso have left a few traces in the Spanish of San Luis. These Mexican immigrants have added another layer of vocabulary brought from the *barrios pobres* (poor neighborhoods) of Mexico. Although Colorado Spanish has been more isolated than other areas in the Southwest, even here this layer of vocabulary, the *pachuquismos,* can be detected. These terms have been adopted by young men in the *barrios* of the Southwest where they have sometimes coined their own terms. It should be remembered, though, that these *pachuquismos* are only one part of the Spanish of the Southwest. *Pachuquismos* such as *simón* for *sí* (yes), *chota* for *policía* (police), and *maderista* (an exaggerator) are not even recognized by many speakers of Southwestern Spanish. These *pachuquismos,* then, are only used among certain groups. The other modern factor involves Spanish radio stations. Songs composed in Mexico are learned in the San Luis Valley via radio stations which broadcast in Spanish. Such radio and television stations may help to maintain the Spanish spoken in the Southwest. Studies have not yet been made in Colorado to determine the effects of such broadcasting.

Let us examine in more detail the current Spanish spoken in the San Luis Valley and discuss historical events as we enter the last quarter of the twentieth century. Basing his study primarily on field work, my student, L. Ronald Ross (pp. 138–155) established several types of vocabulary which characterize this dialect, including Mexicanisms, Nahuatlisms, Pachuquisms, Anglicisms, semantic shifts, regionalisms (created locally), archaisms and a handful of terms borrowed from local Indian languages. By semantic shifts, I mean a semantic change in a lexical item which is internal to the language and not due to an outside influence. Ross (p. 149) mentions *álamo* (Cottonwood tree) which shifted to the generic term for all trees except pine trees. He also mentions (p. 150) *cuerpo* (body) which shifted in meaning to "woman's blouse" in Colorado. The examples we have mentioned deal primarily with vocabulary items since these give a brief but clear sketch of Colorado Spanish. Ross gives a complete description including phonology, vocabulary, and grammar.

In Colorado, there is some disuse of subjunctive after some expressions of doubt (Ross, 103), for example, *No es cierto que Ramón sabe más que Sofía* (It is not true that Ramón knows more than Sofía). Although there is also some disuse of future indicative in other Southwestern dialects, this verb tense is found in Colorado (Ross, 103), for example, *Tal vez vendrá mañana* (Perhaps he will come tomorrow). According to Ross (p. 163), by using *vamos + present participle*, the speaker gives an alternative imperative for first person plural, for example, *Vamos a comer* is used in place of *Comamos* (Let's eat). The verb *régime* with a preposition may, on occasion, not follow standard usage, for example, *trabajar por* is a literal translation of the English "to work for." The use of *calques*, that is, the use of Spanish words with English sentence structures, appears to be infrequent in everyday speech. The high degree of mutual intelligibility and the specific grammatical examples of Colorado Spanish provided by Ross in his dissertation indicate that this dialect is simply one of those classified as rural, that is, *popular* in Spanish terminology.

The impression obtained from listening to a speaker of southern Colorado Spanish is that this dialect is completely Spanish with little if any interference from English. It has so many rural characteristics that a listener, unaware of its origin, would try to place it in rural Spain or Latin America. The very isolation of the speakers of this dialect in remote villages and ranches has contributed to its maintenance. This is especially remarkable when one considers that there has been little direct contact with Mexico by many of these speakers since the midnineteenth century. There are other towns like San Luis in the Culebra Basin where the population is virtually all Mexican

American, where there is little if any outside influence and where life revolves around the family because of the isolation. Spanish is maintained very actively in such towns. Older persons above sixty are usually monolingual speakers of Spanish who may never have traveled outside of the San Luis Valley.

In larger towns such as Monte Vista, where there has been significant racial prejudice, there is a definite loss of Spanish. In such towns, youngsters may have only a passive knowledge of Spanish—understanding but not speaking Spanish. In the fall of 1973, Professor Charles Stansfield administered a placement exam (MLA Cooperative Spanish Form LA Listening Exam) to 177 Mexican-American freshmen at the University of Colorado. He modified the test by having the options spoken rather than read from a test booklet. Judging from this exam, about 15 percent are completely fluent in the regional dialect with very slight English interference. An additional 40 percent can communicate in Spanish but in a labored fashion with definite grammatical mistakes not common to speakers of Spanish; about 20 percent have a passive knowledge of Spanish but do not speak it, and the final 25 percent are monolingual speakers of English. Professor Rodolfo García, who supervises the classes in Spanish taught to Mexican American students, places the number of fluent Spanish speakers at 20 percent and monolingual English speakers at 20 percent, basing his estimates on class observations. His other estimates coincide with the examination results. It is interesting to note that only 15 or 20 percent are completely fluent in the regional dialect. Those who are completely fluent are either from Pueblo, which is in southern Colorado near New Mexico, or from rural areas. Many Chicano students on the Boulder campus who are from Denver also demonstrate a significant loss of Spanish.

The attitudes among younger Chicanos against the maintenance of Spanish is due to those held by the larger society. Until 1975, the State of Colorado had not provided funds for bilingual and bicultural education. Most of the 76,089 Chicano children in the State of Colorado do not yet benefit from such a bicultural education.

What will be the future of Spanish in Colorado and the United States? Will it be lost or maintained? The final answer to both these questions lies in the number and concentration of Mexican Americans, Puerto Ricans, and Cubans in certain cities such as Los Angeles, San Antonio, Chicago, New York, and Miami. Where there is a large concentrated population of the speakers of a language such as in these cities, or in a region such as the San Luis Valley, it is more likely for the language to be maintained. The sheer number of speakers who speak the language in a natural setting helps prevent its loss. In the Southwest, there is constant reinforcement of Spanish because of the proximity to Mexico. In addition, it may be that the current social climate is becoming more beneficial for Spanish maintenance.

The statistics on school age Mexican Americans (*Toward Quality Education for Mexican Americans,* p. 36) give us an idea of the size of the population in the future. In Arizona, Mexican Americans form 20 percent of the school population. In California, the figure is 17 percent; in Colorado it is 14 percent; in New Mexico, it is 40 percent; in Texas it is 23 percent. This is obviously a significant part of the population. One figure quoted for the number of the various Hispanic groups in the United States is 9.2 million (Turner, p. 6). Whether the language of Mexican Americans is maintained will depend on a number of factors, including national policy, demographic growth, and local educational policy. The Spanish language of Colorado, whose history spans four centuries in this region, is important not only because of the unique features it provides for study but also because it is the heritage of a significant part of the population whose ancestors led the way in the Hispanic settlement of Colorado and the Southwest. First came the Native American, then the Spaniards and Mexicans, and finally the North Americans. San Luis Spanish is too rich a language resource to lose; policies favorable to its maintenance must be promoted.

Bibliography

Andrews, John Philip. "History of Rural Spanish Settlement and Land Use in the Upper Culebra Basin of the San Luis Valley, Costilla County, Colorado." M.A. thesis, Boulder: University of Colorado, 1972.

Bancroft, Hubert Howe. *History of Arizona and New Mexico 1530-1888* (A facsimile of the 1889 edition). Albuquerque: Horn and Wallace, Publishers, 1962.

Bentley, Harold W. *A Dictionary of Spanish Terms in English*. New York, 1932.
Boyd-Bowman, Peter. *Léxico hispanoamericano del siglo XVI*. London: Tamesis Books Limited, 1971.
Canfield, Delos Lincoln. *La pronunciación del español en América: Ensayo histórico-descriptivo*. Bogotá: Instituto Caro y Cuervo, 1962.
Espinosa, Aurelio M. *Studies in New Mexican Spanish. Part I: Phonology*. Chicago: The University of Chicago, 1909.
Fernández Gómez, Carlos. *Vocabulario de Cervantes*. Madrid: Real Academia Española, 1962.
Lope Blanch, Juan M. *El español de América*. Madrid: Ediciones Alcalá, 1968.
Perrigo, Lynn I. *The American Southwest, Its Peoples and Cultures*. New York: Holt, Rinehart and Winston, 1971.
Ross, L. Ronald. *La lengua castellana en San Luis, Colorado*. Ph.D. thesis, Boulder: University of Colorado, 1975.
Toward Quality Education for Mexican Americans. Report VI. Washington, D.C.: U.S. Commission on Civil Rights, 1974.
Turner, Paul R., ed. *Bilingualism in the Southwest*. Tucson: The University of Arizona Press, 1973.

Selected Bibliography

Eva Marja Kahiluoto Rudat

Abernethy, Thomas Perkins. *The Burr Conspiracy*. New York: Oxford Press, 1954.

Adams, Eleanor B. "Fray Silvestre and the Obstinate Hopis." *New Mexico Historical Review* 38 (April 1963): 97-138.

Adams, Eleanor B., and Chávez, Fray Angelico, eds. and translators. *The Missions of New Mexico: A Description by Fray Francisco Atanasio Dominguez*. Albuquerque, 1956.

Adams, Robert. *The Architecture and Art of Early Hispanic Colorado*. Boulder: Colorado Associated University Press, 1974.

Alexander, Thomas G., ed. *Essays on the American West, 1973-1974*. Provo, Utah: Brigham Young University, 1975.

Alisky, Marvin. "The Mexican Americans Make Themselves Heard." *The Reporter* 36 (9 Feb. 1967): 45-62.

Almada, Francisco R. *Gobernantes de Chihuahua*. Chihuahua, 1929.

Anderson, Maxwell. *Night over Taos*. New York: Samuel French, 1935.

Andrews, John Philip. "History of Rural Spanish Settlement and Land Use in the Upper Culebra Basin of the San Luis Valley, Costilla County, Colorado." M.A. thesis, University of Colorado, 1972.

Bailey, Jessie B. *Diego de Vargas and the Reconquest of New Mexico*. Albuquerque: University of New Mexico, 1940.

Bancroft, Hubert Howe. *History of Arizona and New Mexico. Works*. Vol. 17. San Francisco: History Co., 1889-1890.

———. *History of Arizona and New Mexico*. 1530-1880 (A facsimile of the 1889 edition). Albuquerque: Horn and Wallace, Publishers, 1962.

Bandelier, Adolph F. A., and Bandelier, Fanny R. *Historical Documents Relating to New Mexico, Nueva Vizcaya, and Approaches Thereto, to 1773*. 3 vols. Washington, D.C.: Carnegie Institution, 1937.

Bartlett, John Russell. *Personal Narrative of Explorations and Incidents in Texas, New Mexico, California, Sonora, and Chihuahua, Connected with the United States Boundary Commission During the Years 1850, 1851, 1852 and 1853*. 2 vols. New York, 1854.

Becker, R. "Diseños." *The American West* 4 (no. 1, Feb. 1967).
Bemis, Samuel Flagg. *John Quincy Adams and the Foundation of American Foreign Policy.* New York: Alfred A. Knopf, 1949.
Benavides, Fray Alonso de. *The Memorial of Fray Alonso de Benavides, 1630.* Translated by Mrs. Edward E. Ayer. Albuquerque: Horn and Wallace, 1965.
Bender, Averam B. *The March of Empire: Frontier Defense in the Southwest.* Lawrence: University of Kansas, 1952.
Bentley, Harold W. *A Dictionary of Spanish Terms in English with Special Reference to the American Southwest.* New York: Columbia University Press, 1932.
Billington, Ray Allen. *The Far Western Frontier, 1830-1860.* New York: Harper and Brothers, 1956.
Bishop, Morris. *The Odyssey of Cabeza de Vaca.* New York: Century Publishing Co., 1933.
Bolton, Herbert Eugene. *Anza's California Expeditions.* 5 vols. Berkeley: University of California, 1930.
──── ed. *Athanase de Mézières and the Louisiana-Texas Frontier, 1768-1780.* 2 vols. Cleveland: Clark, 1914.
──── *Coronado, Knight of the Pueblos and Plains.* New York: McGraw-Hill Book Co., 1949.
────. *Coronado on the Turquoise Trail.* Albuquerque, University of New Mexico Press, 1949.
────. "French Intrusions into New Mexico, 1749-1752." In *The Pacific Ocean in History.* Edited by H. Morse Stephens and Herbert E. Bolton. New York: Macmillan, 1917.
────. *Guide to Materials for the History of the United States in the Principal Archives of Mexico.* Washington, D.C.: Carnegie Institution, 1913.
────. "New Light on Manuel Lisa and the Spanish Fur Trade." *Texas State Historical Association Quarterly* (*Southwestern Historical Quarterly*) 17 (no. 1, July 1913).
────. *Pageant in the Wilderness: The Story of the Escalante Expedition to the Interior Basin, 1776.* Salt Lake City: Utah Historical Society, 1950.
────, ed. "Papers of Zebulon M. Pike, 1806-1807." *American Historical Review* 13 (July 1908).
────. *Rim of Christendom.* New York: The MacMillan Co., 1936.
────. *The Spanish Borderlands.* New Haven, Connecticut: Yale University, 1921.
────, ed. *Spanish Explorations in the Southwest, 1542-1706.* New York: Charles Scribner's Sons, 1916. Reprinted New York: Barnes and Noble, Inc., 1967.

―――. *Texas in the Middle Eighteenth Century.* Berkeley: University of California Press, 1915.
Bolton, Herbert Eugene and Marshall, Thomas Maitland. *The Colonization of North America, 1492-1783.* New York: The MacMillan Co., 1935.
Boyd-Bowman, Peter. *Léxico hispanoamericano del siglo XVI.* London: Tamesis Books Limited, 1971.
Branch, E. Douglas. *The Cowboy and His Interpreters.* New York and London: D. Appleton-Century, Inc., 1926.
Brayer, Herbert O. *William Blackmore: A Case Study in the Economic Development of the West.* 2 vols. Reprint of W. W. Morrow. *Spanish and Mexican Land Grants* (First published San Francisco: Bancroft-Whitney, 1923). Denver: Bradford-Robinson, 1949. Reprint New York: Arno Press, 1974.
Brooks, Philip Coolidge. *Diplomacy and the Borderlands: The Adams-Onís Treaty of 1819.* Berkeley: University of California Press, 1939.
Burma, John H. *Spanish Speaking Groups in the United States.* Durham, North Carolina: Duke University, 1953.
Burpee, Lawrence J. *The Search for the Western Sea.* 2 vols. Toronto: MacMillan, 1935.

Campa, Arthur L. "Los Comanches, A New Mexican Folk Drama." *University of New Mexico Bulletin* Modern Languages Series, 7 (no. 1, April 1, 1942).
―――. *Spanish Folk Poetry in New Mexico.* Albuquerque: University of New Mexico Press, 1940.
―――. "Spanish Folksongs in Metropolitan Denver." *Southern Folklore Quarterly* 24 (no. 3, Sept. 1960).
―――. "Spanish Religious Folktheatre of the Spanish Southwest (First cycle)." *University of New Mexico Bulletin* Modern Language Series, 5, (no. 1, Feb. 15, 1934).
―――. "Spanish Religious Folktheatre in the Southwest (Second cycle)." *University of New Mexico Bulletin* Modern Language Series, 6 (no. 2, June 15, 1934).
―――. *Treasure of the Sangre de Cristos: Tales and Traditions of the Spanish Southwest.* Paintings by Joe Beeler. Norman: University of Oklahoma Press, 1963.
Canfield, Delos Lincoln. *La pronunciación del español en América. Ensayo histórico-descriptivo.* Bogotá: Instituto Caro y Cuervo, 1962.
Carr, Ralph. "The Sangre de Cristo Grant." *The Brand Book* Official Organ of the Westerners, 3 (no. 7, July 1947).

Carroll, H. Bailey, and Haggard, J. Villasana. *Three New Mexico Chronicles.* Albuquerque: Quivira, 1942.
Carter, Clarence Edwin. "The Burr-Wilkinson Intrigue in St. Louis." *Missouri Historical Society Bulletin* 10 (no. 4, pt. I, July 1954).
──────. *Great Britain and the Illinois Country,* 1763-1774. Washington, D.C.: American Historical Assn., 1910.
Castañeda, Carlos E., trans., notes. *The Mexican Side of the Texan Revolution.* by the chief Mexican participants, General Antonio López de Santa Anna, D. Ramón Martínez Caro, General Vicente Filisolo, General José Urrea, General José María Tornel. Dallas: P. L. Turner Co., 1928.
──────. *Our Catholic Heritage in Texas* 1519-1936. 7 vols. Austin: Von Boeckmann-Jones, 1936-58.
Cather, Willa. *Death Comes for the Archbishop.* New York: Alfred A. Knopf, Inc., 1927.
Catlin, George. *North American Indians.* 2 vols. Philadelphia: Leary, Stuart and Co., 1913.
Caughey, John W. *Bernardo de Gálvez in Louisiana,* 1776-1783. Berkeley: University of California, 1934.
──────. *Hubert Howe Bancroft, Historian of the West.* Berkeley: University of California, 1946.
Chapman, Charles E. *Catalogue of Materials in the Archivo General de Indias for the History of the Pacific Coast and the American Southwest.* Berkeley: University of California Press, 1919.
Chávez, Fray Angélico. *My Penitente Land.* Albuquerque: University of New Mexico Press, 1974.
──────. "The Penitentes of New Mexico." *New Mexico Historical Review* 29 (1954): 97-123.
Chittenden, Hiram M. *The American Fur Trade of the Far West.* 3 vols. New York: Francis P. Harper, 1902.
Clark, Ira G. *Then Came the Railroads: The Century from Steam to Diesel in the Southwest.* Norman: University of Oklahoma, 1958.
Cleland, Robert Glass. *The Cattle on the Thousand Hills: Southern California,* 1850-1880. San Marino: Huntington Library, 1941.
──────. *From Wilderness to Empire: A History of California.* Edited and brought down to date by Glenn S. Dumke. New York: Knopf, 1969.
──────. *The Reckless Breed of Men: The Trappers and Fur Traders of the Southwest.* New York: Alfred A. Knopf, Inc., 1950.
Cooper, James Fennimore. *The Prairie. The Works of James Fennimore Cooper.* 32 vols. New York: G. F. Putnam's Sons, 1896.

Córdova, Lorenzo de. *Echoes of the Flute.* Santa Fe: Ancient City Press, 1972.

Cossío, José María de y Tomás Maza Solano. *Romancero popular de la montaña.* Santander: no publisher, no date.

Coues, Elliott, ed. *The Expeditions of Zebulon Montgomery Pike.* 3 vols. New York: Francis P. Harper, 1892.

———. *History of the Expedition Under the Command of Lewis and Clark.* 4 vols. New York: Francis P. Harper, 1893.

Cowan, Robert Granniss. *Ranchos of California: A List of Spanish Concessions 1775-1822, and Mexican Grants 1822-1846.* Fresno, California: Academy Library Guild, 1956.

Cox, Isacc Joselin. *The Early Explorations of Louisiana.* (University Studies, ser. 2, vol. 2, no. 1 [Jan.-Feb. 1906]. Cincinnati: University of Cincinnati Press, 1906.

———. "Opening the Santa Fe Trail." *Missouri Historical Review* 25 (no. 1, Oct. 1930).

Dale, Edward Everett. *Cow Country.* Norman: University of Oklahoma, 1930.

———. *The Range Cattle Industry.* Norman: University of Oklahoma, 1930.

Darley, Alexander M. *The Passionists of the Southwest, or The Holy Brotherhood.* (First published Pueblo, 1893) Reprinted in *The Penitentes of New Mexico.* New York: Arno Press, 1974.

Delgado, Adelardo. *Chicano Movement.* Totinem Press, 1971.

Denhardt, Robert M. *The Horse of the Americas.* Norman: University of Oklahoma Press, 1947.

DeVoto, Bernard. *The Course of Empire.* Boston: Houghton-Mifflin Co., 1952.

DeVoto, Bernard, et al. *1846: The Year of Decision.* Boston: Little, Brown and Company, 1943.

Dickey, Roland F. *New Mexico Village Arts.* Albuquerque: University of New Mexico, 1949.

Dobie, J. Frank. *Coronado's Children.* Dallas: The Southwest Press, 1930.

Doniol, Henri. *Histoire de la Participation de la France à l'Établissement des États-Unis d'Amérique.* 5 vols. Paris, 1886-92.

Douglas, Walter B. *Manuel Lisa* (with hitherto unpublished materials annotated and edited by Abraham P. Nasatir). New York: Argosy-Antiquarian Press, 1964.

Drumm, Stella, ed. *Luttig's Journal of a Fur Trading Expedition on the Upper Missouri, 1812-1813.* St. Louis, Missouri Historical Society,

1920. (New edition by Nasatir; New York, Argosy-Antiquarian Press, 1964.)

Duffus, R. L. *The Santa Fé Trail.* New York: Longmans, Green, 1930.

Dunham, H. H. "New Mexican Land Grants with Special Reference to the Title Papers of the Maxwell Grant." *New Mexico Historical Review* (Jan. 1955).

Dusenberry, William Howard. *The Mexican Mesta: The Administration of Ranching in Colonial Mexico.* Urbana: University of Illinois Press, 1963.

Espinosa, Gilberto. "Los Comanches." *The New Mexico Quarterly* (May 1931): 130–142.

Espinosa, J. Manuel. *Crusaders of the Río Grande: The Story of Don Diego de Vargas.* Chicago: Institute of Jesuit History, 1942.

———. "Journal of the Vargas Expedition into Colorado, 1694." *Colorado Magazine* 16 (May 1939): 81–90.

———. "The Legend of Sierra Azul." *New Mexico Historical Review* 9 (no. 2, April 1934).

Espinoza, Aurelio. "Romancero nuevomejicano." *Revue Hispanique* 40 (June 1917): 97.

———. *Studies in New-Mexican Spanish. Part I: Phonology.* Chicago: University of Chicago, 1909.

Eyre, Alice. *The Famous Frémonts and Their America.* Los Angeles: Fine Arts Press, 1950.

Fergusson, Erna. *Murder and Mystery in New Mexico.* Albuquerque: Merle Armitage, 1948.

———. *New Mexico: A Pageant of Three Peoples.* New York: Alfred A. Knopf, Inc., 1951.

Fernández Gómez, Carlos. *Vocabulario de Cervantes.* Madrid: Real Academia Española, 1962.

Fernando de Taos Grant. Claim No. 125. Microfilm of Manuscripts and Records to New Mexico Land Grants in the Bureau of Land Management, Santa Fe, New Mexico.

Field, Mathew C. "Sketches of Big Timber. Bent's Fort and Milk Fort in 1839." First published in the *New Orleans Picayune* July 14, 1840; reprinted *Colorado Magazine* 14: 102–108.

Folmer, Henri. "Contraband Trade Between Louisiana and New Mexico in the Eighteenth Century." *New Mexico Historical Review* 16 (no. 3, July 1941).

———. *Franco-Spanish Rivalry in North America, 1524–1763.* Glendale, California: Arthur H. Clark Co., 1953.

———. "The Mallet Expedition of 1739 Through Nebraska, Kansas, and Colorado to Santa Fé." *The Colorado Magazine* 16 (no. 5, Sept. 1939): 163-73.

Frémont, John Charles. *Memoirs of My Life: Five Journeys of Western Exploration During the Years 1842, 1843-44, 1845-46-47, 1848-49, 1853-54.* 1 vol. (no more volumes published). Chicago: Belford, Clarke, and Company, 1887.

Galarza, Ernesto. *Mexican American in the Southwest.* Santa Barbara: McNally-Loftin, 1969.

Gannett, Henry. *Boundaries of the United States and of the Several States and Territories* (Bulletin No. 13 of the United States Geological Survey). Washington, D.C.: U.S. Gov. Printing Office, 1885.

Gard, Wayne. *The Chisholm Trail.* Norman: University of Oklahoma, 1954.

———. *Frontier Justice.* Norman: University of Oklahoma, 1949.

Gauthier, Marcel. "De quelques jeux." *Revue Hispanique* 33.

Gilbert, Edmund W. *Exploration of Western America, 1800-1850.* New York: The MacMillan Co., 1933.

Goff, Richard, and McCafree, Robert H. *Century in the Saddle.* Denver: Colorado Cattlemen's Centennial Commission, 1967.

Gomez del Campillo, Miguel. *Relaciones Diplomáticas Entre España y los Estados Unidos.* 2 vols. Madrid: Instituto Gonzalo Fernández de Oviedo, 1946.

Gorham, George C. *Life and Public Services of Edwin M. Stanton.* 2 vols. Boston: Houghton, 1899.

Grebler, Leo, et al. *The Mexican American People: The Nation's Second Largest Minority.* New York: The Free Press, 1970.

Greenleaf, R. E. "Atrisco and Las Ciruelas, 1722-1769." *New Mexico Historical Review* (Jan. 1967).

Gregg, Josiah. *Commerce of the Prairies.* Edited by Max Moorhead. Norman: University of Oklahoma Press, 1954.

Grinnell, George, B. *The Cheyenne Indians.* 2 vols. New Haven: Yale University Press, 1923.

Hackett, Charles Wilson, ed. and trans. *Historical Documents Relating to New Mexico, Nueva Vizcaya and Approaches Thereto, to 1773.* 3 vols. Washington, D.C.: Carnegie Institution, 1923-1937.

———. "New Light on Don Diego de Peñalosa." *The Mississippi Valley Historical Review* 6 (no. 3, Dec. 1919): 313-35.

Hafen, Leroy R. *Colorado and Its People.* 4 vols. New York: Lewis Historical Publishing Co., 1948.

———. *The Overland Mail,* 1849–1866. Cleveland: Arthur H. Clark Co., 1926.

———. "A Winter Rescue March Across the Rockies." *Colorado Magazine* 4 (no. 1, Jan. 1927).

Hafen, Leroy R., and Rister, Carl Coke. *Western America.* New York: Prentice-Hall, Inc., 1941.

Hallenbeck, Cleve. *The Journey of Fray Marcos de Niza.* Dallas: Southern Methodist University, 1949.

Hammond, George P., and Rey, Agapito. *Don Juan de Oñate, Colonizer of New Mexico.* 1595–1628. 2 vols. Albuquerque: University of New Mexico, 1953.

———. *Narratives of the Coronado Expedition* 1540–1542. Albuquerque: University of New Mexico Press, 1940.

Hanke, Lewis. *The Spanish Struggle for Justice in the Conquest of America.* Philadelphia: University of Pennsylvania Press, 1949.

Heap, Gwin Harris. *Central Route to the Pacific.* Edited by Leroy R. Hafen and Anne W. Hafen. Glendale, California: Arthur H. Clark Co., 1957.

Henderson, Alice Corbin. *Brothers of the Light: The Penitentes of the Southwest.* (First published, New York: Harcourt Brace, 1937). Reprinted in *The Penitentes of New Mexico.* New York: Arno Press, 1974.

Hill, J. J. "Spanish and Mexican Exploration." *Utah Historical Quarterly* 3 (no. 1, Jan. 1930).

Hodge, Frederick Webb. "The Narrative of Cabeza de Vaca" *Spanish Explorers in the Southern United States.* New York: Scribner's, 1907.

Hodge, Frederick W. and Lewis, T. H. *Spanish Explorers in the Southern United States,* 1528–1543. New York: Scribner's, 1907.

Horgan, Paul. *Conquistadores in North American History.* New York: Farrar, Strauss, 1963.

———. *Great River: The Rio Grande in North American History.* New York: E. P. Dutton and Co., 1954.

Houck, Louis. *A History of Missouri.* 3 vols. Chicago: Donnelley, 1908.

———. *The Spanish Regime in Missouri.* 2 vols. Chicago: Donnelley, 1909.

Jablow, Joseph. *The Cheyenne in Plains Indian Trade Relations,* 1795–1840. (Monograph of the American Ethnological Society, Vol. 19) New York: J. J. Augustin, 1951.

Jackson, Donald. *Letters of the Lewis and Clark Expedition, with related Documents,* 1733-1854. Urbana: University of Illinois Press, 1962.
James Thomas. *Three Years Among the Indians and Mexicans.* Edited by Walter B. Douglas. St. Louis, Missouri Historical Society, 1916 *Ibid.* (Edited by A. P. Nasatir) Philadelphia, Lippincott, 1962. *Ibid.* (Edited by Milton Milton Quaife). Chicago, Lakeside, 1953.
Jenkins, M. E. *The Baltasar Bacar "Grant": A History of an Encroachment.* Reprint from *El Palacio* 68 (nos. 1 and 2).
Jenkinson, Michael. *Tijerina.* Albuquerque: Paisano Press, 1968.
Jones, Rufus, M. "Flagellation." *Encyclopedia of Religion and Ethics.* Vol. 6 (1967).
Jones, William. *The History of Catholic Education in the State of Colorado.* Washington, D.C.: The Catholic University of America Press, 1955.
Joseph Marie, Sister. *The Role of the Church and the Folk in the Development of the Early Drama in New Mexico.* Philadelphia: University of Pennsylvania Press, 1948.

Keleher, William A. *Turmoil in New Mexico, 1848-1868.* Santa Fe: Rydal Press, 1952.
Kinnaird, Lawrence. "American Penetration into Spanish Louisiana," *New Spain and the Anglo-American West.* Lancaster, Pa., copyright by George P. Hammond, 1932.
Kupper, Winifred. *The Golden Hoof: The Story of the Sheep of the Southwest.* New York: Alfred A. Knopf, Inc., 1945.

Lafora, Nicolás de. *The Frontiers of New Spain.* Edited by Lawrence Kinnaird. Berkeley: Quivira Society, 1958.
Larpenteur, Charles. *Forty Years a Fur Trader.* 2 vols. Edited by Elliot Coues. New York: Francis Harper, 1898.
Lavender, David. *Bent's Fort.* Garden City, New York: Doubleday and Co., 1954.
Lea, Aurora Lucero-White. *Literary Folklore of the Hispanic Southwest.* San Antonio: Naylor Co., 1953.
―――. *Los hispanos: Five Essays on the Folkways of the Hispanos.* New Mexico Series. Denver: Sage Books, 1947.
Lea, Tom. "The Mighty Ranch of Richard King." *Life,* July 8, 1957.
Leonard, Irving A. *Baroque Times in Old Mexico.* Ann Arbor: University of Michigan Press, 1959.
―――. *The Books of the Brave.* Cambridge: Harvard University Press, 1949.

Lockwood, Francis. *The Story of the Spanish Missions of the Middle South West.* Santa Ana, California: Fine Arts Press, 1934.

Loomis, Noel M. and Nasatir, Abraham P. *Pedro Vial and the Roads to Santa Fe.* Norman: University of Oklahoma Press, 1967.

Lope Blanch, Juan M. *El español de América.* Madrid: Ediciones Alcalá, 1968.

Lope de Ubeda, Juan. *Cancionero y vergel de plantas divinas.* Alcalá de Henares, 1588.

López, Olibama. "The Spanish Heritage in the San Luis Valley." M.A. thesis, University of Denver, 1942.

Lowery, Woodbury. *A Descriptive List of Maps of the Spanish Possessions . . .1502–1820.* Washington, D.C.: U.S. Gov. Printing Office, 1912.

Lowrie, S. H. *Culture Conflict in Texas,* 1821–1835. New York: Columbia University, 1932.

Ludwig, Ed., and Santibañez, James. *The Chicanos: Mexican American Voices.* Baltimore: Penguin Books, 1971.

Lummis, Charles F. *The Spanish Pioneers and the California Missions.* Chicago: McClurg, 1929.

McCaleb, Walter F. *The Aaron Burr Conspiracy.* New York: Dodd, Mead, 1903.

McCarty, F. "Land Grant Problems in New Mexico." *Albuquerque Journal* (Sept. 28–Oct. 10, 1969).

McClintock, James H. *Arizona.* Chicago: Th. S. Clarke Publishing Co. 1916.

McWilliams, Carey. *Al norte de México: el conflicto entre "anglos" e hispanos.* Traduccion de Lyn de Cardoza. Mexico: Siglo Veintuno, 1968.

———. *North from Mexico: The Spanish Speaking People of the United States.* (First published, Philadelphia: Lippincott, 1949). Reprint New York: Greenwood Press, 1968.

Marcy, Colonel R. B. *Thirty Years of Army Life on the Border.* New York: Harper and Brothers, Publishers, 1866.

Marshall, James. *Santa Fe: The Railroad That Built an Empire.* New York: Random House, 1945.

Marshall, Thomas Maitland. *A History of the Western Boundary of the Louisiana Purchase,* 1819–1841. Berkeley: University of California Press, 1914.

Matthiessen, Peter. "Profiles: Cesar Chavez." *The New Yorker.* June 21 and June 26, 1969.

Meinig, D. W. *Southwest.* New York: Oxford University Press, 1971.
Mills, George and Grove, Richard. *Lucifer and the Crucifer: The Enigma of the Penitentes.* Colorado Springs: The Taylor Museum, 1966.
Minge, W. A. "Frontier Problems in New Mexico Preceding the Mexican War, 1840-1846." Ph.D. dissert., University of New Mexico, 1965.
Moorhead, Max L. *New Mexico's Royal Road: Trade and Travel on the Chihuahua Trail.* Norman: University of Oklahoma Press, 1958.
Mora, Joseph Jacinto. *Californios: The Sage of Hard-riding Vaqueros. America's Cowboys.* Garden City, N.Y.: Doubleday, 1949.

Nasatir, Abraham P. "Government Employees and Salaries in Spanish Louisiana." *Louisiana Historical Review* 17 (no. 4, Oct. 1946).
———. "The Formation of the Missouri Company." *Missouri Historical Review* 25 (no. 1, Oct. 1930).
———. "Jacques Clamorgan: Colonial Promoter of the Northern Border of New Spain." *New Mexico Historical Review* 17 (no. 2, April 1942).
Nasatir, Abraham P., and Douglas, Walter B. *Manuel Lisa.* New York: Argosy-Antiquarian Press, 1964.
Nava, Julian. *Mexican Americans, Past, Present, Future.* New York: American Book Co., 1969.
Nevins, Allan. *Frémont, Pathmarker of the West.* New York: Appleton-Century Co., 1939.
Norris, Frank. *The Octopus.* New York: Doubleday, Page and Company, 1904.

Ong, Walter J., S.J. *Rhetoric, Romance, and Technology.* Ithaca: Cornell University Press, 1971.
Onís, José de. "Maverick, un americanismo de antecedentes, hispánicos." *Hispania,* 48 (no. 2, May 1963).
——— *Las misiones españolas en los Estados Unidos.* New York: Neff Lithographing Co., 1959.
Onís, Luis de. *Memoir upon the negotiations between Spain and the United States of America, which led to the treaty of 1819.* Translated with notes by Tobias Watkins. Baltimore, 1821.
———. *Memoria sobre las negociaciones entre España y los Estados Unidos de América que dieron motivo al tratado de 1819. Con una noticia sobre la estadística de aquel país. Acompaña un apéndice, que contiene documentos importantes para mayor ilustración del asunto.* Madrid, 1820; Mexico, 1826.

―――. [Verus]. *Observation on the Conduct of our Executive Toward Spain*. Georgetown, D.C., Nov. 12, 1813.

―――. [Verus]. *Observation on the Existing Difference Between the Government of Spain and the U.S.* Philadelphia, 1817.

―――. *Official Correspondence Between D. Luis de Onís and John Quincy Adams*. London, 1818.

Onís Papers. The family archives including records and letters not only of Luis de Onís, but also of his son Mauricio Carlos de Onís who was also a diplomat.

Ortiz, Alfonso. *The Tewa World*. Chicago: University of Chicago Press, 1969.

Otero, Nina. *Old Spain in Our South West*. New York: Harcourt, Brace and Co., 1936.

Paige, Harry W. "Golgatha in New Mexico." *American* 130 (no. 1 A5, Jan. 1974).

Parkman, Francis. *La Salle and the Discovery of the Great West*. Edited by W. R. Taylor. New York: Rinehart and Co., 1956.

Pearce, T. M. "On Regionalism in the Southwest." *The New Mexico Quarterly* 1 (no. 3, Aug. 1931): 197.

The Penitentes of New Mexico. Reprint of: Dorothy Woodward. *The Penitentes of New Mexico* (First published, New Haven, 1935), *The Passionists of the Southwest, or The Holy Brotherhood* (Pueblo, 1893), A. C. Henderson. *Brothers of Light*. (New York: Harcourt Brace, 1937). New York: Arno Press, 1974.

Pereyra, Carlos. "Un americanista genial (Luis de Onís)." *Union Hispano-Americana* 3 (no. 38, 1919): 2–3.

Perrigo, Lynn I. *The American Southwest, Its Peoples and Cultures*. New York: Holt, Rinehart and Winston, 1971.

―――. *Our Spanish Southwest*. Dallas: B. Upshaw, 1960.

Pichardo, Father José Antonio. *Pichardo's Treatise on the Limits of Louisiana and Texas*. 4 vols. Edited by Charles Wilson Hackett. Austin: University of Texas Press, 1931–46.

Pike, Zebulon. *An Account of Expeditions to the Sources of the Mississippi and Through the Eastern Parts of Louisiana to the Sources of the Arkansas, Kansas, La Platte, and Pierre Juan Rivers: Performed by Order of the Government of the United States During the Years 1805, 1806, 1807 and a Tour Through the Interior Parts of New Spain When Conducted Through These Provinces by Order of the Captain General in the Year* 1807. Philadelphia, 1810.

Pino, Pedro. *Exposición sucinta y sencilla de la Provincia del Nuevo México.* Cádiz: Imprenta del Estado Mayor General, 1812.
Place, Edwin B. "A Group of Mystery Plays Found in a Spanish Speaking Region of Southern Colorado." *University of Colorado Studies* 18 (no. 1, Aug. 1930): 1-8.
Priestley, Herbert I. *The Coming of the White Man,* 1492-1848. New York: The MacMillan Co., 1930.
―――. *José de Gálvez.* Berkeley: University of California Press, 1916.
―――. "The Reforms of José de Gálvez in New Spain." *The Pacific Ocean in History.* Edited by H. Morse Stephens and Herbert E. Bolton. New York: MacMillan, 1917.
Purdy, James H. "Ledger Book." Ayer Collection. Newberry Library, Chicago, Illinois.

Rael, Juan. *The New Mexican Alabados.* Stanford University Press, 1951.
Ralliere, J. B. *Cánticos espirituales. Dispuestos en nuevo orden sin añadiduras por un Padre D.K.C.D.J.* El Paso, Texas: Editorial Revista Catolica, 1933.
―――. *Colección de cánticos espirituales.* Tome, New Mexico, 1897.
Ramírez, Jose F. *Mexico During the War with United States.* Edited by W. V. Scholes. Translated by E. B. Scherr. Columbia: University of Missouri, 1950.
Redfield, Robert. *Peasant Society and Culture.* Chicago: University of Chicago Press, 1960.
Reeve, Frank D. "Navaho-Spanish Diplomacy, 1770-1790." *New Mexico Historical Review* 35 (no. 3, July 1960).
Reichard, Gladys A. *Navaho Medicine Man.* New York: J. J. Augustin, 1939.
Richardson, Rupert N. *The Comanche Barrier to South Plains Settlement.* Glendale, California: Arthur H. Clark Co., 1933.
―――. *Texas, the Lone Star State.* Englewood Cliffs, N.J.: Prentice Hall, 1958.
Richman, Irving B. *California under Spain and Mexico,* 1538-1847. Boston: Houghton-Mifflin Co., 1911.
Rickard, Thomas A. *A History of American Mining.* New York: McGraw-Hill, 1932.
Ridge, John R. *The Life and Adventures of Joaquin Marietta.* Norman: University of Oklahoma Press, 1955.
Rister, Carl Coke. *The Comanche Bondage.* Glendale, Calif.: A. H. Clarke Co., 1955.

———. *The Southwestern Frontier, 1865–1881.* Cleveland: Arthur H. Clark Co., 1928.
Rives, George L. *United States and Mexico, 1821–1848.* 2 vols. New York: Scribner's Sons, 1913.
Robertson, James Alexander. *Louisiana Under the Rule of Spain, France, and the United States, 1785–1807.* 2 vols. Cleveland: Clark, 1911.
Robinson, Cecil. *With the Ears of Strangers: The Mexican in American Literature.* Tucson: The University of Arizona Press, 1963.
Robinson, William Wilcox. *Land in California: The Story of Mission Lands, Ranchos, Squatters, Mining Claims, Railroad Grants, Land Scrips and Homesteads.* Berkeley: University of California Press, 1948.
———. *Spanish and Mexican Ranchos of San Fernando Valley.* Los Angeles: Southwest Museum, 1966.
Rojas, Arnold R. *The Vaquero.* Charlotte, N.C.: McNally and Loftin, 1964.
Ross, L. Ronald. "La lengua castellana en San Luis, Colorado." Ph.D. dissert., University of Colorado, 1975.
Rydjord, John. *Foreign Interest in the Independence of New Spain.* Durham, N.C.: Duke University Press, 1935.

Samora, Julián. *La Raza: Forgotten Americans.* University of Notre Dame Press, 1966.
Sancha, Justo de, ed. *Romancero y cancionero sagrados.* Biblioteca de Autores Españoles, vol. 35. Madrid, 1872.
Sánchez, George I. *Forgotten People: A Study of New Mexico.* Albuquerque: University of New Mexico, 1940.
Sandoz, Mari. *The Buffalo Hunters.* New York: Hastings House, 1954.
Sanford, Trent E. *Architecture of the Southwest: Indian, Spanish, American.* New York: W. W. Norton and Co., 1950.
Sexton, R. W. *Spanish Influence on American Architecture and Decoration.* New York: Brentano's, 1927.
Shepherd, William R. *Guide to the Materials for the History of the United States in Spanish Archives.* Washington, D.C.: Carnegie Institution, 1907.
Sonnichsen, Charles L. *The Mescalero Apaches.* Norman: University of Oklahoma, 1958.
Stanley, F. (pseud. Stanley Francis Louis Crocchiola) *Ciudad Santa Fe, Spanish Domination, 1610–1821.* Denver: World Press, 1958.
———. *Desperados of New Mexico.* Denver: World Press, 1953.

———.*The Grant That Maxwell Bought.* Denver: World Press, 1952.
———. *Socorro: The Oasis.* Denver: World Press, 1950.
Stark, Richard B. *Juegos infantiles cantados en Nuevo México.* Santa Fe: Museum of New Mexico Press, 1973.
———. *Music of the Spanish Folk Plays in New Mexico.* Santa Fe: Museum of New Mexico Press, 1969.
Steele, Thomas, S.J. *Santos and Saints.* Albuquerque: Calvin Horn Publisher, 1974.
Swadesh, Frances. "The Social and Philosophical Context of Creativity in New Mexico." *Rocky Mountain Social Science Journal* 9 (1972).
Swan, Howard. *Music in the Southwest, 1825-1950.* San Marino, California: Huntington Library, 1952.

Tate, Bill. *The Penitentes of the Sangre de Cristo.* Truchas: The Tate Gallery, 1966.
Thomas, Alfred Barnaby. *After Coronado.* Norman: University of Oklahoma, 1935.
———. "The First Santa Fe Expedition, 1792-1793." *Chronicles of Oklahoma,* 9 (no. 2, June 1931).
———. "San Carlos, a Comanche Pueblo on the Arkansas River in 1787." *Colorado Magazine* 6:79-91.
———. "Governor Mendinueta's Proposals for the Defense of Mexico, 1772-1778." *New Mexico Historical Review,* 6 (no. 1, Jan. 1931).
Thomas, Chauncey. "Some Characteristics of Jim Baker." *The Colorado Magazine* 4 (no. 4, Aug. 1927).
Tornel, José María. "Texas and the United States of America in their Relations with the Mexican Republic." *The Mexican Side of the Texas Revolution.* Compiled and translated by Carlos Castañeda. Dallas: P. L. Turner Company, 1928.
Toward Quality Education for Mexican Americans. Report VI. Washington, D.C.: U.S. Commission on Civil Rights, 1974.
Towne, Charles W. and Wentworth, Edward N. *Shepherd's Empire.* Norman: University of Oklahoma, 1945.
Turner, Paul R., ed. *Bilingualism in the Southwest.* Tucson, Arizona: The University of Arizona Press, 1973.
Twitchell, Ralph Emerson. *The History of the Military Occupation of the Territory of New Mexico, from 1846 to 1851 by the Government of the United States.* Denver, Colorado: The Smith Brooks Co., 1909.
———. *The Leading Facts of New Mexican History.* 2 vols. Cedar Rapids, Iowa: Torch Press, 1911.

———. *Old Santa Fe: The Story of New Mexico's Ancient Capital.* Santa Fe: New Mexican Publishing Corp., 1925.
———. *The Spanish Archives of New Mexico.* 2 vols. Cedar Rapids, Iowa: The Torch Press, 1914.

VanDiest, Edmond C. "Early History of Costilla County." *Colorado Magazine* 5: 141.
Vandiveer, Clarence A. *The Fur Trade and Early Western Exploration.* Cleveland: Arthur H. Clark Co., 1929.
Vasconcelos, José. *Breve historia de México.* México: Editorial Continental, 1956.
———. *La Cultura en Hispano America.* La Plata, 1934.
———. *La raza cósmica.* Barcelona: Agencia Mundial de Librería, 1925.
Vestal, Stanley. *Kit Carson.* Boston: Houghton-Mifflin Co., 1928.
———. *Mountain Men.* Boston: Houghton-Mifflin Co., 1937.
———. *The Old Santa Fe Trail.* Boston: Houghton-Mifflin Co., 1939.

Wallace, Edward S. *The Great Reconaissance: Soldiers, Artists and Scientists on the Frontier, 1848-1861.* Boston: Little, Brown Co., 1955.
Wallace, Ernest, and Hoebel, E. A. *The Comanches.* Norman: University of Oklahoma, 1952.
Warren, Robert Penn. *The Circus in the Attic and Other Stories.* New York: Harcourt, Brace, 1947.
Weigle, Martha Mary. "Hermanos Penitentes." Michigan, University Microfilm, 1973, pt. 2.
Weigle, Marta. *The Penitentes of the Southwest.* Santa Fe: Ancient City Press, 1970.
Wellman, Paul I. *Death on the Desert: The Fifty Years' War for the Great Southwest.* New York: The MacMillan Co., 1913.
Westphall, Victor. *The Public Domain in New Mexico, 1854-1891.* Albuquerque: University of New Mexico Press, 1965.
Wilkinson, General James. *Memoirs of My Own Times.* 3 vols. Philadelphia, 1816.
Wolf, Eric R. *Peasants.* Englewood Cliffs, N.J.: Prentice Hall, 1966.
———. *Sons of the Shaking Earth.* Chicago: University of Chicago Press, 1959.
Wolle, Muriel Sibell. *The Bonanza Trail: Ghost Towns and Mining Camps f the West.* Bloomington: Indiana University Press, 1953.
Woodward, Dorothy. *The Penitentes of New Mexico.* (First published, New Haven, 1935) Reprint, New York: Arno Press, 1974.

Worcester, Donald E. trans. and ed. *Mexico* (Viceroyalty). *Instructions for Governing the Interior Provinces of New Spain, 1785 by Bernardo de Gálvez.* Berkeley: Quivira, 1951.

Index

Abeyta, Francisco, 172
Abeyta, Lorenzo A., 184
Acacio, San, 120-21, 135
Adams, Governor Billy, 186
Adams, John Quincy, 35, 40
Adán y Eva, 93
Agraciada Golondrina (ballad), 101
Aguilar, Alfonso Faél de, 69
Aguilar, José María, 165
Aguilar, José Ramón, 164
A la Una Yo Nasí (song), 108
Alencáster, Joaquín del Real, 16-17, 111
Alona, Miguel, xxi, 79, 81-82, 85, 87-90
Alona, Mikey. *See* Alona, Miguel
Alvarado, Juan, 57
Angel, the (in Nativity play), 95, 97. *See also* Miguel, Angel
Anthony of Padua, Saint, 119, 165, 178
Anza, Juan Bautista de, 3, 12-14, 99-100
Aparición de la Virgen, La, 94
Apodaca, Mauricio, 185
Apodaca (Viceroy of Mexico), 38
Apostles, the, 144
Aragón, Domingo, 172
Aranz, Fray Dominguez de, 8
Archuleta, Juan de, 6
Arista, Mariano, 56
Armijo, Aduato, 172
Armijo, Governor Manuel, 46, 59-61, 65-66, 73, 76
Arredondo (leader of Royalists' forces), 41
Atencio, Herman J., 186
Austin, Moses, 38, 48
Austin, Stephen, 48-50

Baca, Baltasar, 47
Baca, Felipe, xv, 91, 184
Baca, Lorenzo, 177
Baca, Luis María, 66
Baca, Trinidad, xv
Baker, Jim, 80-82, 84, 87, 90
"Ball, The" (game). *See Pelota, La*
Bandini, Juan, 52
Barabbas, 135
Barela, Arculiano, 104-105
Barela, Casimiro, xxii, 184, 187
Barron, Joseph A., 186
Bartolo (shepherd in Nativity play), 95
Beales, Dr. John Charles, 50
Beaubien, Carlos, xv, 65, 72-76
Beaubien, Narciso, 65, 73, 76
Beaubien, Stephen Louis Lee, 65, 76
"Beautiful Brunette" (song). *See Trigueña Hermosa*
Benavides, Fray Alonso de, 143
Bent, Charles, 66
Bent, Estaban, 66
Bernal, Juan Andrés, 97
Berreyesa, José Reyes, 56
Blackmore, William, 75
"Blind Little Hen, The" (game). *See Gallinita Ciega, La*
Bocanegra (former Mexican Minister of Exterior Relations), 56
Borrego, Epifiano, 174
Borrego, Félix, 174
Borrego, Juan Luis, 172, 174
Borrego, Leandro, 172
Borrego, Salomón, 174
Brewer (Federal Judge), 74
Bucareli, Viceroy Antonio María, 52

Bueno, Padre Estevan, 179
Bueno, Fermín, 172
Bumppo, Natty, 127
Burnet, D. G., 50
Bustos, Tomás, 172

Cachupín, Tomás Vélez, 11
Caín y Abel, 93
Calandria, La (ballad), 102
Calderón, 96
Campa, Dr. Arthur L., 188
Cañute (game), 110
Cárdenas, Abran, 172
Cárdenas, Estevan, 172
Cárdenas, Garcez Lopez de, 32
Cárdenas, Tomás, 172
Carlana (Indian Chief), 10
"Carmelitas", 177-78
Carmen Carmela (song), 107
Carson, Kit, xxi, xxii, 66
Castillero, Andrés, 56
Castrense, the. *See* Luz, Nuestra Señora de la
Catron, Thomas B., 72
Cazulejas (game), 109-10. *See also* Iglesias, Las
Cervantes, 195
Chacón, Eusebio, 68
Chacón, Governor Fernando, 62, 69
Charro, El (ballad), 103
Chaves, José Manuel, 70
Chaves, José María, 71
Chaves, María Josepha, 71
Chávez, Irineo, 68
Chepe Polilla, 98
Choteau, Rene Auguste, 39
Christ, 95, 121, 132-36, 141, 144, 146-49. *See also* Jesus
Christ Child, 96, 119, 121
Christ in the Sepulcher, 122
Chueco, El (game). *See Pelota, La*

Cid, El, 114
Cisneros (current Colorado political official), 189
Clamorgan, James, 39
Clark, 3, 15
Coca, Miguel, 164-66
Coca, Nicolasa, 165
Coca, Pablo, 166
Cofradía de Nuestro Padre Jesús Nazareno, La. *See* Penitentes
Columbus, 19
Comanches, Los, 98
Conquistadora, La (wood carving of the Virgin), 117
Córdova, José J., 181
Córdova, Mauro, 181
Coronado, Francisco Vásquez de, x, xviii, 3-4, 19, 32
Cossío, J. M., 145-46
Costigan, Edward P., 188
"Cradle" (dance). *See Cuna*
"Crook, The" (game). *See Pelota, La; Chueco, El*
Crucifix, the, 122
Crue, Joe La, 187
Cruz, Sor Juana Inés de la, xii
Cueca (dance), 111
Cuerno Verde, 13-14, 98-100
Cuervo y Valdez, Don Franciso, 7
Cuna (dance), 111

Daca mi mujer (play by Lope de Vega), 108
Dama y el Pastor, La (ballad), 102
Dame un abrazo que yo te pido (game), 104
Delgadina (ballad), 101
Devil, 97. *See also* Satan
Diderot, 128
Diego, Juan, 94
Doloritas (wife of Blas Felipe Quintana), 172

Domingo, Felipe, 24
Domingo, Juan, 24
Domínguez, Fray Francisco
  Atanasio, 12, 21-22, 24, 27, 121
Durán y Chávez family, 47

Ecce Homo. *See* Jesús Nazareno
Ecueracapa (successor of Cuerno
  Verde), 14
Edwards, Hayden, 50
Emerson, 127
Enséñame a Amar (song), 106
Escalante, Silvestre Vélez de, 9,
  12-13, 21
Espejo, Antonio de, 4
Esposa Infiel, La (ballad), 101
Estraique de 1910, El (corrido),
  105

Fages, Governor Pedro, 52
Fernández, Don Carlos, 98-99
Figueroa, Governor José, 52
Finn, Huck, 127
Flagellant Brotherhood, 142. *See
  also* Penitentes
Flagellants Society, 142. *See also*
  Penitentes
Foa, Luis, 155
Foix, Luis. *See* Foa, Luis
Francés, Bernal, 101
Francisco, J. M., 184
Francis of Assissi, 134
Frankenstein, by Mary Shelley,
  Monster in, 127
Franklin, 128
Fremont, John Charles, 56-57,
  87
Fuller, Thomas C., 68

Gallegos, Julián, 66
Gallegos, Pascacio, 168
Gallinita Ciega, La (game), 109

Garcés, Father Francisco, 12, 22
García, Fray Andrés, 118
García, Leonizo, 164, 166
García, María Encarnación, 71
García, Reginaldo, 186
García, Samuel, 167
Gerineldo (ballad), 101
God, 131-32
Gonzales (current Colorado
  political official), 189
Gonzales, Francisco, 164
Gonzales, Pedro, 186
González, Captain Juan, 69
Goodale, Tim, Indian wife of, 85,
  90
"Graceful Swallow" (ballad). *See
  Agraciada Golondrina*
Guerrero, A. M., 186
Guitérrez, Gabriel, xv
Guitérrez, Juan N., xv
Gurule, Donaciano, 185

Hayes, President Rutherford B.,
  76
Head, Lafayette, 66
Hermanos Penitentes de la
  Tercera Orden de San Fran-
  cisco, Los, 143. *See also*
  Penitentes
Herod (King), 96
Hibbits, J. H., 164
Hicklin, Zan, 66
Hidalgo, Father Miguel, 40
"Hijas de María", 178
Hilitos de Oro (game). *See
  Quiebro Bolitas de Oro*
Humaña, Antonío Gutiérrez de, 5

Iglesias, Las (game), 109
Immaculate Conception, 119-20

Isidro, St., 178. *See also* Ysidro, San

Jackson (President), 41
Jacques, José María, xvi
Jaramillo, Josefina, xxii
Jarramillo, Nicanora [sic] D., 185
Jesus, 96, 145-46, 148-49, 165. *See also* Christ
Jesús Nazareno, 132-136. *See also* Nazarene Christ
Jesus the Nazarene or Nazarite. *See* Jesús Nazareno
Jimena (Doña), 114
"Joe Weevil." *See Chepe Polilla*
John, Saint, 122, 135
Johnson, Edwin C., 187, 189
Johnson, Jacobo, 172
Johnson, Samuel, 172
Johnston, General Albert S., 79-80
John the Baptist, St., 146. *See also* John, Saint
John the Evangelist, 135. *See also* John, Saint; John the Baptist, St.
Joseph, Saint, 94, 96, 119
Juana María (Indian Midwife), 181
Jusepe (Indian with Leyba de Bonilla party), 5

Kearny, General S. W., 57, 60
King, Richard, 50

"Lady and the Shepherd, The" (ballad). *See Dama y el Pastor, La*
Lady of Mount Carmel, 177-78
Laín, Joaquín, 12
Lalande, Jean Baptiste, 39
Lallemand, General, 38

Lamy (Father), xvi, 121
Lara, José Bernardo Gutiérrez de 40
Larragoite, Mariano, 185
Lássus, Charles Auguste de, xxi, 38
Lássus, Jacques, xxi
Lewis and Clark, 3, 15-16, 19
Leyba de Bonilla, Francisco, 5
Librada, Santa, 135
"Lies." *See Mentiras*

Limantour, J. Y., 55-56
Lindsey, A. I., 165
Lisa, Manuel, 39
Lluvia de Ingleses, Una, 98
López, Bersabé, 165
López, Juan, 9
Lorenzo, Don, 7
Lucero, Andrés, 185-86
Lucero, Juan, 17, 34
Lucero, Lucas, 169
Lucero, Manuel, 184
Lucero, Tomás, 70-71
Luz, Nuestra Señora de la, 118

Mack, Eddie. *See* Quintana, Pedro
Madison (President), 40
Madrid, J. M., 186
Maes, Gaudalupita, 174
Maes, Quirino, 172-74
Maes, Salvador, 173, 180
Maes, Santiago, 173
Mañanitas, Las, 107
Manita Ciega, La (game). *See Gallinta Ciega, La;* "Blind Man's Bluff"
Manzanares, John, 185
Marcy, Captain R. B., 79-90
"Margaret Louse." *See Margarita Piojo*

Margarita Piojo, 98
Marinera (dance). *See Cueca*
Marquez, Lorenzo, 61
Martínez, Antonio, 66
Martínez, Eusebio, 71
Martínez, Francisco, 69-71
Martínez, Joe, 185. *See also* Martínez, José Eliseo
Martínez, José Antonio, 71
Martínez, José Eliseo, 185
Martínez, José Manuel (son of José María), 71
Martínez, Jose Manuel (son of Manuel), 70
Martínez, Jose Maria, 66, 71
Martínez, Julian, 70
Martínez, Manuel, 65, 69-70
Martínez, Maria Antonia, 71
Martínez, Maria de Jesus, 71
Martínez, Maria Dolores, 70
Martínez, Maria Manuela, 70-71
Martínez, Pablo, 172
Martínez, Prudencio, 71
Martínez, Sara, 180
Martínez, Sixto, 71
Martínez, Vincente, 70
Martin (Juan Lucero's interpreter), 17
Marx, Karl, 126
Mary, 94, 96, 135, 147-50. *See also* Virgin, the
Maxwell, Lucian B., 65, 73
Medina, Frank J., 185
Mentiras ("Lies"), 104
Merriwether (Governor), 68
Mestas, Francisco, 164
Mestas, Juan, 174
Micheltorena, Manuel, 56-57
Miera y Pacheco, Bernardo de, 9, 12, 23, 25, 29-30, 118
Miguel, Angel (see also Angel, the), 95

Miguel, San, 117-118
Miranda, Guadalupe, 65, 72
Monroe: President, 35; Secretary, 40
Mora, Pedro, 27
Morelos (Marshall of Northern Mexican Revolutionary Army), 41
Moya, Rosendo, 105
Muñiz, Andrés, 12, 27-28
Murray, William C., 68

Naranja dulce limón partido (game), 104
Nazarene Christ, 119, 122. *See also* Jesús Nazareno
Newton, 128
Nicolás (ballad), 103
Nieto, Juan José, 52
Nieto, Manuel, 52
Niño Perdido, El, 95-97
Nolan, Gervacio, 66
Noriega, Juan N., 186
Nuestra Señora de la Soledád, 135

Ogden, Peter Skene, 30
Oñate, Juan de, 1, 3, 5, 23, 43-44, 66, 153, 193, 197
Onís, Dr. José de, 188, 194
Onís, Luis de, 33, 35-42
Onís, Mauricio Carlos de, 36, 41-42
Ortiz, Antonio José, 62
Osborne, F. J., 68

Passarelli, Franco, 179
Passarelli, Michele, 177
Pastorela, La. See Pastores, Los
Pastores, Los, 94-95
Payo, El (ballad), 103
Pelagianism, 132, 136
Pelham, William, 68

Pelota, La (game), 109
Penitentes, xvi, 120, 122, 134-136, 138, 142-143, 178, 188
Perjura, 107
Peyton, John Rozee, 15
Philip V, 8
Physiocrats, 127
Pico, Governor Pío, 54, 56
Pike, Zebulon, 2-3, 15, 19, 111
Pilate, 134-35, 148
Pino, Pedro Bautista, xi-xiii
Piojo y la Liendre, El (ballad), 104
Pitarrilla (game), 109
Pley, Joseph, 73
Posadas, Las, 94
"Put Your Little Foot" (dance). See *Varsoviana, La*

Quiebro Bolitas de Oro (game), 108
Quijote, El, by Cervantes, 195
Quinn, James H., 73
Quintana, Blas Felipe, 172-73
Quintana, Carmelita, 177
Quintana, Pedro, 186

Reed, Joseph R., 68
Reyes Magos, Los, 96
Reynolds, Matt G., 68
Rielera, La, 107
Rigaud (General), 38
Rivera, Juan María de, 11, 20, 27
Rodríguez, Fray Agustín
Romana (wife of Juan de Jesús Vigil), 172
Romero, Casimiro, 164-65
Romero, Eloy, 180
Romero, Grace, 180
Romero, Jerónimo, 165
Romero, José, 172
Roosevelt, Franklin D., 189
Rosendo Moya (*corrido*), 105

Saint Vrain, Ceran, xxi, 38, 66
Sánchez Chamuscado, Francisco, 4
Sánchez, Demecio, 180
Sánchez, Manuel, 172
Sánchez, Preenciseo, 185
Sandoval, Francisco, 164
Sandoval, Gregorio, 27
Sandoval, Miguel, 98
San José, 94
Santiago, 120-21
Satan, 94-95. See also Devil
Sebastiana (Doña), 122
Sephardic Jews 107-8
"Shepherd, The" (ballad). See *Zagal, El*
"Shower of Englishmen, A." See *Lluvia de Ingleses, Una*
Simms, Ruth Hanna McCormick, 76
Sims, Joseph, 105
Sluss, Harry G., 68
Smith, Jedediah, 30
Solano, Maza, 145-46
Sosa, Gaspar Castaño de, 4
Stearns, Able, 52-53
Stone, Wilbur F., 68

Taney, Chief Justice Roger B., 57
"Teach Me to Love" (song). See *Enséñame a Amar*
Tejas (game), 110
Third Order of St. Francis, 122, 143
Thomas, Governor Charles S., 184
Thoreau, 127
"Tiles" (game). See *Tejas*
Toledo, José Alvarez de, 40
Torres, J. Frank, 186
Trigueña Hermosa (song), 106

Trotier, Charles Hippolyte, 74.
  See also Beaubien, Carlos
Trujillo, Padre Alfonso, 179
Trujillo, Clemente, 184
Trujillo, José Ramón, 171-72
Trujillo, Juan, 171
Trujillo, Pedro Raphael, 185

Ulibarri, Juan de, 2, 7-9, 20
"Unfaithful Wife, The" (ballad).
  See Esposa Infidel, La
Urban VIII, Pope, 143

Vacquero, El (ballad), 103
Vacquero, El (corrido), 106
Vacquero Nicolás, El (ballad), 103
Valdez, Celedón, 66
Valdez, Crescencio, xvi
Valdez (current Colorado political official), 189
Valdez, Francisco de, 8
Valdez, Jesús C., 187
Valdez, Juan, 180
Valdez, Pedro, 91
Valdez, Procopio, 165
Valenciano, Miguel Sánchez, 4
Valentine, Rico, 168
Valle, Francisco Antonio Marin del, 118
Valverde Cosío, Don Antonio, 9-10
Vargas, Diego de, 3, 6-7, 69, 142, 154
Vargas, José de la Luz, 165
Varsoviana, La (dance), 111
Vasquez, Luis, xxi
Vega, Lope de, 108
Vehlein, Joseph, 50
Velásquez, José A., 185
Vial, Jean, 39. See also Vial, Pedro.

Vial, Pedro, xi, 16-17, 34, 39
Vigil, Celedón, 172, 177
Vigil, Charles S., 187
Vigil, Cornelio, 66
Vigil, David, 187
Vigil, Donaciano, 76
Vigil, Fernando, 169
Vigil, Hilario, 172
Vigil, Isidoro, 172
Vigil, José María, 172, 174-75, 177
Vigil, José Urbano, 186-87
Vigil, Juan Bautista (pioneer of Trujillo Creek), 172, 177
Vigil, Juan Bautista (secretary of New Mexican Government), 60-61
Vigil, Juan de Jesús, 169, 171-72
Vigil, Manuel, 172
Vigil, Telésforo, 172
Vigil y Oca, Francisco Montes, 69
Villasur, Pedro de, 11, 20
Virgin, Sorrowing, 121-22
Virgin, the, 94, 119-20, 132, 135, 141, 144-46, 148-50. See also Mary

Walker, Joseph, 30
Watt, James, 128
Wilson, S. J., 50
Wooten, Uncle Richens (Dick), 66
Wordsworth, 127

Ysabelita (wife of José Ramón Trujillo), 171
Ysidro, San, 121. See also Isidoro, St.

Zagal, El (ballad), 103
Zavala, Lorenzo de, 50